First Nation Animism

The New Testament

Hindu Ganesh

The Church of the Holy Sepulcher

Introduction to Religion

A Sourcebook

Sharon Lea Mattila

Babylonian Cosmology

Upper cosmic waters = half of Tiamat, slain by Marduke = abode of Anu

Distance = x

Celestial bodies are in "the roof" of the sky

Abode of Enlil, god of the atmosphere and wind = the lower heaven, called Esharra = the sky

Distance = x

Earth = half of Tiamat = abode of Marduke

The temple of Marduke = the center of the universe

Waters surround and pass under the earth

Subterranean waters = corpse of Apsu, slain by Ea, father of Marduke = abode of Ea

Distance = x

Creation in the Hebrew Bible

The Center of Islam

The Founding Buddha

Jerusalem Today

The Second Temple

Kendall Hunt
publishing company

Contents

Section One
What Is Religion?
A Global, Diverse, and Changing Phenomenon

Upper cosmic waters = half of Tiamat, slain by Marduke = abode of Anu

Celestial bodies are in "the roof" of the sky

Abode of Enlil, god of the atmosphere and wind = the lower heaven, called Esharra = the sky

Earth = half of Tiamat = abode of Marduke

The temple of Marduke = the center of the universe

Subterranean waters = corpse of Apsu, slain by Ea, father of Marduke = abode of Ea

Study Guide/Section One

1. What are the two oldest main branches of Christianity and when did they split? *Cath, Orth/1054*

2. Who was the founder of Protestantism, and when did he post his 95 theses against abuses in the Catholic Church? Before he founded Protestantism, what was he? *Martin Luther, catholic*

3. What does the word "catholic" mean? *Universal*

4. What does the word "orthodox" mean? *right thinking*

5. What main branch of Christianity has by far the most members today? *Catholics*

6. What main branch of Christianity has the fewest members today, and why? *Orthodox, communis*

7. Which religion has the second largest number of adherents after Christianity? *Islam*

8. Where did Christianity originate? *Israel*

9. Where did Islam originate? *Saudi Arabia*

10. Which religions, discussed in this course, originated in India? *Hinduism*

11. Which religions originated in China and Japan? *Shintoism (buddhist), Buddism Taoism/daoism & confucianism*

12. What is the difference between an atheist and an agnostic?

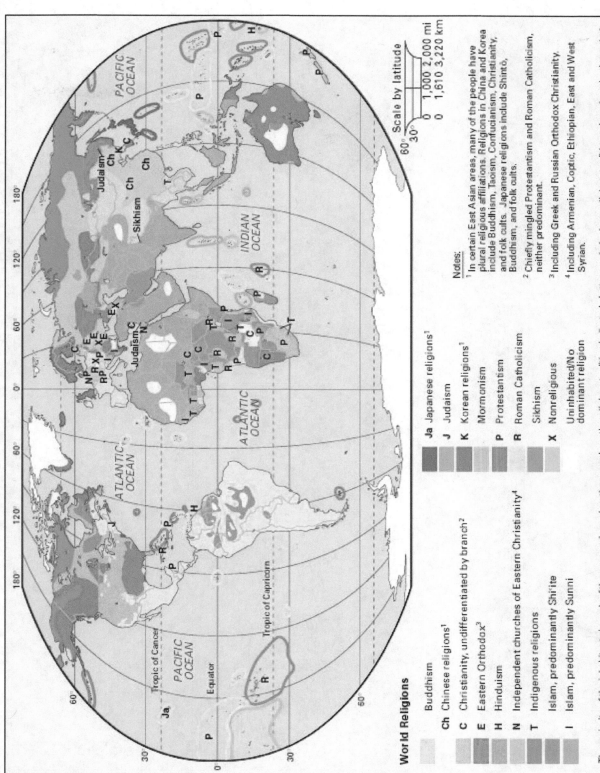

World Religions

	Buddhism
Ch	Chinese religions[1]
C	Christianity, undifferentiated by branch[2]
E	Eastern Orthodox[3]
H	Hinduism
N	Independent churches of Eastern Christianity[4]
T	Indigenous religions
I	Islam, predominantly Shi'ite
I	Islam, predominantly Sunni
Ja	Japanese religions[1]
J	Judaism
K	Korean religions[1]
	Mormonism
P	Protestantism
R	Roman Catholicism
	Sikhism
X	Nonreligious
	Uninhabited/No dominant religion

Scale by latitude

0   1,000   2,000 mi
0   1,610   3,220 km

Notes:

1. In certain East Asian areas, many of the people have plural religious affiliations. Religions in China and Korea include Buddhism, Taoism, Confucianism, Christianity, and folk cults. Japanese religions include Shintō, Buddhism, and folk cults.

2. Chiefly mingled Protestantism and Roman Catholicism, neither predominant.

3. Including Greek and Russian Orthodox Christianity.

4. Including Armenian, Coptic, Ethiopian, East and West Syrian.

© 2003 Encyclopædia Britannica, Inc.

The majority of the inhabitants in each of the areas coloured on the map share the religious tradition indicated. Letter symbols show religious traditions shared not by the majority but by at least 25 percent of the inhabitants within areas no smaller than 1,000 square miles. Therefore minority religions of city dwellers have generally not been represented.

Section Two
An Example of a North American Animistic Religion
The Kwakiutl Tribe
of the Pacific North West

Section Two/In-Class Group Assignment on

I Heard the Owl Call My Name

1. There is something that Keetah does that presents one of the greatest challenges to Mark's Christian values that he encounters while among the people of Kingcome. What does she do and *why* does she do it? 3 points

2. How had the people of Kingcome buried their dead in old times, and what had happened to their old burial site?

3. Two potlatch feasts and ceremonies are described at some length in the book—one at Gilford Island, which most of the village attends, and one in Kingcome itself, held in honor of Jim. Briefly describe what happens at these potlatches. 141

Related Questions for Class Discussion

1. Do you understand what Keetah does and do you agree with how Mark handles it? Why or why not?

2. If you had grown up in Kingcome, with whom do you think you would most identify—Gordon, Jim, or Keetah?

Bonus Question

According to the Encylopaedia Britannica, "The world of the Ojibwa tribe of North America was animated by a great number of eternal spirits (manitous), all of about equal rank, represented in trees, food plants, birds, animals, celestial bodies, winds, and wonders of every description. Beside these esteemed spirits were other categories, which were dreaded: ghosts, monsters, and the windigo, a crazed man-eating ogre who brought madness (a cannibalistic psychosis)." [**animism**. (2009). In *Encyclopædia Britannica*. Retrieved August 19, 2009, from Encyclopædia Britannica Online: http://0-search.eb.com.uncclc.coast.uncwil.edu/eb/article-38103].

What important features does the world of the Kwakiutl (of which the people of Kingcome are a part) share with the world of the Ojibwa?

Maps and Photographs Relating to the Assigned Novel, *I Heard the Owl Call My Name,* by Margaret Craven

These have been adapted by Sharon Lea Mattila from "The Southern Kwakiutl, Tribal Boundaries and Village Settlements," in Audrey Hawthorn, *Art of the Kwakiutl Indians and Other Northwest Coast Tribes* (Seattle: University of Washington Press, 1967) 6; Figure 89, and Plates IV, V.B, XX, XXI, and XXIII, in Audrey Hawthorn, *Kwakiutl Art* (Vancouver: Douglas & McIntyre, 1979).

The guides to pronunciation provided below are from the "Pronunciation Guide" in the *2009/2010 Guide to Aboriginal Organizations and Services in British Columbia* (a province of Canada).

Introduction

by Sharon Lea Mattila

The people of Kingcome described in *I Heard the Owl Call My Name* have a very long history. They are part of a very old aboriginal culture of coastal fishers along the Pacific coast of both Canada and the northern United States. They belong to a linguistic group called the Kwakiutl (pronounced, *kwa-cue-tul*), whose language is Kwak'wala. They are located in British Columbia, Canada, in the northern part of Vancouver Island and along the adjacent part of the mainland up to an area a bit north of there. The Haisla (pronounced *highs-la*) tribe is the northernmost group among them.

The band of the Kwakiutl to which the people of Kingcome belong is called the Tsawataineuk (pronounced, *za-wah-day-nook*), or "people of the oolachon country." The oolachon (also spelt eulachon) is a special fish that has a run in Kingcome Inlet, from which the people make their beloved gleena or oolachon oil, the oil into which they dip their dried fish at feasts.

Potlatch is a Chinook word, meaning "to give." Potlatches are lavish feasts, held for various occasions including the handing on of family privileges. Dances are held and gifts are generously distributed to the guests. The dances are very theatrical, involving many characters from nature and myth. The dancers often wear elaborate masks when portraying these characters, some of which are shown on the following pages. Such masks are a very important part of Kwakiutl art and culture.

The white missionaries and authorities of the nineteenth century disapproved of the potlatch, and in 1884, it was made illegal. It nevertheless continued, because it was so interwoven with the fabric of Kwakiutl society. In 1921, the authorities interrupted a potlatch taking place at Alert Bay. Several participants were imprisoned, and the masks of the dancers were confiscated and taken to the National Museum. In 1951, the ban was repealed.

Included in the following pages is a mask of Tsonokwa. She is a giantess, who lives in the faraway mountains and woods, and sometimes in the sea. She is a threatening and horrid creature, who loves to collect children into a basket on her back, in order to take them home to eat. Because she is vain, stupid, and clumsy, however, the children usually outwit her.

She is also a bringer of wealth and good fortune, a role that is very important at potlatches. In this role, she usually appears as a male, and usually has locks of human hair. It is probably the male version of this mask that is meant by the "giant mask," referred to in the book. Gordon's family owns one, finely carved and "black with red lips." In the case of Gordon's family's mask, the hair is that of his great-grandmother, and they had been offered $3,000 for it but had refused to sell it. It is this mask that Gordon's uncle, after having been made drunk by the fiancé of Keetah's sister, sells to him for $50, causing Keetah and her family to leave the village in shame. They fear that perhaps Keetah's sister knew about this act of her fiancé's, and had been part of it, and therefore, they feel responsible. Hence, Mrs. Hudson's prediction comes true that they would be ashamed of Keetah's sister. Her prediction also comes true that the outside world would destroy Keetah's sister.

Also on the following pages are a number of Hamatsa masks. The Hamatsa dance complex originated among the Haisla, a northern Kwakiutl group. A full-fledged Hamatsa has to have danced for twelve years. The Hamatsa is a kind of wild, animal-like, cannibal man, and the ceremony involves his taming to the point of becoming human again. The novice must disappear into the woods for a few days when initiated, as mentioned happened to Jim in the book. The "Hamatsa cry" is "*haap*" ("eat"), and the dancer in his frenzy attempts to bite people in the room.

In addition to the Hamatsa himself, the complex cast of characters involved in this dramatic ritual includes a number of bird-monsters that are terrifying eaters of human flesh. These include the raven, but also a number of mythical birds. One of the latter is the *hokwokw*, a bird-monster with an extraordinarily long beak. Another is called the Crooked Beak, and has a peculiar, curved beak.

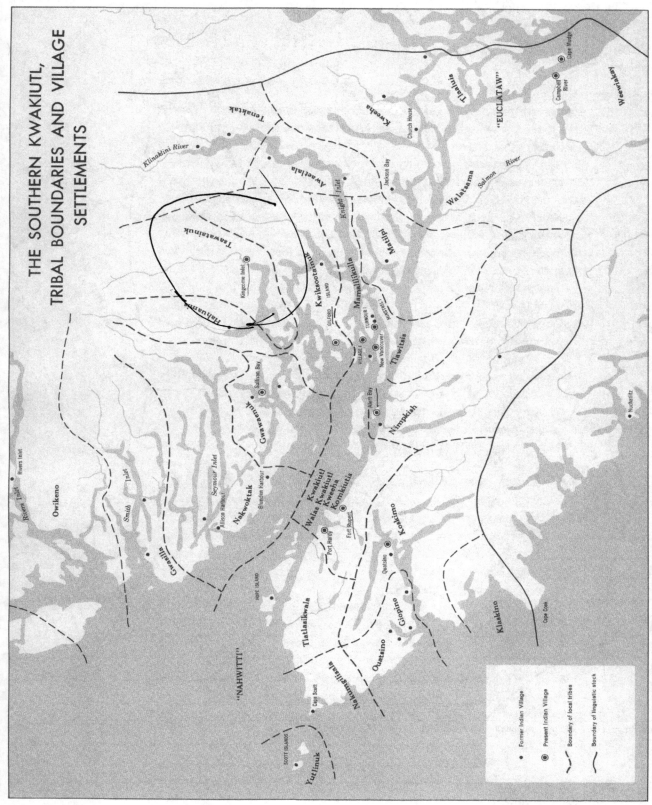

THE SOUTHERN KWAKIUTL,
TRIBAL BOUNDARIES AND VILLAGE
SETTLEMENTS

Rivers Inlet

Owikeno

Smith Inlet

Gwasilla

Seymour Inlet

Allison Harbour

Blunden Harbour

Nakwoktak

SCOTT ISLANDS

Yutlinuk

"NAHWITTI"

Cape Scott

HOPE ISLAND

Nakumgilisala

Tlatlasikwala

Koskimo

Quatsino

Quatsino

Giopino

Klaskino

Cape Cook

Port Hardy

Fort Rupert

Walas Kwakiutl
Kwakiutl
Kweeha
Komkiutis

Gwawaenuk

Sullivan Bay

Kwiksootainuk

Hahuamis

Kingcome Inlet

Tsawatainuk

Klinaklini River

Tenaktak

Awaetlala

Knight Inlet

GILFORD
ISLAND

TURNOUR I.

MINSTREL I.

VILLAGE

New Vancouver

Alert Bay

Mamalilikulla

TURNOUR I.

Matilpi

Tlawitsis

Nimpkish

Jackson Bay

Salmon River

Walatsma

Church House

Kweeha

Tsaaluis

"EUCLATAW"

Campbell
River

Cape Mudge

Weewiakey

Nuchatlitz

Former Indian Village
Present Indian Village
Boundary of local tribes
Boundary of linguistic stock

Courtesy of Audrey & Harry Hawthron Library & Archives, UBC Museum of Anthropology

9

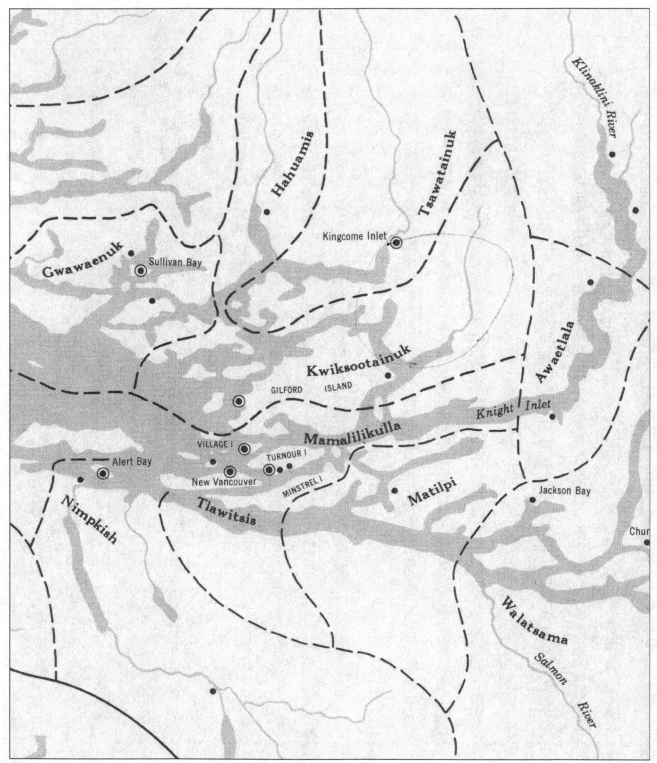

Klinaklini River

Hahuamis

Tsawatainuk

Kingcome Inlet

Awaetlala

Gwawaenuk   Sullivan Bay

Kwiksootainuk

GILFORD   ISLAND

Knight   Inlet

Mamalilikulla

VILLAGE I

Jackson Bay

Alert Bay   TURNOUR I

New Vancouver   Matilpi

MINSTREL I   Chur

Nimpkish   Tlawitsis

Walatsama

Salmon

River

Courtesy of Audrey & Harry Hawthron Library & Archives, UBC Museum of Anthropology

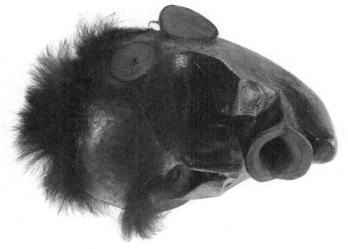

Tsonokwa mask from Fort Rupert, made of wood, with its hair and eyebrows made out of bear hide.

Tsonokwa mask with bird on top.

Moon mask from Kingcome.

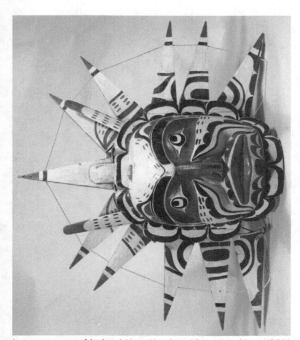

Sun Mask from Kingcome.

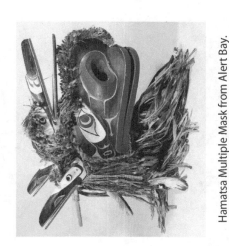

Hamatsa Multiple Mask from Alert Bay. (A large Crooked Beak, topped by a raven and a Hokwokw.)

Section Three

The Ancient Near East and First Temple Judaism

From Polytheism to Henotheism to Monolatry to Monotheism

waters = half of Tiamat,
Marduke = abode of Anu

bodies are in "the roof" of the sky

Abode of Enlil, god of the atmosphere
and wind = the lower heaven, called
Esharra = the sky

Distance = x

Earth = half of
Tiamat = abode
of Marduke

The temple of
Marduke = the
center of the
universe

Water
surround
and pass
under the
earth

Subterranean waters = corpse of Apsu,
slain by Ea, father of Marduke
= abode of Ea

Distance = x

ט וַיֹּאמֶר אֱלֹהִים יִקָּווּ הַמַּיִם מִתַּחַת הַשָּׁמַיִם אֶל־מָקוֹם אֶחָד
י וְתֵרָאֶה הַיַּבָּשָׁה וַיְהִי־כֵן: וַיִּקְרָא אֱלֹהִים ׀ לַיַּבָּשָׁה אֶרֶץ וּלְמִקְוֵה
הַמַּיִם קָרָא יַמִּים וַיַּרְא אֱלֹהִים כִּי־טוֹב: וַיֹּאמֶר אֱלֹהִים תַּדְשֵׁא
הָאָרֶץ דֶּשֶׁא עֵשֶׂב מַזְרִיעַ זֶרַע עֵץ פְּרִי עֹשֶׂה פְּרִי לְמִינוֹ אֲשֶׁר
יא זַרְעוֹ־בוֹ עַל־הָאָרֶץ וַיְהִי־כֵן: וַתּוֹצֵא הָאָרֶץ דֶּשֶׁא עֵשֶׂב מַזְרִיעַ
זֶרַע לְמִינֵהוּ וְעֵץ עֹשֶׂה־פְּרִי אֲשֶׁר זַרְעוֹ־בוֹ לְמִינֵהוּ וַיַּרְא אֱלֹהִים
יב כִּי־טוֹב: וַיְהִי־עֶרֶב וַיְהִי־בֹקֶר יוֹם שְׁלִישִׁי:
וַיֹּאמֶר אֱלֹהִים יְהִי מְאֹרֹת בִּרְקִיעַ הַשָּׁמַיִם לְהַבְדִּיל בֵּין הַיּוֹם
וּבֵין הַלָּיְלָה וְהָיוּ לְאֹתֹת וּלְמוֹעֲדִים וּלְיָמִים וְשָׁנִים: וְהָיוּ
מְאוֹרֹת בִּרְקִיעַ הַשָּׁמַיִם לְהָאִיר עַל־הָאָרֶץ וַיְהִי־כֵן: וַיַּעַשׂ
יים אֶת־שְׁנֵי הַמְּאֹרֹת הַגְּדֹלִים אֶת־הַמָּאוֹר הַגָּדֹל לְמֶמְ
אֶת־הַמָּאוֹר הַקָּטֹן לְמֶמְשֶׁלֶת הַלַּיְלָה וְאֵת הַכּוֹ
אֱלֹהִים בִּרְקִיעַ הַשָּׁמַיִם לְהָאִיר עַל־הָאָרֶ
לְהַבְדִּיל בֵּין הָאוֹר וּבֵין הַח

Study Guide/Section Three

1. Define the following terms (make sure your definitions are clear): Polytheism, Henotheism, Monolatry, and Monotheism.

2. Explain, on the basis of the reading from 2 Chronicles, why after the death of Solomon the ten northern tribes formed their own kingdom, called Israel, while only the southern tribes of Benjamin and Judah remained under the rule of the Davidic dynasty.

3. Explain, on the basis of your reading of the excerpts from 2 Kings, how we know that the ancient northern kingdom of Israel throughout its entire history was henotheistic, and never strictly monolatrous.

4. What happened to the Northern kingdom of Israel in 722 BCE, according to 2 Kings?

5. Cite (i.e., quote, with the reference provided) two passages from the excerpts from 2 Kings that explain why, according to the author of 2 Kings, Josiah's Reform in ca. 621 BCE was not enough to prevent the Babylonian Exile (586 BCE).

6. What did the prophet Jeremiah advise the people of Judah to do just before the Babylonians destroyed the First Temple?

7. Second Isaiah or Deutero-Isaiah (Isaiah 40:1–55:13) was written toward the end of the Babylonian Exile. We know this because it proclaims Cyrus of Persia, who conquered Babylonia and allowed the exiles to return to Jerusalem in about 539/538 BCE, to be Yahweh's *Messiah*, or "anointed [one]" (Isaiah 45:1). Second Isaiah is clearly monotheistic. Cite at least three passages from this passage to show why this is so.

8. Describe the main features of the Babylonian creation epic, the *Enuma Elish*, including how the high god, Marduk, creates the universe.

9. What was the state of the universe before creation in both the Priestly Account of Creation and in the *Enuma Elish*?

10. What is the structure of the universe after it is created in both the Priestly Account and the *Enuma Elish*? In other words, what is their shared *cosmology*?

11. How does their *cosmogony* differ? That is, what are the differences in how these two creation stories explain the "birth" or "origin" of the universe, or how the universe came to have the structure it was understood by both accounts to have?

12. How does God create in the Priestly Account of creation? How does He create in the Yahwist narrative?

13. In what order are men, women, and animals created in the Priestly Account? In what order are they created in the Yahwist narrative?

14. In which of the two biblical creation accounts is God more anthropomorphic and why? Provide some examples to back your argument.

15. The Hebrew word *ha* is the definite article "the." Based on the translations provided for both the Priestly and Yahwist accounts of creation, what range of meanings are there for the Hebrew word *adam* or, with the definite article, *ha-adam*? What does the word *ha-adamah* mean?

16. Based on the above-mentioned translations, what do the Hebrew words *mayim* and *shamayim* mean? What do you notice about the connection between these two words? Why do you think they are thus connected?

17. Based on the translation of the Yahwist account of creation, what do the Hebrew words *īsh* and *īshah* mean?

18. Is the serpent or snake Satan or the devil?

19. Why has Yahweh's prohibition against eating from the tree of the knowledge of good and evil been one of the most difficult to interpret?

20. Explain why it is in fact quite clear in the Yahwist narrative that the man and his woman (or wife) were *not* created immortal by Yahweh God.

The patriarchal period:
Abraham, Issac, Jacob,
+ Jozpeph

HISTORICAL TIME-LINE / SECTION THREE

1250—
1000 BCE
Bronze Age

A people called "Israel" arise in the Hill Country of Palestine; this is the time of the books of **Joshua** and **Judges**, when these people were divided into **twelve tribes**.

1000 BCE

After a brief reign by Saul, **David** becomes king of the twelve tribes and **conquers Jerusalem**.

✱ Hrh of the covent into the city

950 BCE

David's son, **Solomon**, builds the **First Jerusalem Temple**.

922 BCE

Upon Solomon's death, the **northern tribes** rebel against Solomon's son and **form a new kingdom, Israel; while Judah** (together with Benjamin) remains under the rule of David's descendants.

722/21
BCE

The **Assyrian Empire destroys the northern kingdom of Israel** and exiles *→ worshipping mcm Gods* many of the people they do not kill; archaeological excavations attest to severe depopulation in the region at this time. These are **"the lost tribes of Israel."**

701 BCE

Jerusalem, under king Hezekiah, withstands the siege of the **Assyrians**. Hence, **Judah continues to exist as a small nation** paying tribute to the Assyrian Empire. During the long reign of **Manasseh**, Hezekiah's son, **Judah remains henotheistic.**

can only worship Yahweh

621 BCE

Josiah, king of Judah and grandson of Manasseh, **institutes a reform based on the "book of the law" (i.e., a form of Deuteronomy),** found in the Jerusalem temple. His reform does not last after his death.

586 BCE

after his death went back to old ways

Zedekiah, against the advice of both **Jeremiah** and Ezekiel, rebels against the **Babylonians** who had imposed tribute on the kingdom of Judah in about 597 BCE. The Egyptians come to Jerusalem's assistance but do not remain. Once they are gone, the **Babylonians return, destroy the First Temple** and the city and **exile many of the people** = the **Babylonian Exile.**

539 BCE

King **Cyrus of Persia**, declared Yahweh's **Messiah** by **Second Isaiah**, allows the Jews to return to Jerusalem to **rebuild their Temple**.

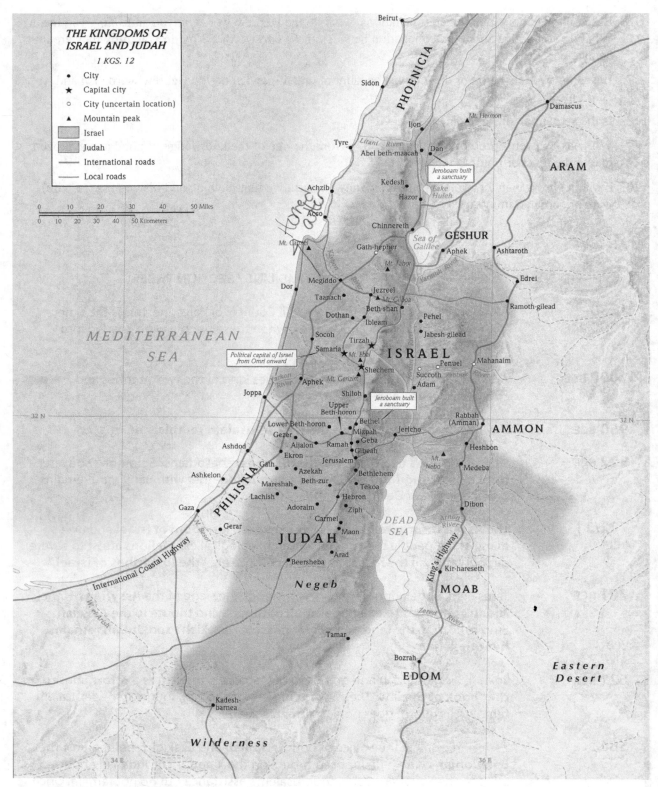

Map of the Divided Kingdom of Israel and Judah

From *Holman Bible Atlas* by Thomas C. Brisco. Copyright © 1998 by Broadman & Holman. Reprinted by permission.

FIRST TEMPLE PERIOD
(950—586 BCE):

During this time, there were two important developments: 1) in worship and belief—from **henotheism** to **monolatry** to **monotheism**; 2) in the rules concerning where sacrifice to Yahweh could take place.

As reflected in the Covenant Code in the book of Exodus, in the earlier period, **sacrifice to Yahweh was permitted wherever an appropriate altar was erected** (Shiloh, Bethel, Dan, Beer-Sheba, etc., and numerous high places). It was only when "the book of the law" or some form of the book of Deuteronomy was discovered, that **the Jerusalem Temple became the only place where sacrifices to Yahweh could take place**.

The **northern kingdom of Israel** was **henotheistic** and had multiple centers of worship to the high god, Yahweh, throughout its entire history (922—722 BCE).

The **southern kingdom of Judah** was likewise **henotheistic** and had multiple centers of Yahwistic worship throughout the major part of its history (922—586 BCE), although it underwent an important, albeit temporary, **monolatrous reform under Josiah** in 621 BCE.

Josiah's reform involved *two very important changes* from the earlier practices that had taken place throughout the northern and southern kingdoms: 1) **Yahweh alone was to be worshipped (monolatry)**; and 2) **one could sacrifice to Yahweh only at the Jerusalem Temple (centralization of the cult)**.

After Josiah dies, his successors revert back to henotheism. Soon after this the **Babylonians destroy the First Temple**. The **Arc of the Covenant is lost**.

During the **Babylonian Exile** of 586—539 BCE, however, the religion became increasingly **monotheistic**. The Jewish exiles interpreted what had happened as **the just punishment of Yahweh** for their worship of other gods. The author of **Deutero-Isaiah (or Second Isaiah)**—who proclaimed Cyrus, the Persian, to be Yahweh's "Messiah," because in 539 BCE Cyrus allowed the exiles to return to Jerusalem to rebuild the Second Temple—wrote some of our very earliest, unambiguously **monotheistic** declarations.

Excerpts from the Hebrew Bible*

Henotheistic and/or Monolatrous Declarations

Henotheistic *(margin handwritten note)*

Mono *(margin handwritten note)*

Exodus 15:10-12: "You blew with your wind, the sea covered them [i.e., the Egyptians who attempted to pursue the Jews after they had crossed over when Moses parted the sea]; they sank like lead in the mighty waters. Who is like you among the gods, O Yahweh? Who is like you, majestic in holiness, awesome in praises, working wonders? You stretched out your right hand, the earth swallowed them."

Exodus 18:11: "Now I know that the Yahweh is greater than all other gods, for he did this to those who had treated Israel arrogantly."

Exodus 20:3-5 / Deuteronomy 5:7-9: "You shall have no other gods before (or besides) me . . . for I Yahweh your God am a jealous God"

Psalm 82:1: "God stands in the divine council; in the midst of the gods he passes judgment."

Psalm 86:8: "There is no one like you among the gods, O Yahweh, nor are there any works like yours."

Psalm 97:9: "For you O Yahweh are the most high over all the Earth. You are exalted far above all gods."

Multiple Sanctuaries and Altars to Yahweh

[Note: According to the book of Exodus, the people may worship Yahweh anywhere where they build a simple altar to him and invoke or remember his name. The law code in Exodus, called the Covenant Code, dates to before Josiah's Reform in 621 BCE (see below). In this earlier period, when animals were slaughtered for their meat, they were also offered to Yahweh at one of the many altars or sanctuaries devoted to his worship].

Exodus 20:24: "You need make for me only an altar of earth and sacrifice on it your burnt offerings and your offerings of well-being, your sheep and your oxen; in every place where I cause my name to be remembered I will come to you and bless you."

Key Historical Events

2 Chronicles 9:30

[30]Solomon reigned in Jerusalem over all Israel for forty years. [31]Solomon slept with his ancestors and was buried in the city of his father David; and his son Rehoboam succeeded him.

The Northern Kingdom of Israel Splits Off
from the Southern Kingdom of Judah (922 BCE)

2 Chronicles 10:1–19

[1]Rehoboam went to Shechem for all Israel had come to Shechem to make him king. [2]When Jeroboam son of Nebat heard of it (for he was in Egypt, where he had fled from King Solomon), then Jeroboam returned from Egypt. [3]They sent and called him; and Jeroboam and all Israel came and said to Rehoboam, [4]'Your father made our yoke heavy. Now therefore lighten the hard service of your father and his heavy yoke that he placed on us, and we will serve you.' [5]He said to them, 'Come to me again in three days.' So the people went away.

[6]Then King Rehoboam took counsel with the older men who had attended his father Solomon while he was still alive, saying, 'How do you advise me to answer this people?' [7]They answered him, 'If you will be kind to this people and please them, and speak good words to them, then they will be your servants for ever.' [8]But he rejected

the advice that the older men gave him, and consulted the young men who had grown up with him and now attended him. [9]He said to them, 'What do you advise that we answer this people who have said to me, "Lighten the yoke that your father put on us"?' [10]The young men who had grown up with him said to him, 'Thus should you speak to the people who said to you, "Your father made our yoke heavy, but you must lighten it for us"; tell them, "My little finger is thicker than my father's loins. [11]Now, whereas my father laid on you a heavy yoke, I will add to your yoke. My father disciplined you with whips, but I will discipline you with scorpions."'

[12]So Jeroboam and all the people came to Rehoboam the third day, as the king had said, 'Come to me again the third day.' [13]The king answered them harshly. King Rehoboam rejected the advice of the older men; [14]he spoke to them in accordance with the advice of the young men, 'My father made your yoke heavy, but I will add to it; my father disciplined you with whips, but I will discipline you with scorpions.' [15]So the king did not listen to the people, because it was a turn of affairs brought about by God so that Yahweh might fulfil his word, which he had spoken by Ahijah the Shilonite to Jeroboam son of Nebat.

[16]When all Israel saw that the king would not listen to them, the people answered the king,

'What share do we have in David?
We have no inheritance in the son of Jesse.
Each of you to your tents, O Israel!
Look now to your own house, O David.'

So all Israel departed to their tents. [17]But Rehoboam reigned over the people of Israel who were living in the cities of Judah. [18]When King Rehoboam sent Hadoram, who was taskmaster over the forced labor, the people of Israel stoned him to death. King Rehoboam hurriedly mounted his chariot to flee to Jerusalem. [19]So Israel has been in rebellion against the house of David to this day.

The End of the Northern Kingdom of Israel (722 BCE)

2 Kings 17, with a few verses removed

[1]In the twelfth year of King Ahaz of Judah, Hoshea son of Elah began to reign in Samaria over Israel; he reigned nine years. [2]He did what was evil in the sight of Yahweh, yet not like the kings of Israel who were before him. [3]King Shalmaneser of Assyria came up against him; Hoshea became his vassal, and paid him tribute. [4]But the king of Assyria found treachery in Hoshea; for he had sent messengers to King So of Egypt, and offered no tribute to the king of Assyria, as he had done year by year; therefore the king of Assyria confined him and imprisoned him. [5]Then the king of Assyria invaded all the land and came to Samaria; for three years he besieged it. [6]In the ninth year of Hoshea the king of Assyria captured Samaria; he carried the Israelites away to Assyria. He placed them in Halah, on the Habor, the river of Gozan, and in the cities of the Medes. [7]This occurred because the people of Israel had sinned against Yahweh their God, who had brought them up out of the land of Egypt from under the hand of Pharaoh king of Egypt. They had worshiped other gods [8]and walked in the customs of the nations whom Yahweh drove out before the people of Israel, and in the customs that the kings of Israel had introduced. [9]The people of Israel secretly did things that were not right against Yahweh their God. They built for themselves high places at all their towns, from watchtower to fortified city; [10]they set up for themselves pillars and statues of Asherah on every high hill and under every green tree; [11]there they made offerings on all the high places, as the nations did whom Yahweh carried away before them. They did wicked things, provoking Yahweh to anger; [12]they served idols, of which Yahweh had said to them, "You shall not do this." [13]Yet Yahweh warned Israel and Judah by every prophet and every seer, saying, "Turn from your evil ways and keep my commandments and my statutes, in accordance with all the law that I commanded your ancestors and that I sent to you by my servants the prophets." [14]They would not listen but were stubborn, as their ancestors had been, who did not believe in Yahweh their God. [15]They despised his statutes, and his covenant that he made with their ancestors, and the warnings that he gave them. They went after false idols and became false; they followed the nations that were around them, concerning whom Yahweh had commanded them that they should not do as they did. [16]They rejected all the commandments of Yahweh their God and made for themselves cast images of two calves; they made an Asherah, worshiped all

the host of heaven, and served Baal. [17]They made their sons and their daughters pass through fire; they used divination and augury; and they sold themselves to do evil in the sight of Yahweh, provoking him to anger. [18]Therefore Yahweh was very angry with Israel and removed them out of his sight; none was left but the tribe of Judah alone. [19]Judah also did not keep the commandments of Yahweh their God but walked in the customs that Israel had introduced. [20]Yahweh rejected all the descendants of Israel; he punished them and gave them into the hand of plunderers, until he had banished them from his presence. [21]When he had torn Israel from the house of David, they made Jeroboam son of Nebat king. Jeroboam drove Israel from following Yahweh and made them commit great sin. [22]The people of Israel continued in all the sins that Jeroboam committed; they did not depart from them [23]until Yahweh removed Israel out of his sight, as he had foretold through all his servants the prophets. So Israel was exiled from their own land to Assyria until this day.

. . .

[33]So they worshiped Yahweh but also served their own gods, after the manner of the nations from among whom they had been carried away. [34]To this day they continue to practice their former customs. They do not worship Yahweh and they do not follow the statutes or the ordinances or the law or the commandment that Yahweh commanded the children of Jacob, whom he named Israel. [35]Yahweh had made a covenant with them and commanded them, "You shall not worship other gods or bow yourselves to them or serve them or sacrifice to them, [36]but you shall worship Yahweh, who brought you out of the land of Egypt with great power and with an outstretched arm; you shall bow yourselves to him, and to him you shall sacrifice. [37]The statutes and the ordinances and the law and the commandment that he wrote for you, you shall always be careful to observe. You shall not worship other gods; [38]you shall not forget the covenant that I have made with you. You shall not worship other gods, [39]but you shall worship Yahweh your God; he will deliver you out of the hand of all your enemies." [40]They would not listen, however, but they continued to practice their former custom. [41]So these nations worshiped Yahweh, but also served their carved images; to this day their children and their children's children continue to do as their ancestors did.

Hezekiah of Judah Rebels against Assyria around the Time Israel is Destroyed (ca. 722 BCE)

2 Kings 18:1-12, with a few verses removed

[1]In the third year of King Hoshea son of Elah of Israel, Hezekiah son of King Ahaz of Judah began to reign. [2]He was twenty-five years old when he began to reign; he reigned twenty-nine years in Jerusalem. His mother's name was Abi daughter of Zechariah. . . . [7b]He rebelled against the king of Assyria and would not serve him. [8]He attacked the Philistines as far as Gaza and its territory, from watchtower to fortified city. [9]In the fourth year of King Hezekiah, which was the seventh year of King Hoshea son of Elah of Israel, King Shalmaneser of Assyria came up against Samaria, besieged it, [10]and at the end of three years, took it [in 722 BCE]. In the sixth year of Hezekiah, which was the ninth year of King Hoshea of Israel, Samaria was taken. [11]The king of Assyria carried the Israelites away to Assyria, settled them in Halah, on the Habor, the river of Gozan, and in the cities of the Medes, [12]because they did not obey the voice of Yahweh their God but transgressed his covenant — all that Moses the servant of Yahweh had commanded; they neither listened nor obeyed.

King Sennacherib of Assyria Invades Judah and Besieges Jerusalem (ca. 705–701 BCE)

2 Kings 18:13-19:37, with a few verses removed

[13]In the fourteenth year of King Hezekiah, King Sennacherib of Assyria came up against all the fortified cities of Judah and captured them. [14]King Hezekiah of Judah sent to the king of Assyria at Lachish, saying, 'I have done wrong; withdraw from me; whatever you impose on me I will bear.' The king of Assyria demanded of King Hezekiah of Judah three hundred talents of silver and thirty talents of gold. [15]Hezekiah gave him all the silver that was found in the house of Yahweh and in the treasuries of the king's house. [16]At that time Hezekiah

stripped the gold from the doors of the temple of Yahweh, and from the doorposts that King Hezekiah of Judah had overlaid, and gave it to the king of Assyria. [17]The king of Assyria sent the Tartan [lit., the chief commander], the Rabsaris [lit., the chief eunuch], and the Rabshakeh [lit., the chief butler] with a great army from Lachish to King Hezekiah at Jerusalem. They went up and came to Jerusalem. When they arrived, they came and stood by the conduit of the upper pool, which is on the highway to the Fuller's Field. [18]When they called for the king, there came out to them Eliakim son of Hilkiah, who was in charge of the palace, and Shebnah the secretary, and Joah son of Asaph, the recorder.

[19]The Rabshakeh [lit., the chief butler] said to them, 'Say to Hezekiah: Thus says the great king, the king of Assyria: On what do you base this confidence of yours? [20]Do you think that mere words are strategy and power for war? On whom do you now rely, that you have rebelled against me? [21]See, you are relying now on Egypt, that broken reed of a staff, which will pierce the hand of anyone who leans on it. Such is Pharaoh king of Egypt to all who rely on him. [22]But if you say to me, "We rely on Yahweh our God," is it not he whose high places and altars Hezekiah has removed, saying to Judah and to Jerusalem, "You shall worship before this altar in Jerusalem"? [23]Come now, make a wager with my master the king of Assyria: I will give you two thousand horses, if you are able on your part to set riders on them. [24]How then can you repulse a single captain among the least of my master's servants, when you rely on Egypt for chariots and for horsemen? [25]Moreover, is it without Yahweh that I have come up against this place to destroy it? Yahweh said to me, Go up against this land, and destroy it.'

[26]Then Eliakim son of Hilkiah, and Shebnah, and Joah said to the Rabshakeh [lit., the chief butler], 'Please speak to your servants in the Aramaic language, for we understand it; do not speak to us in the language of Judah within the hearing of the people who are on the wall.' [27]But the Rabshakeh [lit., the chief butler] said to them, 'Has my master sent me to speak these words to your master and to you, and not to the people sitting on the wall, who are doomed with you to eat their own dung and to drink their own urine?'

[28]Then the Rabshakeh [lit., the chief butler] stood and called out in a loud voice in the language of Judah, 'Hear the word of the great king, the king of Assyria! [29]Thus says the king: "Do not let Hezekiah deceive you, for he will not be able to deliver you out of my hand. [30]Do not let Hezekiah make you rely on Yahweh by saying, Yahweh will surely deliver us, and this city will not be given into the hand of the king of Assyria." [31]Do not listen to Hezekiah; for thus says the king of Assyria: "Make your peace with me and come out to me; then every one of you will eat from your own vine and your own fig tree, and drink water from your own cistern, [32]until I come and take you away to a land like your own land, a land of grain and wine, a land of bread and vineyards, a land of olive oil and honey, that you may live and not die. Do not listen to Hezekiah when he misleads you by saying, Yahweh will deliver us. [33]Has any of the gods of the nations ever delivered its land out of the hand of the king of Assyria? [34]Where are the gods of Hamath and Arpad? Where are the gods of Sepharvaim, Hena, and Ivvah? Have they delivered Samaria out of my hand? [35]Who among all the gods of the countries have delivered their countries out of my hand, that Yahweh should deliver Jerusalem out of my hand?" '

[36]But the people were silent and answered him not a word, for the king's command was, 'Do not answer him.' [37]Then Eliakim son of Hilkiah, who was in charge of the palace, and Shebna the secretary, and Joah son of Asaph, the recorder, came to Hezekiah with their clothes torn and told him the words of the Rabshakeh [lit., the chief butler].

Hezekiah Consults the Prophet Isaiah (ca. 701 BCE)

2 Kings 19

[1]When King Hezekiah heard it, he tore his clothes, covered himself with sackcloth, and went into the house of Yahweh. [2]And he sent Eliakim, who was in charge of the palace, and Shebna the secretary, and the senior priests, covered with sackcloth, to the prophet Isaiah son of Amoz. [3]They said to him, 'Thus says Hezekiah, This day is a day of distress, of rebuke, and of disgrace; children have come to birth, and there is no strength to bring them forth. [4]It may be that Yahweh your God heard all the words of the Rabshakeh [lit., the chief butler], whom his master the king of Assyria has sent to mock the living God, and will rebuke the words that Yahweh your God has heard; therefore lift up your prayer for the remnant that is left.' [5]When the servants of King Hezekiah came to Isaiah, [6]Isaiah said to them, 'Say to your master, "Thus says Yahweh: Do not be afraid because of the words that you have heard, with which the servants of the king of Assyria have reviled me. [7]I myself will put a spirit in him, so that he shall hear a rumor and return to his own land; I will cause him to fall by the sword in his own land." '

Sennacherib's Threat

[8]The Rabshakeh [lit., the chief butler] returned, and found the king of Assyria fighting against Libnah; for he had heard that the king had left Lachish. [9]When the king heard concerning King Tirhakah of Ethiopia, 'See, he has set out to fight against you', he sent messengers again to Hezekiah, saying, [10]'Thus shall you speak to King Hezekiah of Judah: Do not let your God on whom you rely deceive you by promising that Jerusalem will not be given into the hand of the king of Assyria. [11]See, you have heard what the kings of Assyria have done to all lands, destroying them utterly. Shall you be delivered? [12]Have the gods of the nations delivered them, the nations that my predecessors destroyed, Gozan, Haran, Rezeph, and the people of Eden who were in Telassar? [13]Where is the king of Hamath, the king of Arpad, the king of the city of Sepharvaim, the king of Hena, or the king of Ivvah?'

Hezekiah's Prayer in the Jerusalem Temple (ca. 701 BCE)

[14]Hezekiah received the letter from the hand of the messengers and read it; then Hezekiah went up to the house of Yahweh and spread it before Yahweh. [15]And Hezekiah prayed before Yahweh, and said: 'O Yahweh the God of Israel, who are enthroned upon the cherubim, . . . [16]Incline your ear, O Yahweh, and hear; open your eyes, O Yahweh, and see; hear the words of Sennacherib, which he has sent to mock the living God. [17]Truly, O Yahweh, the kings of Assyria have laid waste the nations and their lands, [18]and have hurled their gods into the fire . . . [19]So now, O Yahweh our God, save us, I pray you, from his hand . . .'

[20]Then Isaiah son of Amoz sent to Hezekiah, saying, 'Thus says Yahweh, the God of Israel: I have heard your prayer to me about King Sennacherib of Assyria. [21]This is the word that Yahweh has spoken concerning him:

. . .

28 Because you have raged against me
    and your arrogance has come to my ears,
I will put my hook in your nose
    and my bit in your mouth;
I will turn you back on the way
    by which you came.
. . .

[32]'Therefore thus says Yahweh concerning the king of Assyria: He shall not come into this city, shoot an arrow there, come before it with a shield, or cast up a siege-ramp against it. [33]By the way that he came, by the same he shall return; he shall not come into this city, says Yahweh. [34]For I will defend this city to save it, for my own sake and for the sake of my servant David.'

Sennacherib's Defeat (701 BCE) and Death (681 BCE)

[35]That very night the angel of Yahweh set out and struck down one hundred and eighty-five thousand in the camp of the Assyrians; when morning dawned, they were all dead bodies. [36]Then King Sennacherib of Assyria left, went home, and lived at Nineveh. [37]As he was worshipping in the house of his god Nisroch, his sons Adrammelech and Sharezer killed him with the sword, and they escaped into the land of Ararat. His son Esar-haddon succeeded him.

King Manasseh of Judah (698/87–642 BCE)

2 Kings 21

[1]Manasseh was twelve years old when he began to reign; he reigned fifty-five years in Jerusalem. His mother's name was Hephzibah. [2]He did what was evil in the sight Yahweh, following the abominable practices of the nations that Yahweh drove out before the people of Israel. [3]For he rebuilt the high places that his father Hezekiah had destroyed; he erected altars for Baal, made an Asherah, as King Ahab of Israel had done, worshiped all the host of heaven, and served them. [4]He built altars in the house of Yahweh, of which Yahweh had said, "In

[handwritten: sacrificed]

Jerusalem I will put my name." [5]He built altars for all the host of heaven in the two courts of the house of Yahweh. [6]He made his son pass through fire; he practiced soothsaying and augury, and dealt with mediums and with wizards. He did much evil in the sight of Yahweh, provoking him to anger. [7]The carved image of Asherah that he had made he set in the house of which Yahweh said to David and to his son Solomon, "In this house, and in Jerusalem, which I have chosen out of all the tribes of Israel, I will put my name forever; [8]I will not cause the feet of Israel to wander any more out of the land that I gave to their ancestors, if only they will be careful to do according to all that I have commanded them, and according to all the law that my servant Moses commanded them." [9]But they did not listen; Manasseh misled them to do more evil than the nations had done that Yahweh destroyed before the people of Israel.

Prediction of the Babylonian Exile *[handwritten: – Judah is destroyed]*

[10]Yahweh said by his servants the prophets, [11]"Because King Manasseh of Judah has committed these abominations, has done things more wicked than all that the Amorites did, who were before him, and has caused Judah also to sin with his idols; [12]therefore thus says Yahweh, the God of Israel, I am bringing upon Jerusalem and Judah such evil that the ears of everyone who hears of it will tingle. [13]I will stretch over Jerusalem the measuring line for Samaria, and the plummet for the house of Ahab; I will wipe Jerusalem as one wipes a dish, wiping it and turning it upside down. [14]I will cast off the remnant of my heritage, and give them into the hand of their enemies; they shall become a prey and a spoil to all their enemies, [15]because they have done what is evil in my sight and have provoked me to anger, since the day their ancestors came out of Egypt, even to this day."

Death of Mannasseh and Reign of Amon (642–640 BCE)

[16]Moreover Manasseh shed very much innocent blood, until he had filled Jerusalem from one end to another, besides the sin that he caused Judah to sin so that they did what was evil in the sight of Yahweh. [17]Now the rest of the acts of Manasseh, all that he did, and the sin that he committed, are they not written in the Book of the Annals of the Kings of Judah? [18]Manasseh slept with his ancestors, and was buried in the garden of his house, in the garden of Uzza. His son Amon succeeded him. [19]Amon was twenty-two years old when he began to reign; he reigned two years in Jerusalem. His mother's name was Meshullemeth daughter of Haruz of Jotbah. [20]He did what was evil in the sight of Yahweh, as his father Manasseh had done. [21]He walked in all the ways in which his father walked, served the idols that his father served, and worshiped them; [22]he abandoned Yahweh, the God of his ancestors, and did not walk in the way of Yahweh. [23]The servants of Amon conspired against him, and killed the king in his house. [24]But the people of the land killed all those who had conspired against King Amon, and the people of the land made his son Josiah king in place of him. [25]Now the rest of the acts of Amon that he did, are they not written in the Book of the Annals of the Kings of Judah? [26]He was buried in his tomb in the garden of Uzza; then his son Josiah succeeded him.

King Josiah of Judah (640–609 BCE)

2 Kings 22

[1]Josiah was eight years old when he began to reign; he reigned thirty one years in Jerusalem. His mother's name was Jedidah daughter of Adaiah of Bozkath. [2]He did what was right in the sight of Yahweh, and walked in all the way of his father David; he did not turn aside to the right or to the left. [3]In the eighteenth year of King Josiah, the king sent Shaphan son of Azaliah, son of Meshullam, the secretary, to the house of Yahweh, saying, [4]"Go up to the high priest Hilkiah, and have him count the entire sum of the money that has been brought into the house of Yahweh, which the keepers of the threshold have collected from the people; [5]let it be given into the hand of the workers who have the oversight of the house of Yahweh; let them give it to the workers who are at the house of Yahweh, repairing the house, [6]that is, to the carpenters, to the builders, to the masons; and let them use it to buy timber and quarried stone to repair the house. [7]But no accounting shall be asked from them for the money that is delivered into their hand, for they deal honestly." [8]The high priest Hilkiah said to Shaphan the secretary, "I have found the book of the law [probably the book of Deuteronomy] in the house of Yahweh."

When Hilkiah gave the book to Shaphan, he read it. [9]Then Shaphan the secretary came to the king, and reported to the king, "Your servants have emptied out the money that was found in the house, and have delivered it into the hand of the workers who have oversight of the house of Yahweh." [10]Shaphan the secretary informed the king, "The priest Hilkiah has given me a book." Shaphan then read it aloud to the king. [11]When the king heard the words of the book of the law, he tore his clothes. [12]Then the king commanded the priest Hilkiah, Ahikam son of Shaphan, Achbor son of Micaiah, Shaphan the secretary, and the king's servant Asaiah, saying, [13]"Go, inquire of Yahweh for me, for the people, and for all Judah, concerning the words of this book that has been found; for great is the wrath of Yahweh that is kindled against us, because our ancestors did not obey the words of this book, to do according to all that is written concerning us."

Why This Book of the Law Was Probably Deuteronomy

[Throughout Deuteronomy, the people are now commanded, not only to worship Yahweh alone, but also to offer sacrifices to Yahweh only in the Jerusalem Temple; although at the same time permission is now granted for the secular slaughter of animals for meat in other locations].

   Deuteronomy 12:13-16, 26-27: "Take care that you do not offer your burnt offerings at any place you happen to see. But only at the place that Yahweh will choose in one of your tribes [i.e., Jerusalem in the tribe of Judah]—there you shall offer your burnt offerings and there you shall do everything I command you. Yet whenever you desire you may slaughter and eat meat within any of your towns, according to the blessing that Yahweh your God has given you…The blood, however, you must not eat; you shall pour it out on the ground like water….But the sacred donations that are due from you, and your votive gifts, you shall bring to the place that Yahweh will choose i.e., the Jerusalem Temple. You shall present your whole burnt offerings, both the meat and the blood, on the altar of Yahweh your God; the blood of your other sacrifices shall be poured out on the altar of Yahweh your God, but the meat you may eat."

Huldah Predicts the Babylonian Exile but That It Will Happen after Josiah's Death

2 Kings 22

[14]So the priest Hilkiah, Ahikam, Achbor, Shaphan, and Asaiah went to the prophetess Huldah the wife of Shallum son of Tikvah, son of Harhas, keeper of the wardrobe; she resided in Jerusalem in the Second Quarter, where they consulted her. [15]She declared to them, "Thus says Yahweh, the God of Israel: Tell the man who sent you to me, [16]Thus says Yahweh, I will indeed bring disaster on this place and on its inhabitants — all the words of the book that the king of Judah has read. [17]Because they have abandoned me and have made offerings to other gods, so that they have provoked me to anger with all the work of their hands, therefore my wrath will be kindled against this place, and it will not be quenched. [18]But as to the king of Judah, who sent you to inquire of Yahweh, thus shall you say to him, Thus says Yahweh, the God of Israel: Regarding the words that you have heard, [19]because your heart was penitent, and you humbled yourself before Yahweh, when you heard how I spoke against this place, and against its inhabitants, that they should become a desolation and a curse, and because you have torn your clothes and wept before me, I also have heard you, says Yahweh. [20]Therefore, I will gather you to your ancestors, and you shall be gathered to your grave in peace; your eyes shall not see all the disaster that I will bring on this place." They took the message back to the king.

Josiah's Reform (ca. 622 BCE)

2 Kings 23

[1]Then the king directed that all the elders of Judah and Jerusalem should be gathered to him. [2]The king went up to the house of Yahweh, and with him went all the people of Judah, all the inhabitants of Jerusalem, the priests, the prophets, and all the people, both small and great; he read in their hearing all the words of the

book of the covenant that had been found in the house of Yahweh. [3]The king stood by the pillar and made a covenant before Yahweh, to follow Yahweh, keeping his commandments, his decrees, and his statutes, with all his heart and all his soul, to perform the words of this covenant that were written in this book. All the people joined in the covenant. [4]The king commanded the high priest Hilkiah, the priests of the second order, and the guardians of the threshold, to bring out of the temple of Yahweh all the vessels made for Baal, for Asherah, and for all the host of heaven; he burned them outside Jerusalem in the fields of the Kidron, and carried their ashes to Bethel. [5]He deposed the idolatrous priests whom the kings of Judah had ordained to make offerings in the high places at the cities of Judah and around Jerusalem; those also who made offerings to Baal, to the sun, the moon, the constellations, and all the host of the heavens. [6]He brought out the image of Asherah from the house of Yahweh, outside Jerusalem, to the Wadi Kidron, burned it at the Wadi Kidron, beat it to dust and threw the dust of it upon the graves of the common people. [7]He broke down the houses of the male temple prostitutes that were in the house of Yahweh, where the women did weaving for Asherah. [8]He brought all the priests out of the towns of Judah, and defiled the high places where the priests had made offerings, from Geba to Beersheba; he broke down the high places of the gates that were at the entrance of the gate of Joshua the governor of the city, which were on the left at the gate of the city. [9]The priests of the high places, however, did not come up to the altar of Yahweh in Jerusalem, but ate unleavened bread among their kindred. [10]He defiled Topheth, which is in the valley of Ben-hinnom, so that no one would make a son or a daughter pass through fire as an offering to Molech. [11]He removed the horses that the kings of Judah had dedicated to the sun, at the entrance to the house of Yahweh, by the chamber of the eunuch Nathan-melech, which was in the precincts; then he burned the chariots of the sun with fire. [12]The altars on the roof of the upper chamber of Ahaz, which the kings of Judah had made, and the altars that Manasseh had made in the two courts of the house of Yahweh, he pulled down from there and broke in pieces, and threw the rubble into the Wadi Kidron. [13]The king defiled the high places that were east of Jerusalem, to the south of the Mount of Destruction, which King Solomon of Israel had built for Astarte the abomination of the Sidonians, for Chemosh the abomination of Moab, and for Milcom the abomination of the Ammonites. [14]He broke the pillars in pieces, cut down the statues of Asherahs, and covered the sites with human bones. [15]Moreover, the altar at Bethel, the high place erected by Jeroboam son of Nebat, who caused Israel to sin — he pulled down that altar along with the high place. He burned the high place, crushing it to dust; he also burned the Asherah. [16]As Josiah turned, he saw the tombs there on the mount; and he sent and took the bones out of the tombs, and burned them on the altar, and defiled it, according to the word of Yahweh that the man of God proclaimed, when Jeroboam stood by the altar at the festival; he turned and looked up at the tomb of the man of God who had predicted these things. [17]Then he said, "What is that monument that I see?" The people of the city told him, "It is the tomb of the man of God who came from Judah and predicted these things that you have done against the altar at Bethel." [18]He said, "Let him rest; let no one move his bones." So they let his bones alone, with the bones of the prophet who came out of Samaria. [19]Moreover, Josiah removed all the shrines of the high places that were in the towns of Samaria, which kings of Israel had made, provoking Yahweh to anger; he did to them just as he had done at Bethel. [20]He slaughtered on the altars all the priests of the high places who were there, and burned human bones on them. Then he returned to Jerusalem. [21]The king commanded all the people, "Keep the passover to Yahweh your God as prescribed in this book of the covenant." [22]No such passover had been kept since the days of the judges who judged Israel, even during all the days of the kings of Israel and of the kings of Judah; [23]but in the eighteenth year of King Josiah this passover was kept to Yahweh in Jerusalem. [24]Moreover Josiah put away the mediums, wizards, teraphim, idols, and all the abominations that were seen in the land of Judah and in Jerusalem, so that he established the words of the law that were written in the book that the priest Hilkiah had found in the house of Yahweh. [25]Before him there was no king like him, who turned to Yahweh with all his heart, with all his soul, and with all his might, according to all the law of Moses; nor did any like him arise after him.

Josiah's Reform Was Not Enough to Prevent the Babylonian Exile

[26]Still Yahweh did not turn from the fierceness of his great wrath, by which his anger was kindled against Judah, because of all the provocations with which Manasseh had provoked him. [27]Yahweh said, "I will remove Judah also out of my sight, as I have removed Israel; and I will reject this city that I have chosen, Jerusalem, and the house of which I said, my name shall be there."

Josiah Dies

[28]Now the rest of the acts of Josiah, and all that he did, are they not written in the Book of the Annals of the Kings of Judah? [29]In his days Pharaoh Neco king of Egypt went up to the king of Assyria to the river Euphrates. King Josiah went to meet him; but when Pharaoh Neco met him at Megiddo, he killed him. [30]His servants carried him dead in a chariot from Megiddo, brought him to Jerusalem, and buried him in his own tomb. The people of the land took Jehoahaz son of Josiah, anointed him, and made him king in place of his father.

Josiah's Successors Abandon His Reforms

[31]Jehoahaz was twenty-three years old when he began to reign; he reigned three months in Jerusalem. His mother's name was Hamutal daughter of Jeremiah of Libnah. [32]He did what was evil in the sight of Yahweh, just as his ancestors had done. [33]Pharaoh Neco confined him at Riblah in the land of Hamath, so that he might not reign in Jerusalem, and imposed tribute on the land of one hundred talents of silver and a talent of gold. [34]Pharaoh Neco made Eliakim son of Josiah king in place of his father Josiah, and changed his name to Jehoiakim. But he took Jehoahaz away; he came to Egypt, and died there. [35]Jehoiakim gave the silver and the gold to Pharaoh, but he taxed the land in order to meet Pharaoh's demand for money. He exacted the silver and the gold from the people of the land, from all according to their assessment, to give it to Pharaoh Neco. [36]Jehoiakim was twenty-five years old when he began to reign; he reigned eleven years in Jerusalem. His mother's name was Zebidah daughter of Pedaiah of Rumah. [37]He did what was evil in the sight of Yahweh, just as all his ancestors had done.

The Sole Remaining Kingdom of Judah is Overrun by Enemies (608–597 BCE)

2 Kings 24:1-25:1

[1]In his days King Nebuchadnezzar of Babylon came up; Jehoiakim became his servant for three years; then he turned and rebelled against him. [2]Yahweh sent against him bands of the Chaldeans [i.e., Babylonians], bands of the Arameans, bands of the Moabites, and bands of the Ammonites; he sent them against Judah to destroy it, according to the word of Yahweh that he spoke by his servants the prophets. [3]Surely this came upon Judah at the command of Yahweh, to remove them out of his sight, for the sins of Manasseh, for all that he had committed, [4]and also for the innocent blood that he had shed; for he filled Jerusalem with innocent blood, and Yahweh was not willing to pardon. [5]Now the rest of the deeds of Jehoiakim, and all that he did, are they not written in the Book of the Annals of the Kings of Judah? [6]So Jehoiakim slept with his ancestors; then his son Jehoiachin succeeded him. [7]The king of Egypt did not come again out of his land, for the king of Babylon had taken over all that belonged to the king of Egypt from the Wadi of Egypt to the River Euphrates.

Reign and Captivity of Jehoiachin (597 BCE)

[8]Jehoiachin was eighteen years old when he began to reign; he reigned for three months in Jerusalem. His mother's name was Nehushta daughter of Elnathan of Jerusalem. [9]He did what was evil in the sight of Yahweh, just as his father had done.

[10]At that time the servants of King Nebuchadnezzar of Babylon came up to Jerusalem, and the city was besieged. [11]King Nebuchadnezzar of Babylon came to the city, while his servants were besieging it; [12]King Jehoiachin of Judah gave himself up to the king of Babylon, himself, his mother, his servants, his officers, and his palace officials. The king of Babylon took him prisoner in the eighth year of his reign.

Capture of Jerusalem by the Babylonians (597 BCE)

[13]He [Nebuchadnezzar] carried off all the treasures of the house of Yahweh, and the treasures of the king's house; he cut in pieces all the vessels of gold in the temple of Yahweh, which King Solomon of Israel had

made, all this as Yahweh had foretold. [14]He carried away all Jerusalem, all the officials, all the warriors, ten thousand captives, all the artisans and the smiths; no one remained, except the poorest people of the land. [15]He carried away Jehoiachin to Babylon; the king's mother, the king's wives, his officials, and the elite of the land, he took into captivity from Jerusalem to Babylon. [16]The king of Babylon brought captive to Babylon all the men of valor, seven thousand, the artisans and the smiths, one thousand, all of them strong and fit for war. [17]The king of Babylon made Mattaniah, Jehoiachin's uncle, king in his place, and changed his name to Zedekiah.

Zedekiah Reigns Over Judah (597–586 BCE)

[18]Zedekiah was twenty-one years old when he began to reign; he reigned for eleven years in Jerusalem. His mother's name was Hamutal daughter of Jeremiah of Libnah. [19]He did what was evil in the sight of Yahweh, just as Jehoiakim had done. [20]Indeed, Jerusalem and Judah so angered Yahweh that he expelled them from his presence.

The Fall and Captivity of Judah

Zedekiah rebelled against the king of Babylon. [21]And in the ninth year of his reign, in the tenth month, on the tenth day of the month, King Nebuchadnezzar of Babylon came with all his army against Jerusalem, and laid siege to it; they built siege-works against it all round.

Jeremiah's Sign of the Yoke (during Zedekiah's Rebellion Between 597 and 586 BCE)

Jeremiah 27:1—28:17

[27]In the beginning of the reign of King Zedekiah son of Josiah of Judah, this word came to Jeremiah from Yahweh. [2]Thus Yahweh said to me: Make yourself a yoke of straps and bars, and put them on your neck. [3]Send word to the king of Edom, the king of Moab, the king of the Ammonites, the king of Tyre, and the king of Sidon by the hand of the envoys who have come to Jerusalem to King Zedekiah of Judah. [4]Give them this charge for their masters: Thus says Yahweh of hosts, the God of Israel: This is what you shall say to your masters: [5]It is I who by my great power and my outstretched arm have made the earth, with the people and animals that are on the earth, and I give it to whomsoever I please. [6]Now I have given all these lands into the hand of King Nebuchadnezzar of Babylon, my servant, and I have given him even the wild animals of the field to serve him. [7]All the nations shall serve him and his son and his grandson, until the time of his own land comes; then many nations and great kings shall make him their slave.

[8]But if any nation or kingdom will not serve this king, Nebuchadnezzar of Babylon, and put its neck under the yoke of the king of Babylon, then I will punish that nation with the sword, with famine, and with pestilence, says Yahweh, until I have completed its destruction by his hand. [9]You, therefore, must not listen to your prophets, your diviners, your dreamers, your soothsayers, or your sorcerers, who are saying to you, 'You shall not serve the king of Babylon.' [10]For they are prophesying a lie to you, with the result that you will be removed far from your land; I will drive you out, and you will perish. [11]But any nation that will bring its neck under the yoke of the king of Babylon and serve him, I will leave on its own land, says Yahweh, to till it and live there.

[12]I spoke to King Zedekiah of Judah in the same way: Bring your necks under the yoke of the king of Babylon, and serve him and his people, and live. [13]Why should you and your people die by the sword, by famine, and by pestilence, as Yahweh has spoken concerning any nation that will not serve the king of Babylon? [14]Do not listen to the words of the prophets who are telling you not to serve the king of Babylon, for they are prophesying a lie to you. [15]I have not sent them, says Yahweh, but they are prophesying falsely in my name, with the result that I will drive you out and you will perish, you and the prophets who are prophesying to you.

[16]Then I spoke to the priests and to all this people, saying, Thus says Yahweh: Do not listen to the words of your prophets who are prophesying to you, saying, 'The vessels of Yahweh's house will soon be brought back from Babylon', for they are prophesying a lie to you. [17]Do not listen to them; serve the king of Babylon and live. Why should this city become a desolation? [18]If indeed they are prophets, and if the word of Yahweh is with them, then let them intercede with Yahweh of hosts, that the vessels left in the house of Yahweh, in the house of the king of Judah, and in Jerusalem may not go to Babylon. [19]For thus says Yahweh of hosts concerning the pillars, the sea, the stands, and the rest of the vessels that are left in this city, [20]which King Nebuchadnezzar of Babylon did not take away when he took into exile from Jerusalem to Babylon King Jeconiah son of Jehoiakim of Judah, and all the nobles of Judah and Jerusalem— [21]thus says Yahweh of hosts, the God of Israel, concerning the vessels left in the house of Yahweh, in the house of the king of Judah, and in Jerusalem: [22]They shall be carried to Babylon, and there they shall stay, until the day when I give attention to them, says Yahweh. Then I will bring them up and restore them to this place.

[28]In that same year, at the beginning of the reign of King Zedekiah of Judah, in the fifth month of the fourth year, the prophet Hananiah son of Azzur, from Gibeon, spoke to me in the house of Yahweh, in the presence of the priests and all the people, saying, [2]'Thus says Yahweh of hosts, the God of Israel: I have broken the yoke of the king of Babylon. [3]Within two years I will bring back to this place all the vessels of Yahweh's house, which King Nebuchadnezzar of Babylon took away from this place and carried to Babylon. [4]I will also bring back to this place King Jeconiah son of Jehoiakim of Judah, and all the exiles from Judah who went to Babylon, says Yahweh, for I will break the yoke of the king of Babylon.'

[5]Then the prophet Jeremiah spoke to the prophet Hananiah in the presence of the priests and all the people who were standing in the house of Yahweh; [6]and the prophet Jeremiah said, 'Amen! May Yahweh do so; may Yahweh fulfil the words that you have prophesied, and bring back to this place from Babylon the vessels of the house of Yahweh, and all the exiles. [7]But listen now to this word that I speak in your hearing and in the hearing of all the people. [8]The prophets who preceded you and me from ancient times prophesied war, famine, and pestilence against many countries and great kingdoms. [9]As for the prophet who prophesies peace, when the word of that prophet comes true, then it will be known that Yahweh has truly sent the prophet.'

[10]Then the prophet Hananiah took the yoke from the neck of the prophet Jeremiah, and broke it. [11]And Hananiah spoke in the presence of all the people, saying, 'Thus says Yahweh: This is how I will break the yoke of King Nebuchadnezzar of Babylon from the neck of all the nations within two years.' At this, the prophet Jeremiah went his way.

[12]Some time after the prophet Hananiah had broken the yoke from the neck of the prophet Jeremiah, the word of Yahweh came to Jeremiah: [13]Go, tell Hananiah, Thus says Yahweh: You have broken wooden bars only to forge iron bars in place of them! [14]For thus says Yahweh of hosts, the God of Israel: I have put an iron yoke on the neck of all these nations so that they may serve King Nebuchadnezzar of Babylon, and they shall indeed serve him; I have even given him the wild animals. [15]And the prophet Jeremiah said to the prophet Hananiah, 'Listen, Hananiah, Yahweh has not sent you, and you made this people trust in a lie. [16]Therefore thus says Yahweh: I am going to send you off the face of the earth. Within this year you will be dead, because you have spoken rebellion against Yahweh.'

[17]In that same year, in the seventh month, the prophet Hananiah died.

The Destruction of Jerusalem and the Temple and the Beginning of the Babylonian Exile (586 BCE)

2 Kings 25:1-21

[1]And in the ninth year of his [Zedekiah's] reign, in the tenth month, on the tenth day of the month, King Nebuchadnezzar of Babylon came with all his army against Jerusalem, and laid siege to it; they built siege-works against it all round. [2]So the city was besieged until the eleventh year of King Zedekiah. [3]On the ninth day of the fourth month the famine became so severe in the city that there was no food for the people of the land. [4]Then a breach was made in the city wall; the king with all the soldiers fled by night by the way of the gate between the

two walls, by the king's garden, though the Chaldeans [i.e., the Babylonians] were all round the city. They went in the direction of the Arabah. [5]But the army of the Chaldeans [i.e., the Babylonians] pursued the king, and overtook him in the plains of Jericho; all his army was scattered, deserting him. [6]Then they captured the king and brought him up to the king of Babylon at Riblah, who passed sentence on him. [7]They slaughtered the sons of Zedekiah before his eyes, then put out the eyes of Zedekiah; they bound him in fetters and took him to Babylon.

[8]In the fifth month, on the seventh day of the month—which was the nineteenth year of King Nebuchadnezzar, king of Babylon—Nebuzaradan, the captain of the bodyguard, a servant of the king of Babylon, came to Jerusalem. [9]He burned the house of Yahweh, the king's house, and all the houses of Jerusalem; every great house he burned down. [10]All the army of the Chaldeans [i.e., the Babylonians] who were with the captain of the guard broke down the walls around Jerusalem. [11]Nebuzaradan the captain of the guard carried into exile the rest of the people who were left in the city and the deserters who had defected to the king of Babylon— all the rest of the population. [12]But the captain of the guard left some of the poorest people of the land to be vine-dressers and tillers of the soil.

[13]The bronze pillars that were in the house of Yahweh, as well as the stands and the bronze sea that were in the house of Yahweh, the Chaldeans [i.e., the Babylonians] broke in pieces, and carried the bronze to Babylon. [14]They took away the pots, the shovels, the snuffers, the dishes for incense, and all the bronze vessels used in the temple service, [15]as well as the fire pans and the basins. What was made of gold the captain of the guard took away for the gold, and what was made of silver, for the silver. [16]As for the two pillars, the one sea, and the stands, which Solomon had made for the house of Yahweh, the bronze of all these vessels was beyond weighing. [17]The height of one pillar was eighteen cubits, and on it was a bronze capital; the height of the capital was three cubits; lattice-work and pomegranates, all of bronze, were on the capital all round. The second pillar had the same, with the lattice-work.

[18]The captain of the guard took the chief priest Seraiah, the second priest Zephaniah, and the three guardians of the threshold; [19]from the city he took an officer who had been in command of the soldiers, and five men of the king's council who were found in the city; the secretary who was the commander of the army who mustered the people of the land; and sixty men of the people of the land who were found in the city. [20]Nebuzaradan the captain of the guard took them, and brought them to the king of Babylon at Riblah. [21]The king of Babylon struck them down and put them to death at Riblah in the land of Hamath. So Judah went into exile out of its land.

Excerpt from Second Isaiah Regarding Cyrus, King of Persia, Predicting that He Will Allow the Exiled Jews to Return to Jerusalem Around 639 BCE

Isaiah 44:24–45:23

24 Thus says Yahweh, your Redeemer,
    who formed you in the womb:
I am Yahweh, who made all things,
    who alone stretched out the heavens,
    who by myself spread out the earth;
25 who frustrates the omens of liars,
    and makes fools of diviners;
who turns back the wise,
    and makes their knowledge foolish;
26 who confirms the word of his servant,
    and fulfils the prediction of his messengers;
who says of Jerusalem, 'It shall be inhabited',
    and of the cities of Judah, 'They shall be rebuilt,
    and I will raise up their ruins';

27 who says to the deep, 'Be dry—
    I will dry up your rivers';
28 who says of Cyrus, 'He is my shepherd,
    and he shall carry out all my purpose';
and who says of Jerusalem, 'It shall be rebuilt',
    and of the temple, 'Your foundation shall be laid.'

Cyrus, Yahweh's Messiah

45 Thus says Yahweh to his Messiah [lit., his anointed], to Cyrus,
    whose right hand I have grasped
to subdue nations before him
    and strip kings of their robes,
to open doors before him—
    and the gates shall not be closed:
2 I will go before you
    and level the mountains,
I will break in pieces the doors of bronze
    and cut through the bars of iron,
3 I will give you the treasures of darkness
    and riches hidden in secret places,
so that you may know that it is I, Yahweh,
    the God of Israel, who call you by your name.
4 For the sake of my servant Jacob,
    and Israel my chosen,
I call you by your name,
    I surname you, though you do not know me.
5 I am Yahweh, and there is no other;
    besides me there is no god.
    I arm you, though you do not know me,
6 so that they may know, from the rising of the sun
    and from the west, that there is no one besides me;
    I am Yahweh, and there is no other.
7 I form light and create darkness,
    I make weal and create woe;
    I Yahweh do all these things.
8 Shower, O heavens, from above,
    and let the skies rain down righteousness;
let the earth open, that salvation may spring up,
    and let it cause righteousness to sprout up also;
    I Yahweh have created it.

9 Woe to you who strive with your Maker,
    earthen vessels with the potter!
Does the clay say to the one who fashions it, 'What are you making?'
    or 'Your work has no handles'?
10 Woe to anyone who says to a father, 'What are you begetting?'
    or to a woman, 'With what are you in labour?'
11 Thus says Yahweh,
    the Holy One of Israel, and its Maker:

Will you question me about my children,
   or command me concerning the work of my hands?
12 I made the earth,
   and created humankind upon it;
it was my hands that stretched out the heavens,
   and I commanded all their host.
13 I have aroused Cyrus in righteousness,
   and I will make all his paths straight;
he shall build my city
   and set my exiles free,
not for price or reward,
   says Yahweh of hosts.
14 Thus says Yahweh:
The wealth of Egypt and the merchandise of Ethiopia,
   and the Sabeans, tall of stature,
shall come over to you and be yours,
   they shall follow you;
   they shall come over in chains and bow down to you.
They will make supplication to you, saying,
   'God is with you alone, and there is no other;
   there is no god besides him.'
15 Truly, you are a God who hides himself,
   O God of Israel, the Saviour.
16 All of them are put to shame and confounded,
   the makers of idols go in confusion together.
17 But Israel is saved by Yahweh
   with everlasting salvation;
you shall not be put to shame or confounded
   to all eternity.

18 For thus says Yahweh,
who created the heavens
   (he is God!),
who formed the earth and made it
   (he established it;
he did not create it a chaos,
   he formed it to be inhabited!):
I am Yahweh, and there is no other.
19 I did not speak in secret,
   in a land of darkness;
I did not say to the offspring of Jacob,
   'Seek me in chaos.'
I Yahweh speak the truth,
   I declare what is right.

20 Assemble yourselves and come together,
   draw near, you survivors of the nations!
They have no knowledge—
   those who carry about their wooden idols,
and keep on praying to a god
   that cannot save.

21 Declare and present your case;
    let them take counsel together!
Who told this long ago?
    Who declared it of old?
Was it not I, Yahweh?
    There is no other god besides me,
a righteous God and a Saviour;
    there is no one besides me.

22 Turn to me and be saved,
    all the ends of the earth!
    For I am God, and there is no other.
23 By myself I have sworn,
    from my mouth has gone forth in righteousness
    a word that shall not return:
'To me every knee shall bow,
    every tongue shall swear.'

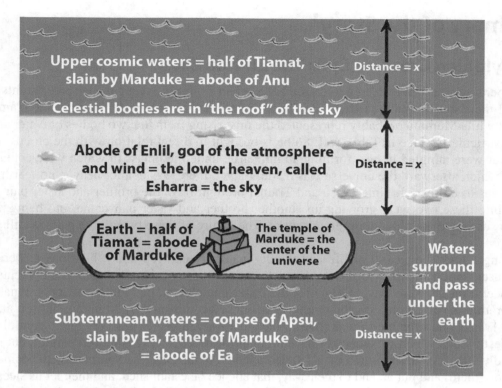

The Cosmology of the Babylonian Creation Epic, the *Enuma Elish*
© Sharon Lea Mattila

[handwritten notes:]
Done separate / the water from water

1. Water
2. Dome
3. Dry land
4. light: sun
moon: stars
5. Birds + fish = evening + morning
6. land animals / humankind

**The Cosmology of the Priestly Account of Creation
(Genesis 1)**
From BANDSTRA. *Reading of the Old Testament*, 1E. © 1995 Wadsworth, a part of
Cengage Learning, Inc. Reproduced by permission. www.cengage.com/permissions

[handwritten note:]
Thought the earth was flat!

A Summary of the Story[*]

The Babylonian Creation Epic: The Enuma Elish

The epic opens with a brief reference to the time when nothing except the divine parents, Apsû and Tiâmat, and their son Mummu existed. Apsû was the primeval sweet-water ocean, and Tiâmat the salt-water ocean, while Mummu probably represented the mist rising from the two bodies of water and hovering over them, particularly since in Tablet VII: 86 he is brought in direct relation with the clouds. These three types of water were mingled in one, forming an immense, undefined mass in which were contained all the elements of which afterward the universe was made. As yet, there was neither heaven nor earth, not even a reed marsh was to be seen. In time, Apsû and Tiâmat brought forth the brother and sister pair Laḫmu and Laḫâmu. While these two were growing up, another brother and sister pair came into being, Anshar and Kishar, who surpassed the older children in stature. The nature of these two divine pairs is still a matter for conjecture.

The younger gods, being full of life and vitality, naturally enjoyed noisy, hilarious gatherings. These, however, caused serious distress to their old, inactive, and rest-loving parents and grandparents, Apsû and Tiâmat. Peaceful means were tried to diminish the disturbing clamor, but without success. Finally, Apsû, in utter exasperation, resolved on a drastic course of action. Accompanied by Mummu, his son and vizier, he went before Tiâmat and submitted a plan to her which made her motherly heart cry out in painful rage: "Why should we destroy that which we ourselves have brought forth? Their way is indeed painful, but let us take it good-naturedly!" But Apsû, supported by his vizier, adhered to his expressed purpose with adamant tenacity: "I will destroy (them) and put an end to their way, that silence be established, and then let us sleep!"

At the break of the news, the gods were filled with consternation and ran about aimlessly. Finally, they quieted down and sat in silent gloom, without anyone being able to suggest a way of deliverance. Fortunately, in that dark hour there was found one who was master even of Apsû; it was Ea, "the one of supreme under-standing, the skilful, (and) wise," the god of magic. He made a magic circle of some kind around the gods, as a protection against attack, and then composed an overpowering, holy incantation. He recited it and caused it to descend, as a soporific force, upon Apsû. As Ea recited his incantation, Apsû succumbed to the power of the spell and sank into a profound sleep. And as Apsû was lying there, suffused with sleep, Ea removed his royal tiara and his supernatural radiance and clothed himself therewith. After he had thus come into possession of Apsû's might and splendor, he slew the father of all the gods and imprisoned his vizier, gaining his victory chiefly through the application of authority or power inherent in the spoken word, the magic of the spell. Tiâmat remained unmolested, since she had not been in sympathy with Apsû's designs. Upon the slain Apsû, Ea subsequently established a spacious abode. He named it "Apsû" and appointed it for shrines for himself and for other deities. There he and his wife, Damkina, dwelt in splendor.

There also it was that Marduk, "the wisest of the gods," was born, the one who was destined some day to deliver the gods from an even more dreadful foe and to become the head of the vast Babylonian pantheon. "He who begot him was Ea, his father. Damki[na], his mother, was she who bore him. He sucked the breasts of goddesses" and thus imbibed additional divine power and qualities. Marduk was an imposing figure, endowed with flashing eyes and awe-inspiring majesty. When his father beheld him, "he rejoiced, he beamed, his heart was filled with joy." Evidently by means of magic, Ea then conferred upon his son double equality with the gods, which manifested itself in the two faces of Marduk and the doubled dimensions of his members, so that "he was exalted among the gods."

In the meantime, Tiâmat was disturbed, doubtless because of the violent death of her husband. Day and night, she restlessly moved about. Her restlessness mounted as some of the gods, led by Kingu (cf. Tablet VI: 23–30), in their wickedness instigated her to avenge the death of her spouse. Tiâmat yielded and decided on war against the gods who were either responsible for or in sympathy with the murder of her husband.

The rebel gods now publicly seceded and went over to the side of Tiâmat; they raged and plotted, not resting day or night; "they held a meeting and planned the conflict." Tiâmat, on her part, gave birth to eleven kinds of monster serpents and ferocious dragons for the impending contest; she exalted Kingu to be her new spouse, she entrusted

[*] From Alexander Heidel, "The Babylonian Genesis: The Story of Creation." Copyright © 1951 by University of Chicago. Reprinted by permission.

him with the high command of the battle, gave him dominion over all the gods, and presented him with the coveted tablet of destinies with all its magic powers. A formidable demonic host had suddenly sprung into existence.

It was not until Tiâmat was almost ready for the assault that someone informed Ea of the imminent peril. When Ea, the wise and skilful, the hero who had vanquished Apsû, heard of the impending danger, he was benumbed with fear and dismay. When he had thought the matter over and had regained his composure, he went to Anshar, his grandfather, and "communicated to him all that Tiâmat had planned" and the preparations she had made, repeating word for word the report which he himself had received. Anshar was moved to expressions of deepest grief and grave concern and appealed to Ea to proceed against the foe. Ea obeyed the voice of his grandfather, but the venture, though undertaken by him who had achieved such a decisive victory over Apsû, ended in failure. Anshar then turned to his son Anu, urging him to try peaceful measures, saying: "[Go a]nd stand thou before Tiâmat, [that] her spirit [become quiet and] her heart calm down. [If] she does not hearken to thy word, speak our [word(?)] to her, that she may be quieted." Anu went, armed with his own authority and that of the leader of the gods. But, unlike Apsû, Tiâmat could not be overcome by any amount of mere authority or any degree of mere magic power; she had to be conquered through the application of physical force. Anu returned in terror, asking to be relieved of the task. Anshar lapsed into silence, looking upon the ground and shaking his head. "All the Anunnaki were assembled at the place. Their lips were closed, [they sat in] silence." Never before had the gods been in such a plight. The picture is painted in extremely dark and somber colors to make the greatness of the subsequent victory all the more evident.

In this moment of supreme crisis, a happy thought occurred to Anshar; he remembered the prowess of valiant Marduk, who in some way had already proved his valor (cf. Tablet II: 95) and who certainly would not fail. Marduk was summoned into the presence of Ea, to be instructed by his father, and then appeared before Anshar. When Anshar saw the young Marduk, abounding in strength and radiating confidence, "his heart was filled with joy; he kissed his lips, his fear was removed," while Marduk assured him: "[Anshar], be not silent, (but) open thy lips; I will go and accomplish all that is in thy heart! [My father, c]reator, be glad and rejoice; soon thou shalt trample upon the neck of Tiâmat!" There was no doubt in anyone's mind that Marduk, despite his youth, could save the gods from their powerful enemy. Moreover, Marduk was ready to go to battle and deliver the gods from disaster. But he demanded a high price—supreme and undisputed authority among the gods. Anshar agreed to the terms (cf. Tablet III: 65–66), but the decision had to be confirmed by the gods in their assembly.

Anshar therefore dispatched Kaka, his vizier, to Laḫmu and Laḫâmu and all the other gods who were living at a great distance and, consequently, had as yet no knowledge of the impending struggle. Kaka was to inform the gods of the gravity of the situation and to summon them into the presence of Anshar. After a few prefatory remarks, Anshar gave Kaka a verbatim repetition of the account of Tiâmat's hostile activities and charged him to repeat the message word for word to Laḫmu and Laḫâmu. Kaka went and repeated Anshar's speech in every detail.[1] Upon learning of the sudden and unparalleled crisis, the gods were perplexed and horrified, they cried aloud and wailed painfully. They departed and entered into the presence of Anshar, filling the Court of Assembly. They kissed one another as they met, and then sat down to a banquet, which Anshar had prepared to put the gods in the right frame of mind. "The sweet wine dispelled their fears; [their] bod[ies] swelled as they drank the strong drink. Exceedingly carefree were they, their spirit was exalted; for Marduk, their avenger, they decreed the destiny."

After the feast, the gods erected a lordly throne-dais for Marduk, and the young god sat down before his fathers to receive sovereignty. In a solemn speech, the gods conferred upon him the powers of the supreme position in the pantheon and gave him "kingship over the totality of the whole universe." To determine whether Marduk actually had this power, the gods made a test. They placed a garment in their midst. At his command, the garment was destroyed; again at his command, the garment was restored to its former condition. When the gods beheld the efficacy of his word, they rejoiced and paid homage, acclaiming Marduk king of the gods. They invested him with the royal insignia, the scepter, the throne, and the royal robe(?), adding thereto "an irresistible weapon smiting the enemy," with the plea: "Go and cut off the life of Tiâmat!"

Marduk departed to prepare for the fray. He made a bow, put an arrowhead on the arrow, and grasped a club in his right hand; the bow and quiver he hung at his side; like the stormgod, he caused lightning to precede him; he filled his body with a blazing flame; he made a net and had the four winds, the gift of Anu, carry it for him; as a further aid, he created seven winds of his own; he raised the rain-flood and mounted his irresistible, terrible storm chariot, drawn by four frightful mythological creatures. Clad in a terrifying coat of mail, with an overpowering brightness about his head, and supplied with various apotropaic means, Marduk then set out to meet the seemingly invincible Ti'âmat, the gods milling around him.

The mere appearance of Marduk, arrayed in all his terrifying might and dazzling splendor, threw Kingu and his helpers into confusion. Ti'âmat alone remained unperturbed, greeting Marduk with awful taunts and apparently a loud roar to frighten the youthful god. But Marduk was of tougher fiber than his father Ea and his grandfather Anu. Without being in the least disturbed, he denounced Ti'âmat in trenchant terms for her wicked measures and challenged her to a duel! "When Ti'âmat heard this, she became like one in a frenzy (and) lost her reason. She cried out loud (and) furiously," shaking to her very foundations! But she accepted the challenge, and the two pressed on to single combat. Marduk spread out his net and enmeshed her. "When Ti'âmat opened her mouth to devour him, he drove in the evil wind, in order that (she should) not (be able) to close her lips." As the raging winds distended her body, Marduk shot an arrow through her open mouth; it struck her heart and destroyed her life. Having thus killed Ti'âmat, he cast down her carcass and victoriously stood upon it. When her followers saw that their leader was dead, they dispersed and tried to flee. But none escaped.

The enemy gods were imprisoned and deprived of their weapons. Marduk took from Kingu the tablet of destinies, sealed it with his own seal, to prove his ownership and to legalize his claim to it, and fastened it on his breast. After having strengthened his hold upon the captive gods, he returned to Ti'âmat, split her skull with his unsparing club, cut her arteries, and caused the north wind to carry her blood southward to out-of-the-way places. Finally, he divided the colossal body of Ti'âmat into two parts to create the universe. With one half of her corpse he formed the sky, with the other he fashioned the earth, and then established Anu, Enlil, and Ea in their respective domains.

Next, he created stations in the sky for the great gods; he organized the calendar, by setting up stellar constellations to determine, by their rising and setting, the year, the months, and the days; he built gates in the east and in the west for the sun to enter and to depart; in the very center of the sky he fixed the zenith; he caused the moon to shine forth and entrusted the night to her. After some detailed orders to the moon, the tablet dealing with the creation and organization of the heavenly bodies breaks off.

The imprisoned gods, who had joined the ranks of Ti'âmat, were made the servants of the victors, for whose sustenance they had to provide. However, their menial task proved so burdensome that they asked Marduk for relief. As Marduk listened to the words of the captive gods, he resolved to create man and to impose on him the service which the defeated deities had to render. In consultation with Ea, it was then decided to kill the ringleader of the rebels, to create mankind with his blood, and to set the captive gods free. In a solemn court Kingu was indicted. He it was who "created the strife," who "caused Ti'âmat to revolt and prepare for battle." Accordingly, Kingu was bound and brought before Ea. With the aid of certain gods, Ea severed his arteries and created mankind with his blood, acting on the ingenious plans of Marduk. Man now had to take over the work of the defeated army of gods and feed the host of Babylonian divinities.

Next, Marduk divided the totality of the Anunnaki, a name which in the early period seems to have been a general designation for all the gods of heaven and earth. Marduk set three hundred of them in the heavens, and three hundred he assigned to the earth, allotting to each group their appropriate tasks.

As a token of gratitude for their deliverance at the hands of Marduk, the Anunnaki built the city of Babylon and Marduk's great temple Esagila with its stagetower. Then the gods, after a joyful banquet, in solemn assembly, recited the fifty names of Marduk. As the gods had previously met in the Court of Assembly to invest Marduk with supreme regal power and authority before he set out against Ti'âmat, so they were gathered again in the same place to confer upon him fifty titles with all the attributes and abilities of the various gods of the pantheon, thus making "his way pre-eminent," in further appreciation of all that Marduk had done.

The poem closes with an epilogue urging the people to study these names, to hold them in remembrance, and to rejoice in Marduk, that it may be well with them.[2]

---

[1] The constant verbatim repetition of the description of Ti'âmat's preparations for war is fully consonant with the style of the Babylonian poets, as we can discern from the Gilgamesh Epic and other literary productions. The same stylistic feature is observable in the epical literature of Ras Shamra (see H. L. Ginsberg in the *Bulletin of the American Schools of Oriental Research*, No. 84 [1941], pp. 12–13).

The Object of the Epic

Enûma elish is the principal source of our knowledge of Mesopotamian cosmology. While the various other creation stories treat of certain aspects of the cosmos, *Enûma elish* gives us an account of the origin and the order of the universe as a whole. The universe, in its component parts, begins with the gods, who represent cosmic elements or forces in nature (although the character of some of the gods is still uncertain), and is organized and completed through the creative activities of Marduk, the author of the present world order.

Yet, *Enûma elish* is not primarily a creation story at all. If we were to put together all the lines which treat of creation, including the theogony and even granting that most of the missing portion of Tablet V deals with works of creation, they would cover not even two of the seven tablets but only about as much space as is devoted to Marduk's fifty names in Tablets VI and VII. The brief and meager account of Marduk's acts of creation is in sharp contrast to the circumstantial description of his birth and growth, his preparations for battle, his conquest of Tiâmat and her host, and the elaborate and pompous proclamation and explanation of his fifty names. If the creation of the universe were the prime purpose of the epic, much more emphasis should have been placed on this point.

As it is, there can be no doubt that, in its present form, *Enûma elish* is first and foremost a literary monument in honor of Marduk as the champion of the gods and the creator of heaven and earth. Its prime object is to offer cosmological reasons for Marduk's advancement from the position as chief god of Babylon to that of head of the entire Babylonian pantheon. This was achieved by attributing to him the defeat of Tiâmat and the creation and maintenance of the universe. The description of the birth of the gods and of the subsequent struggle between Ea and Apsû and the account of origin of the universe were added mainly for the purpose of furthering the cause of Marduk; the former was included as the antecedent to Marduk's conflict with Tiâmat and his accession to supreme power among the gods, while the latter, the story of the creation of the universe, was added not so much for the sake of giving an account of how all things came into being, but chiefly because it further served to enhance the glory of Marduk and helped to justify his claim to sovereignty over all things visible and invisible.

Next to the purpose of singing the praises of Marduk comes the desire, on the part of the Babylonian priests, who were responsible for the composition of this epic, to sing the praises of Babylon, the city of Marduk, and to strengthen her claim to supremacy over all the cities of the land. Babylon's claim to supremacy was justified already by the fact that it was Babylon's god who had conquered Tiâmat and had created and organized the universe. It was further supported by tracing Babylon's origin back to the very beginnings of time and by attributing her foundation to the great Anunnaki themselves, who built Babylon as a dwelling place for Marduk and the gods in general (Tablet VI: 45–73). Our epic is thus not only a religious treatise but also a political one.

Excerpt from the *Enûma elish,* Tablet IV, lines 121-146

121. He took from him the tablet of destinies, which was not his rightful possession.

122. He sealed (it) with (his) seal and fastened (it) on his breast.[3]

123. After he had vanquished (and) subdued his enemies,

124. Had overpowered the arrogant foe like a bull(?),

125. Had fully established Anshar's victory over the enemy,

126. Had attained the desire of Nudimmud,[4] the valiant Marduk

---

[2] This summary has benefited to some degree from Thorkild Jacobsen's observations in Frankfort, Wilson, Jacobsen, and Irwin, *The Intellectual Adventure of Ancient Man* (Chicago, 1947), pp. 170–83.

[3] *Lit.*: he seized (it) with his breast.

[4] Marduk carried out his father's plan and thus succeeded where Ea had failed.

127. Strengthened his hold upon the captive gods;

128. And then he returned to Ti'âmat, whom he had subdued.

129. The lord trod upon the hinder part of Ti'âmat,

130. And with his unsparing club he split (her) skull.

131. He cut the arteries of her blood

132. And caused the north wind to carry (it) to out-of-the-way places.

133. When his fathers[5] saw (this), they were glad and rejoiced

134. (And) sent him dues (and) greeting-gifts.

135. The lord rested, examining her dead body,

136. To divide the abortion[6] (and) to create ingenious things (therewith).

137. He split her open like a mussel(?) into two (parts);

138. Half of her he set in place and formed the sky (therewith) as a roof.

139. He fixed the crossbar (and) posted guards;

140. He commanded them not to let her waters escape.[7]

141. He crossed the heavens and examined the regions.

142. He placed himself opposite the *Apsû,* the dwelling of Nudimmud.

143. The lord measured the dimensions of the *Apsû,*

144. And a great structure, its[8] counterpart, he established, (namely,) Esharra,

145. The great structure Esharra which he made as a canopy.[9]

146. Anu, Enlil, and Ea he (then) caused to inhabit their residences.[10]

[5] I.e., Anshar, Ea, and the other older gods.
[6] See Thureau-Dangin in *Revue d'assyriologie,* XIX (1922), 81 f. The monstrous corpse of Ti'âmat is here compared to a thing as repulsive as an abortion.
[7] I.e., the waters of Ti'âmat which were contained in that half of her body which Marduk used in the construction of the sky.
[8] I.e., the counterpart of the *Apsû.*
[9] Esharra in this passage is a poetic designation of the earth, which is pictured as a great structure, in the shape of a canopy, placed over the *Apsû.* For this interpretation see Jensen, *Die Kosmologie der Babylonier* (Strassburg, 1890), pp. 195–201, and *Assyrisch-babylonische Mythen und Epen* (Berlin, 1900), pp. 344f.; Morris Jastrow, Jr., *The Religion of Babylonia and Assyria* (Boston, 1898), pp. 430–32. The import of the second half of this line cannot be that Marduk at this time created the sky, for the sky was made already in 1. 138.
[10] Now that heaven and earth were completed, Anu, Enlil, and Ea, at the instance of Marduk, occupied their residences, which must not be confused with the stations mentioned in the next tablet, for these were set up later, as is evident from Tablet V:7–8. Anu occupied the sky, Enlil the air and the surface of the earth, and Ea the sweet waters in and on the earth. Enlil was god not only of the air but also of the surface of the earth, as is attested by the fact that in the Gilgamesh Epic, Tablet XI:41, Babylonia (or a certain area thereof) is called "the land of Enlil," and by his titles "lord of the land," "lord of the whole land," "lord of the lands," and "king of the lands." Before the creation of the earth, Ea lived in his *Apsû,* the building of which is recorded in Tablet I. Now he took possession of those areas which he occupied in historic times, viz., all the sweet waters on and below the surface of the earth, his realm embracing the waters in the underground strata, the wells and springs, the rivers, lagoons, and marshes.

The Priestly Account of Creation*    only 1 God

Genesis 1:1-2:3

(The NRSV translation of the Hebrew, with some modifications by Sharon Lea Mattila)

1 [1]In the beginning when God began to create the heavens (Heb. *ha-shamayim*) and the earth, [2]the earth was a formless void and darkness covered the face of the deep, while a wind (or breath) of God swept over the face of the waters (Heb. *ha-mayim*).

[3]Then God said, "Let there be light"; and there was light. [4]And God saw that the light was good; and God separated the light from the darkness. [5]God called the light Day, and the darkness he called Night. And there was evening and there was morning, one day.

[6]And God said, "Let there be a dome in the midst of the waters (Heb. *ha-mayim*), and let it separate the waters (Heb. *ha-mayim*) from the waters (Heb. *ha-mayim*)." [7]So God made the dome and separated the waters (Heb. *ha-mayim*) that were under the dome from the waters (Heb. *ha-mayim*) that were above the dome. And it was so. [8]God called the dome heavens (Heb. *shamayim*). And there was evening and there was morning, the second day.

[9]And God said, "Let the waters (Heb. *ha-mayim*) under the heavens (Heb. *ha-shamayim*) be collected together into one place, and let the dry land appear." And it was so. [10]God called the dry land Earth, and the collection of the waters (Heb. *ha-mayim*) that were gathered together he called Seas. And God saw that it was good. [11]Then God said, "Let the earth put forth vegetation: plants yielding seed, and fruit trees of every kind on earth that bear fruit with the seed in it." And it was so. [12]The earth brought forth vegetation: plants yielding seed of every kind, and trees of every kind bearing fruit with the seed in it. And God saw that it was good. [13]And there was evening and there was morning, the third day.

[14]And God said, "Let there be lights in the dome of the heavens (Heb. *ha-shamayim*) to separate the day from the night; and let them be for signs and for seasons and for days and years, [15]and let them be lights in the dome of the heavens (Heb. *ha-shamayim*) to give light upon the earth." And it was so. [16]God made the two great lights—the greater light to rule the day and the lesser light to rule the night—and the stars. [17]God set them in the dome of the heavens (Heb. *ha-shamayim*) to give light upon the earth, [18]to rule over the day and over the night, and to separate the light from the darkness. And God saw that it was good. [19]And there was evening and there was morning, the fourth day.

[20]And God said, "Let the waters (Heb. *ha-mayim*) bring forth swarms of living creatures, and let birds fly above the earth across the dome of the heavens (Heb. *ha-shamayim*)." [21]So God created the great sea monsters and every living creature that moves, of every kind, with which the waters (Heb. *ha-mayim*) swarm, and every winged bird of every kind. And God saw that it was good. [22]God blessed them, saying, "Be fruitful and multiply and fill the waters (Heb. *ha-mayim*) in the seas, and let birds multiply on the earth." [23]And there was evening and there was morning, the fifth day.

[24]And God said, "Let the earth bring forth living creatures of every kind: cattle and creeping things and wild animals of the earth of every kind." And it was so. [25]God made the wild animals of the earth of every kind, and the cattle of every kind, and everything that creeps upon the ground of every kind. And God saw that it was good.

[26]Then God said, "Let us make humankind (Heb. *adam*) in our image, according to our likeness; and let them have dominion over the fish of the sea, and over the birds of the air, and over the cattle, and over all the wild animals of the earth, and over every creeping thing that creeps upon the earth." [27]So God created humankind (Heb. *ha-adam*) in his image, in the image of God he created them; male and female he created them. [28]God blessed them, and God said to them, "Be fruitful and multiply, and fill the earth and subdue it; and have dominion over the fish of the sea and over the birds of the air and over every living thing that moves upon the earth."

[29]God said, "See, I have given you every plant yielding seed that is upon the face of all the earth, and every tree with seed in its fruit; you shall have them for food. [30]And to every beast of the earth, and to every bird

of the air, and to everything that creeps on the earth, everything that has the breath of life, I have given every green plant for food." And it was so. [31]God saw everything that he had made, and indeed, it was very good. And there was evening and there was morning, the sixth day.

2[1]Thus the heavens (Heb. *ha-shamayim*) and the earth were finished, and all their multitude. [2]And on the seventh day God finished the work that he had done, and he rested on the seventh day from all the work that he had done. [3]So God blessed the seventh day and hallowed it, because on it God rested from all the work that he had done in creation.

The Yahwist Account of Creation*

2[4]These are the generations of the heavens (Heb. *ha-shamayim*) and the earth when they were created. In the day that Yahweh God made earth and heavens (Heb. *shamayim*), [5]when no plant of the field was yet in the earth and no herb of the field had yet sprung up—for Yahweh God had not caused it to rain upon the earth, and there was no human being (Heb. *adam*) to work (or till) the ground (Heb. *ha-adamah*); [[6]but a stream would rise from the earth, and water the whole face of the ground (*probably a later interpolation, for then there would indeed have been plants already springing up from the ground*)]; [7]then Yahweh God formed the human being (Heb. *ha-adam*) of dust from the ground (Heb. *ha-adamah*), and breathed into his nostrils the breath of life; and the human being (Heb. *ha-adam*) became a living being.

[8]And Yahweh God planted a garden in Eden, in the east; and there he put the human being (Heb. *ha-adam*) whom he had formed. [9]Out of the ground (Heb. *ha-adamah*) Yahweh God made to grow every tree that is pleasant to the sight and good for food, the tree of life also in the midst of the garden, and the tree of the knowledge of good and evil. [10]A river flows out of Eden to water the garden, and from there it divides and becomes four branches. [11]The name of the first is Pishon; it is the one that flows around the whole land of Havilah, where there is gold; [12]and the gold of that land is good; bdellium and onyx stone are there. [13]The name of the second river is Gihon; it is the one that flows around the whole land of Cush. [14]The name of the third river is the Tigris, which flows east of Assyria. And the fourth river is the Euphrates.   Babylonia

[15]Yahweh God took the human being (Heb. *ha-adam*) and put him in the garden of Eden to till it and keep it.

[16]And Yahweh God commanded the human being (Heb. *ha-adam*), "You may freely eat of every tree of the garden; [17]but of the tree of the knowledge of good and evil you shall not eat, for in the day that you eat of it you shall die."

[18]Then Yahweh God said, "It is not good that the human being (Heb. *ha-adam*) should be alone; I will make him a helper as his partner." [19]So out of the ground (Heb. *ha-adamah*) Yahweh God formed every animal of the field and every bird of the air, and brought them to the human being (Heb. *ha-adam*) to see what he would call them; and whatever the human being (Heb. *ha-adam*) called every living creature, that was its name. [20]The human being (Heb. *ha-adam*) gave names to all cattle, and to the birds of the air, and to every animal of the field; but for the human being (Heb. *ha-adam*) there was not found a helper as his partner.

[21]So Yahweh God caused a deep sleep to fall upon the human being (Heb. *ha-adam*), and he slept; then he took one of his ribs and closed up its place with flesh. [22]And the rib that Yahweh God had taken from the human being (Heb. *ha-adam*) He made into a woman (Heb. *īshah*) and brought her to the human being (Heb. *ha-adam*). [23]Then the human being (Heb. *ha-adam*) said, "This one at last is bone of my bones and flesh of my flesh; this one shall be called Woman (Heb. *īshah*), for out of a man (Heb. *īsh*) this one was taken." [24]Therefore a man (Heb. *īsh*) leaves his father and his mother and clings to his wife (literally, "his woman," or his *īshah*), and they become one flesh. [25]And the human being (Heb. *ha-adam*) and his wife (lit. "his woman") were both naked, and were not ashamed.

3[1]Now the serpent was more crafty than all of the animals of the field that Yahweh God had made. He said to the woman (Heb. *ha-īshah*), "Did God say, 'You shall not eat from any tree in the garden'?" [2]The woman (Heb. *ha-īshah*) said to the serpent, "We may eat of the fruit of the trees in the garden; [3]but God said, 'You shall not eat of the fruit of the tree that is in the middle of the garden, nor shall you touch it, or you shall die.' " [4]But the serpent said to the woman (Heb. *ha-īshah*), "You will not die; [5]for God knows that when you eat of it your eyes will be opened, and you will be like God, knowing good and evil." → True

[6]So when the woman (Heb. *ha-īshah*) saw that the tree was good for food, and that it was a delight to the eyes, and that the tree was to be desired to make one wise, she took of its fruit and ate; and she also gave some to her husband (literally, "to her man," her *īsh*), who was with her, and he ate. [7]Then the eyes of both were opened, and they knew that they were naked; and they sewed fig leaves together and made loincloths for themselves. [8]They heard the sound of Yahweh God walking in the garden at the time of the evening breeze, and the human being (Heb. *ha-adam*) and his wife (his *īshah*) hid themselves from the presence of Yahweh God among the trees of the garden.

[9]But Yahweh God called to the human being (Heb. *ha-adam*), and said to him, "Where are you?" [10]He said, "I heard the sound of you in the garden, and I was afraid, because I was naked; and I hid myself."

[11]He said, "Who told you that you were naked? Have you eaten from the tree of which I commanded you not to eat?" [12]The human being (Heb. *ha-adam*) said, "The woman (Heb. *ha-īshah*) whom you gave to be with me, she gave me fruit from the tree, and I ate." [13]Then Yahweh God said to the woman (Heb. *ha-īshah*), "What is this that you have done?" The woman (Heb. *ha-īshah*) said, "The serpent tricked me, and I ate."

[14]Yahweh God said to the serpent, "Because you have done this, cursed are you among all animals and among all wild creatures; upon your belly you shall go, and dust you shall eat all the days of your life. [15]I will put enmity between you and the woman (Heb. *ha-īshah*), and between your offspring and hers; he will strike your head, and you will strike his heel."

[16]To the woman (Heb. *ha-īshah*) he said, "I will greatly increase your pangs in childbearing; in pain you shall bring forth children, yet your desire shall be for your husband (literally, "your man," your *īsh*), and he shall rule over you."

[17]And to the human being (Heb. *ha-adam*) he said, "Because you have listened to the voice of your wife (literally, "your woman," your *īshah*), and have eaten of the tree about which I commanded you, 'You shall not eat of it,' cursed is the ground (Heb. *ha-adamah*) because of you; in toil you shall eat of it all the days of your life; [18]thorns and thistles it shall bring forth for you; and you shall eat the plants of the field. [19]By the sweat of your face you shall eat bread until you return to the ground (Heb. *ha-adamah*), for out of it you were taken; you are dust, and to dust you shall return."

[20]The human being (Heb. *ha-adam*) named his wife (his *īshah*) Eve, because she was the mother of all living.

[21]And Yahweh God made garments of skins for the human being (Heb. *ha-adam*) and for his wife (his *īshah*), and clothed them.

[22]Then Yahweh God said, "See, the human being (Heb. *ha-adam*) has become like one of us, knowing good and evil; and now, he might reach out his hand and take also from the tree of life, and eat, and live forever"— [23]therefore Yahweh God sent him forth from the garden of Eden, to till the ground (Heb. *ha-adamah*) from which he was taken. [24]He drove out the human being (Heb. *ha-adam*); and at the east of the garden of Eden he placed the cherubim, and a sword flaming and turning to guard the way to the tree of life.

4 [1]Now the human being (Heb. *ha-adam*) knew his wife (his *īshah*) Eve, and she conceived and bore Cain, saying, "I have produced a man (Heb. *īsh*) with the help of Yahweh." [2]Next she bore his brother Abel. Now Abel was a keeper of sheep, and Cain a tiller of the ground. [3]In the course of time Cain brought to Yahweh an offering of the fruit of the ground, [4]and Abel for his part brought of the firstlings of his flock, their fat portions. And Yahweh had regard for Abel and his offering, [5]but for Cain and his offering he had no regard. So Cain was very angry, and his countenance fell.

Section Four

The Emergence of the Concept of an Afterlife in Second Temple Judaism and Its Further Development in Christianity

From Sheol to the Divine Comedy

Study Guide/Section Four

Texts from the Old Testament (Dating from the First Temple Period to the Persian and Early Hellenistic Periods of the Second Temple; That Is, Prior to 165 BCE):

1. Summarize the rewards and punishments listed near the end of the Torah (Deuteronomy 28) for those who obey the covenant of Yahweh versus those who disobey. Are any of these promised in an afterlife?

2. How do the excerpts from Psalm 88 and Ecclesiastes (or Qoheleth) describe Sheol? Cite (i.e., write out within quotation marks) the relevant passages.

3. What is the "evil in all that happens under the sun," according to Qoheleth, the author of Ecclesiastes?

4. Cite (i.e., write out within quotation marks) two passages from Job that reflect a clear lack of belief in any afterlife. Does Job appear to regard this in the same way as does Qoheleth?

5. Cite passages from Job showing how he disagrees with Deuteronomy regarding the rewards of the just and the punishment of the wicked, and that this is for him an issue of theodicy.

Texts from the Time of the Maccabean Revolt (ca. 165 BCE and a Bit Later):

1. What kind of resurrection do those dying for keeping the law anticipate in reward for their obedience, according to 2 Maccabees?

2. Are the wicked raised, according to 2 Maccabees?

3. How are the wicked punished in 2 Maccabees, and when does this happen?

4. Compare and contrast the fate of the good vs. the fate of the wicked found in Daniel 12:1-3.

5. What kind of resurrection do the righteous experience, according to the book of Daniel?

6. Why do scholars believe that the notion of an afterlife arose specifically around the time of the Maccabean Revolt?

Texts from the New Testament Period (First Century CE):

1. Compare and contrast the views of the Sadducees, Pharisees, and Essenes on the afterlife. Pay special attention to how each sect conceives of the relationship between the body and the soul.

2. Describe Jesus's view of the afterlife, as reflected in the excerpts from the Gospels in Synopsis.

3. How does Paul describe the resurrection of the dead in Christ in 1 Corinthians 15? How does he conceive of the relationship between the body and the soul?

4. How does the book of Revelation describe the afterlife?

Dante's Divine Comedy: A Major Text from the Middle Ages (1308–1321 CE)

Read the excerpt from Dante's Inferno, together with the scholarly notes on this excerpt provided, and also examine the diagrams of his Hell, his Cosmos, and his Purgatory. Further information will also be provided in class that will be necessary to answer these questions.

1. How does Dante fit Hell, Mount Purgatory, and the various levels of Paradise into the cosmology of the Middle Ages?

2. What are the main divisions of Dante's Hell?

3. Why is Dante's Hell divided in this way?

4. What figure from the New Testament do you think is down in the lowest circle of Dante's Hell, and why would he be there?

5. Who goes to Purgatory, and why?

6. Why is Virgil, Dante's guide, not able to guide Dante past Purgatory into Heaven?

SECOND TEMPLE PERIOD
(520 BCE—70 CE):

Throughout this period, **Judaism is strictly monotheistic** and **one can sacrifice to God only in Jerusalem**, despite the fact that there is a large Diaspora Jewish community. Hence, people make the pilgrimage to Jerusalem from all over the Greco-Roman world, and from Babylonia.

There is nothing in the Holy of Holies.

The Persians and the Greeks after them allow the Jews to practice their religion, but around 165 BCE **Antiochus IV Epiphanes** tries to force the Jews to abandon their religion, worship pagan gods, and eat pork. This instigates the **Maccabean Revolt** reflected in the **Book of Daniel** and in **1—2 Maccabees**.

The **belief in an afterlife** in Judaism appears to have begun at around this time, and the issue seems to have been one of **theodicy.** How could the only, all-powerful God allow his people to suffer in this way, not for disobeying his covenant (as in the case of the Babylonian Exile), but **for obeying his covenant**? Hence, the rewards for obedience are now promised in an afterlife. Both the **Book of Daniel** and **2 Maccabees** reflect a belief in an afterlife, albeit these two texts hold quite different concepts of what this will entail and who will participate.

By the time of **Jesus** about 165 years later, the belief in an afterlife has undergone further development. However, not all Jews believed in an afterlife. The **Essenes** and the **Pharisees** accepted the idea, while the **Sadducees** rejected the notion.

The **apostle Paul** further develops the notion of an afterlife, linking it to the **resurrection of Jesus** and arguing for a **general bodily resurrection of the dead**.

In 66-70 CE, the Jews rebel against Rome. **The Second Temple is destroyed in 70 CE** and has never been rebuilt.

With the temple gone, **Judaism becomes Rabbinic Judaism**, based in the **synagogues**.

Excerpts from the Hebrew Bible Dating from the Period Prior to the Maccabean Revolt of 165 BCE*

1. The Blessings and Curses of the Torah (Deuteronomy 28)

Blessings for Keeping Torah

[28]If you will only obey Yahweh your God, by diligently observing all his commandments that I am commanding you today, Yahweh your God will set you high above all the nations of the earth; [2]all these blessings shall come upon you and overtake you, if you obey Yahweh your God:

[3]Blessed shall you be in the city, and blessed shall you be in the field.

[4]Blessed shall be the fruit of your womb, the fruit of your ground, and the fruit of your livestock, both the increase of your cattle and the issue of your flock.

[5]Blessed shall be your basket and your kneading-bowl.

[6]Blessed shall you be when you come in, and blessed shall you be when you go out.

[7]Yahweh will cause your enemies who rise against you to be defeated before you; they shall come out against you one way, and flee before you seven ways. [8]Yahweh will command the blessing upon you in your barns, and in all that you undertake; he will bless you in the land that Yahweh your God is giving you. [9]Yahweh will establish you as his holy people, as he has sworn to you, if you keep the commandments of Yahweh your God and walk in his ways. [10]All the peoples of the earth shall see that you are called by the name of Yahweh, and they shall be afraid of you. [11]Yahweh will make you abound in prosperity, in the fruit of your womb, in the fruit of your livestock, and in the fruit of your ground in the land that Yahweh swore to your ancestors to give you. [12]Yahweh will open for you his rich storehouse, the heavens, to give the rain of your land in its season and to bless all your undertakings. You will lend to many nations, but you will not borrow. [13]Yahweh will make you the head, and not the tail; you shall be only at the top, and not at the bottom—if you obey the commandments of Yahweh your God, which I am commanding you today, by diligently observing them, [14]and if you do not turn aside from any of the words that I am commanding you today, either to the right or to the left, following other gods to serve them.

Curses for Not Keeping Torah

[15]But if you will not obey Yahweh your God by diligently observing all his commandments and decrees, which I am commanding you today, then all these curses shall come upon you and overtake you:

[16]Cursed shall you be in the city, and cursed shall you be in the field.

[17]Cursed shall be your basket and your kneading-bowl.

[18]Cursed shall be the fruit of your womb, the fruit of your ground, the increase of your cattle, and the issue of your flock.

[19]Cursed shall you be when you come in, and cursed shall you be when you go out.

[20]Yahweh will send upon you disaster, panic, and frustration in everything you attempt to do, until you are destroyed and perish quickly, on account of the evil of your deeds, because you have forsaken me. [21]Yahweh will make the pestilence cling to you until it has consumed you from the land that you are entering to possess. [22]Yahweh will afflict you with consumption, fever, inflammation, with fiery heat and drought, and with blight

and mildew; they shall pursue you until you perish. [23]The sky over your head shall be bronze, and the earth under you iron. [24]Yahweh will change the rain of your land into powder, and only dust shall come down upon you from the sky until you are destroyed.

[25]Yahweh will cause you to be defeated before your enemies; you shall go out against them one way and flee before them seven ways. You shall become an object of horror to all the kingdoms of the earth. [26]Your corpses shall be food for every bird of the air and animal of the earth, and there shall be no one to frighten them away. [27]Yahweh will afflict you with the boils of Egypt, with ulcers, scurvy, and itch, of which you cannot be healed. [28]Yahweh will afflict you with madness, blindness, and confusion of mind; [29]you shall grope about at noon as blind people grope in darkness, but you shall be unable to find your way; and you shall be continually abused and robbed, without anyone to help. [30]You shall become engaged to a woman, but another man shall lie with her. You shall build a house, but not live in it. You shall plant a vineyard, but not enjoy its fruit. [31]Your ox shall be butchered before your eyes, but you shall not eat of it. Your donkey shall be stolen in front of you, and shall not be restored to you. Your sheep shall be given to your enemies, without anyone to help you. [32]Your sons and daughters shall be given to another people, while you look on; you will strain your eyes looking for them all day but be powerless to do anything. [33]A people whom you do not know shall eat up the fruit of your ground and of all your labours; you shall be continually abused and crushed, [34]and driven mad by the sight that your eyes shall see. [35]Yahweh will strike you on the knees and on the legs with grievous boils of which you cannot be healed, from the sole of your foot to the crown of your head. [36]Yahweh will bring you, and the king whom you set over you, to a nation that neither you nor your ancestors have known, where you shall serve other gods, of wood and stone. [37]You shall become an object of horror, a proverb, and a byword among all the peoples where Yahweh will lead you.

[38]You shall carry much seed into the field but shall gather little in, for the locust shall consume it. [39]You shall plant vineyards and dress them, but you shall neither drink the wine nor gather the grapes, for the worm shall eat them. [40]You shall have olive trees throughout all your territory, but you shall not anoint yourself with the oil, for your olives shall drop off. [41]You shall have sons and daughters, but they shall not remain yours, for they shall go into captivity. [42]All your trees and the fruit of your ground the cicada shall take over. [43]Aliens residing among you shall ascend above you higher and higher, while you shall descend lower and lower. [44]They shall lend to you but you shall not lend to them; they shall be the head and you shall be the tail.

[45]All these curses shall come upon you, pursuing and overtaking you until you are destroyed, because you did not obey Yahweh your God, by observing the commandments and the decrees that he commanded you. [46]They shall be among you and your descendants as a sign and a portent for ever.

[47]Because you did not serve Yahweh your God joyfully and with gladness of heart for the abundance of everything, [48]therefore you shall serve your enemies whom Yahweh will send against you, in hunger and thirst, in nakedness and lack of everything. He will put an iron yoke on your neck until he has destroyed you. [49]Yahweh will bring a nation from far away, from the end of the earth, to swoop down on you like an eagle, a nation whose language you do not understand, [50]a grim-faced nation showing no respect to the old or favor to the young. [51]It shall consume the fruit of your livestock and the fruit of your ground until you are destroyed, leaving you neither grain, wine, and oil, nor the increase of your cattle and the issue of your flock, until it has made you perish. [52]It shall besiege you in all your towns until your high and fortified walls, in which you trusted, come down throughout your land; it shall besiege you in all your towns throughout the land that Yahweh your God has given you. [53]In the desperate straits to which the enemy siege reduces you, you will eat the fruit of your womb, the flesh of your own sons and daughters whom Yahweh your God has given you. [54]Even the most refined and gentle of men among you will begrudge food to his own brother, to the wife whom he embraces, and to the last of his remaining children, [55]giving to none of them any of the flesh of his children whom he is eating, because nothing else remains to him, in the desperate straits to which the enemy siege will reduce you in all your towns. [56]She who is the most refined and gentle among you, so gentle and refined that she does not venture to set the sole of her foot on the ground, will begrudge food to the husband whom she embraces, to her own son, and to her own daughter, [57]begrudging even the after birth that comes out from between her thighs, and the children that she bears, because she is eating them in secret for lack of anything else, in the desperate straits to which the enemy siege will reduce you in your towns.

[58]If you do not diligently observe all the words of this law that are written in this book, fearing this glorious and awesome name, Yahweh your God, [59]then Yahweh will overwhelm both you and your offspring with severe and lasting afflictions and grievous and lasting maladies. [60]He will bring back upon you all the diseases of Egypt, of which you were in dread, and they shall cling to you. [61]Every other malady and affliction, even though not recorded in the book of this law, Yahweh will inflict on you until you are destroyed. [62]Although once you were as numerous as the stars in heaven, you shall be left few in number, because you did not obey Yahweh your God. [63]And just as Yahweh took delight in making you prosperous and numerous, so Yahweh will take delight in bringing you to ruin and destruction; you shall be plucked off the land that you are entering to possess. [64]Yahweh will scatter you among all peoples, from one end of the earth to the other; and there you shall serve other gods, of wood and stone, which neither you nor your ancestors have known. [65]Among those nations you shall find no ease, no resting-place for the sole of your foot. There Yahweh will give you a trembling heart, failing eyes, and a languishing spirit. [66]Your life shall hang in doubt before you; night and day you shall be in dread, with no assurance of your life. [67]In the morning you shall say, 'If only it were evening!' and at evening you shall say, 'If only it were morning!'—because of the dread that your heart shall feel and the sights that your eyes shall see. [68]Yahweh will bring you back in ships to Egypt, by a route that I promised you would never see again; and there you shall offer yourselves for sale to your enemies as male and female slaves, but there will be no buyer.

2. Psalm 88

Prayer of a Man Near Death for a Prolonged Life

1 O Yahweh, God of my salvation,
when, at night, I cry out in your presence,
2 let my prayer come before you;
incline your ear to my cry.

3 For my soul is full of troubles,
and my life draws near to Sheol.
4 I am counted among those who go down to the Pit;
I am like those who have no help,
5 like those forsaken among the dead,
like the slain that lie in the grave,
like those whom you remember no more,
for they are cut off from your hand.
6 You have put me in the depths of the Pit,
in the regions dark and deep.
7 Your wrath lies heavy upon me,
and you overwhelm me with all your waves.
Selah

8 You have caused my companions to shun me;
you have made me a thing of horror to them.
I am shut in so that I cannot escape;
9 my eye grows dim through sorrow.
Every day I call on you, O Yahweh;
I spread out my hands to you.
10 Do you work wonders for the dead?
Do the shades rise up to praise you?
Selah
11 Is your steadfast love declared in the grave,
or your faithfulness in Abaddon (lit., "Destruction")?

12 Are your wonders known in the darkness,
or your saving help in the land of forgetfulness?

13 But I, O Yahweh, cry out to you;
in the morning my prayer comes before you.
14 O Yahweh, why do you cast me off?
Why do you hide your face from me?
15 Wretched and close to death from my youth up,
I suffer your terrors; I am desperate.
16 Your wrath has swept over me;
your dread assaults destroy me.
17 They surround me like a flood all day long;
from all sides they close in on me.
18 You have caused friend and neighbor to shun me;
my companions are in darkness.

3. Excerpts from Ecclesiastes or the Book of Qoheleth

Ecclesiastes 2:13-17

[13]Then I saw that wisdom excels folly as light excels darkness.
[14]The wise have eyes in their head,
but fools walk in darkness.

Yet I perceived that the same fate befalls all of them. [15]Then I said to myself, 'What happens to the fool will happen to me also; why then have I been so very wise?' And I said to myself that this also is vanity. [16]For there is no enduring remembrance of the wise or of fools, seeing that in the days to come all will have been long forgotten. How can the wise die just like fools? [17]So I hated life, because what is done under the sun was grievous to me; for all is vanity and a chasing after wind.

Ecclesiastes 3:18-20

[18]I said in my heart with regard to human beings that God is testing them to show that they are but animals. [19]For the fate of humans and the fate of animals is the same; as one dies, so dies the other. They all have the same breath, and humans have no advantage over the animals; for all is vanity. [20]All go to one place; all are from the dust, and all turn to dust again.

Ecclesiastes 9:1-10

[9]All this I laid to heart, examining it all, how the righteous and the wise and their deeds are in the hand of God; whether it is love or hate one does not know. Everything that confronts them [2]is vanity since the same fate comes to all, to the righteous and the wicked, to the good and the evil, to the clean and the unclean, to those who sacrifice and those who do not sacrifice. As are the good, so are the sinners; those who swear are like those who shun an oath. [3]This is an evil in all that happens under the sun, that the same fate comes to everyone. Moreover, the hearts of all are full of evil; madness is in their hearts while they live, and after that they go to the dead. [4]But whoever is joined with all the living has hope, for a living dog is better than a dead lion. [5]The living know that they will die, but the dead know nothing; they have no more reward, and even the memory of them is lost. [6]Their love and their hate and their envy have already perished; never again will they have any share in all that happens under the sun.

[7]Go, eat your bread with enjoyment, and drink your wine with a merry heart; for God has long ago approved what you do. [8]Let your garments always be white; do not let oil be lacking on your head. [9]Enjoy life with the wife whom you love, all the days of your vain life that are given you under the sun, because that is your portion in life and in your toil at which you toil under the sun. [10]Whatever your hand finds to do, do with your might; for there is no work or thought or knowledge or wisdom in Sheol, to which you are going.

4. Excerpts from the Book of Job

Job 1

Part of the framing narrative, composed in prose

[1]There was once a man in the land of Uz whose name was Job. That man was blameless and upright, one who feared God and turned away from evil. [2]There were born to him seven sons and three daughters. [3]He had seven thousand sheep, three thousand camels, five hundred yoke of oxen, five hundred donkeys, and very many slaves, so that this man was the greatest of all the people of the east. [4]His sons used to go and hold feasts in one another's houses in turn; and they would send and invite their three sisters to eat and drink with them. [5]And when the feast days had run their course, Job would send and sanctify them, and he would rise early in the morning and offer burnt-offerings according to the number of them all; for Job said, 'It may be that my children have sinned, and cursed God in their hearts.' This is what Job always did.

[6]One day the sons of God came to present themselves before Yahweh, and the Accuser (Heb., *ha-satan*) also came among them. [7]Yahweh said to the Accuser (Heb., *ha-satan*), 'Where have you come from?' The Accuser (Heb., *ha-satan*) answered Yahweh, 'From going to and fro on the earth, and from walking up and down on it.' [8]Yahweh said to the Accuser (Heb., *ha-satan*), 'Have you considered my servant Job? There is no one like him on the earth, a blameless and upright man who fears God and turns away from evil.' [9]Then the Accuser (Heb., *ha-satan*) answered Yahweh, 'Does Job fear God for nothing? [10]Have you not put a fence around him and his house and all that he has, on every side? You have blessed the work of his hands, and his possessions have increased in the land. [11]But stretch out your hand now, and touch all that he has, and he will curse you to your face.' [12]Yahweh said to the Accuser (Heb., *ha-satan*), 'Very well, all that he has is in your power; only do not stretch out your hand against him!' So the Accuser (Heb., *ha-satan*) went out from the presence of Yahweh.

[13]One day when his sons and daughters were eating and drinking wine in the eldest brother's house, [14]a messenger came to Job and said, 'The oxen were ploughing and the donkeys were feeding beside them, [15]and the Sabeans fell on them and carried them off, and killed the slaves with the edge of the sword; I alone have escaped to tell you.' [16]While he was still speaking, another came and said, 'The fire of God fell from heaven and burned up the sheep and the slaves, and consumed them; I alone have escaped to tell you.' [17]While he was still speaking, another came and said, 'The Chaldeans [i.e., the Babylonians] formed three columns, made a raid on the camels and carried them off, and killed the slaves with the edge of the sword; I alone have escaped to tell you.' [18]While he was still speaking, another came and said, 'Your sons and daughters were eating and drinking wine in their eldest brother's house, [19]and suddenly a great wind came across the desert, struck the four corners of the house, and it fell on the young people, and they are dead; I alone have escaped to tell you.'

[20]Then Job arose, tore his robe, shaved his head, and fell on the ground and worshipped. [21]He said, 'Naked I came from my mother's womb, and naked shall I return there; Yahweh gave, and Yahweh has taken away; blessed be the name of Yahweh.'

[22]In all this Job did not sin or charge God with wrongdoing.

Job 2

[1]One day the sons of God came to present themselves before Yahweh, and the Accuser (Heb., *ha-satan*) also came among them to present himself before Yahweh. [2]Yahweh said to the Accuser (Heb., *ha-satan*), 'Where have you come from?' The Accuser (Heb., *ha-satan*) answered Yahweh, 'From going to and fro on the earth, and from walking up and down on it.' [3]Yahweh said to the Accuser (Heb., *ha-satan*), 'Have you considered my servant Job? There is no one like him on the earth, a blameless and upright man who fears God and turns away from evil. He still persists in his integrity, although you incited me against him, to destroy him for no reason.' [4]Then the Accuser (Heb., *ha-satan*) answered Yahweh, 'Skin for skin! All that people have they will give to save their lives. [5]But stretch out your hand now and touch his bone and his flesh, and he will curse you to your face.' [6]Yahweh said to the Accuser (Heb., *ha-satan*), 'Very well, he is in your power; only spare his life.'

[7]So the Accuser (Heb., *ha-satan*) went out from the presence of Yahweh, and inflicted loathsome sores on Job from the sole of his foot to the crown of his head. [8]Job took a potsherd with which to scrape himself, and sat among the ashes.

[9]Then his wife said to him, 'Do you still persist in your integrity? Curse God, and die.' [10]But he said to her, 'You speak as any foolish woman would speak. Shall we receive the good at the hand of God, and not receive the bad?' In all this Job did not sin with his lips.

[11]Now when Job's three friends heard of all these troubles that had come upon him, each of them set out from his home—Eliphaz the Temanite, Bildad the Shuhite, and Zophar the Naamathite. They met together to go and console and comfort him. [12]When they saw him from a distance, they did not recognize him, and they raised their voices and wept aloud; they tore their robes and threw dust in the air upon their heads. [13]They sat with him on the ground for seven days and seven nights, and no one spoke a word to him, for they saw that his suffering was very great.

End of the prose narrative. The poem begins in Chapter 3.

Job 14

Excerpted from the poem

1 'A mortal, born of woman, few of days and full of trouble,
2 comes up like a flower and withers,
flees like a shadow and does not last.
3 Do you fix your eyes on such a one?
Do you bring me into judgment with you?
4 Who can bring a clean thing out of an unclean?
No one can.
5 Since their days are determined,
and the number of their months is known to you,
and you have appointed the bounds that they cannot pass,
6 look away from them, and desist,
that they may enjoy, like laborers, their days.

7 'For there is hope for a tree,
if it is cut down, that it will sprout again,
and that its shoots will not cease.
8 Though its root grows old in the earth,
and its stump dies in the ground,
9 yet at the scent of water it will bud
and put forth branches like a young plant.
10 But mortals die, and are laid low;
humans expire, and where are they?
11 As waters fail from a lake,
and a river wastes away and dries up,
12 so mortals lie down and do not rise again;
until the heavens are no more, they will not awake
or be roused out of their sleep.))
13 O that you would hide me in Sheol,
that you would conceal me until your wrath is past,
that you would appoint me a set time, and remember me!
14 If mortals die, will they live again?
All the days of my service I would wait
until my release should come.

15 You would call, and I would answer you;
you would long for the work of your hands.
16 For then you would number my steps,
you would not keep watch over my sin;
17 my transgression would be sealed up in a bag,
and you would cover over my iniquity.

18 'But the mountain falls and crumbles away,
and the rock is removed from its place;
19 the waters wear away the stones;
the torrents wash away the soil of the earth;
so you destroy the hope of mortals.
20 You prevail forever against them, and they pass away;
you change their countenance, and send them away.
21 Their children come to honor, and they do not know it;
they are brought low, and it goes unnoticed.
22 They feel only the pain of their own bodies,
and mourn only for themselves.'

Job 21

Exerpted from the poem; Job replies to his friend, Zophar the Naamathite, who has argued in Chapter 20 that the prosperity of the wicked is short-lived and they inevitably receive just retribution from God.

1 Then Job answered:
2 'Listen carefully to my words,
and let this be your consolation.
3 Bear with me, and I will speak;
then after I have spoken, mock on.
4 As for me, is my complaint addressed to mortals?
Why should I not be impatient?
5 Look at me, and be appalled,
and lay your hand upon your mouth.
6 When I think of it I am dismayed,
and shuddering seizes my flesh.
7 Why do the wicked live on,
reach old age, and grow mighty in power?
8 Their children are established in their presence,
and their offspring before their eyes.
9 Their houses are safe from fear,
and no rod of God is upon them.
10 Their bull breeds without fail;
their cow calves and never miscarries.
11 They send out their little ones like a flock,
and their children dance around.
12 They sing to the tambourine and the lyre,
and rejoice to the sound of the pipe.
13 They spend their days in prosperity,
and in peace they go down to Sheol.
14 They say to God, "Leave us alone!
We do not desire to know your ways.

15 What is the Almighty that we should serve him?
And what profit do we get if we pray to him?"
16 Is not their prosperity indeed in their hand?
The plans of the wicked are repugnant to me.

17 'How often is the lamp of the wicked put out?
How often does calamity come upon them?
How often does God distribute pains in his anger?
18 How often are they like straw before the wind,
and like chaff that the storm carries away?
19 You say, "God stores up their iniquity for their children."
Let it be paid back to them, so that they may know it.
20 Let their own eyes see their destruction,
and let them drink of the wrath of the Almighty.
21 For what do they care for their household after them,
when the number of their months is cut off?
22 Will any teach God knowledge,
seeing that he judges those that are on high?
23 One dies in full prosperity,
being wholly at ease and secure,
24 his loins full of milk
and the marrow of his bones moist.
25 Another dies in bitterness of soul,
never having tasted of good.
26 They lie down alike in the dust,
and the worms cover them.

27 'Oh, I know your thoughts,
and your schemes to wrong me.
28 For you say, "Where is the house of the prince?
Where is the tent in which the wicked lived?"
29 Have you not asked those who travel the roads,
and do you not accept their testimony,
30 that the wicked are spared on the day of calamity,
and are rescued on the day of wrath?
31 Who declares their way to their face,
and who repays them for what they have done?
32 When they are carried to the grave,
a watch is kept over their tomb.
33 The clods of the valley are sweet to them;
everyone will follow after,
and those who went before are innumerable.
34 How then will you comfort me with empty nothings?
There is nothing left of your answers but falsehood.'

Job 38

Excerpted from the poem

1 Then Yahweh answered Job out of the whirlwind:
2 'Who is this that darkens counsel by words without knowledge?

3 Gird up your loins like a man,
I will question you, and you shall declare to me.

4 'Where were you when I laid the foundation of the earth?
Tell me, if you have understanding.
5 Who determined its measurements—surely you know!
Or who stretched the line upon it?
6 On what were its bases sunk,
or who laid its cornerstone
7 when the morning stars sang together
and all the sons of God shouted for joy?

8 'Or who shut in the sea with doors
when it burst out from the womb?—
9 when I made the clouds its garment,
and thick darkness its swaddling band,
10 and prescribed bounds for it,
and set bars and doors,
11 and said, "Thus far shall you come, and no farther,
and here shall your proud waves be stopped"?

12 'Have you commanded the morning since your days began,
and caused the dawn to know its place,
13 so that it might take hold of the skirts of the earth,
and the wicked be shaken out of it?
14 It is changed like clay under the seal,
and it is dyed like a garment.
15 Light is withheld from the wicked,
and their uplifted arm is broken.

16 'Have you entered into the springs of the sea,
or walked in the recesses of the deep?
17 Have the gates of death been revealed to you,
or have you seen the gates of deep darkness?
18 Have you comprehended the expanse of the earth?
Declare, if you know all this.

19 'Where is the way to the dwelling of light,
and where is the place of darkness,
20 that you may take it to its territory
and that you may discern the paths to its home?
21 Surely you know, for you were born then,
and the number of your days is great!

22 'Have you entered the storehouses of the snow,
or have you seen the storehouses of the hail,
23 which I have reserved for the time of trouble,
for the day of battle and war?
24 What is the way to the place where the light is distributed,
or where the east wind is scattered upon the earth?

25 'Who has cut a channel for the torrents of rain,
and a way for the thunderbolt,
26 to bring rain on a land where no one lives,
on the desert, which is empty of human life,
27 to satisfy the waste and desolate land,
and to make the ground put forth grass?

28 'Has the rain a father,
or who has begotten the drops of dew?
29 From whose womb did the ice come forth,
and who has given birth to the hoar-frost of heaven?
30 The waters become hard like stone,
and the face of the deep is frozen.

31 'Can you bind the chains of the Pleiades [i.e., the Big Dipper],
or loose the cords of Orion?
32 Can you lead forth the Mazzaroth [i.e., the constellations of the Zodiac] in their season,
or can you guide the Bear with its children?
33 Do you know the ordinances of the heavens?
Can you establish their rule on the earth?

34 'Can you lift up your voice to the clouds,
so that a flood of waters may cover you?
35 Can you send forth lightnings, so that they may go
and say to you, "Here we are"?
36 Who has put wisdom in the inward parts,
or given understanding to the mind?
37 Who has the wisdom to number the clouds?
Or who can tilt the water skins of the heavens,
38 when the dust runs into a mass
and the clods cling together?

39 'Can you hunt the prey for the lion,
or satisfy the appetite of the young lions,
40 when they crouch in their dens,
or lie in wait in their covert?
41 Who provides for the raven its prey,
when its young ones cry to God,
and wander about for lack of food?
. . .

Job 40

[Excerpted from the poem]

1 And Yahweh said to Job:
2 'Shall a fault-finder contend with the Almighty?
Anyone who argues with God must respond.'

3 Then Job answered Yahweh:
4 'See, I am of small account; what shall I answer you?

I lay my hand on my mouth.
5 I have spoken once, and I will not answer;
twice, but will proceed no further.'

6 Then Yahweh answered Job out of the whirlwind:
7 'Gird up your loins like a man;
I will question you, and you declare to me.
8 Will you even put me in the wrong?
Will you condemn me that you may be justified?
9 Have you an arm like God,
and can you thunder with a voice like his?

. . .

Job 42

1 Then Job answered Yahweh:
2 'I know that you can do all things,
and that no purpose of yours can be thwarted.
3 "Who is this that hides counsel without knowledge?"
Therefore I have uttered what I did not understand,
things too wonderful for me, which I did not know.
4 "Hear, and I will speak;
I will question you, and you declare to me."
5 I had heard of you by the hearing of the ear,
but now my eye sees you;
6 therefore I despise myself,
and repent in dust and ashes.'

The framing prose narrative resumes

[7]After Yahweh had spoken these words to Job, Yahweh said to Eliphaz the Temanite: 'My wrath is kindled against you and against your two friends; for you have not spoken of me what is right, as my servant Job has. [8]Now therefore take seven bulls and seven rams, and go to my servant Job, and offer up for yourselves a burnt-offering; and my servant Job shall pray for you, for I will accept his prayer not to deal with you according to your folly; for you have not spoken of me what is right, as my servant Job has done.' [9]So Eliphaz the Temanite and Bildad the Shuhite and Zophar the Naamathite went and did what Yahweh had told them; and Yahweh accepted Job's prayer.

Job's Fortunes Are Restored Twofold

[10]And Yahweh restored the fortunes of Job when he had prayed for his friends; and Yahweh gave Job twice as much as he had before. [11]Then there came to him all his brothers and sisters and all who had known him before, and they ate bread with him in his house; they showed him sympathy and comforted him for all the evil that Yahweh had brought upon him; and each of them gave him a piece of money and a gold ring. [12]Yahweh blessed the latter days of Job more than his beginning; and he had fourteen thousand sheep, six thousand camels, a thousand yoke of oxen, and a thousand donkeys. [13]He also had seven sons and three daughters. [14]He named the first Jemimah, the second Keziah, and the third Keren-happuch. [15]In all the land there were no women so beautiful as Job's daughters; and their father gave them an inheritance along with their brothers. [16]After this Job lived for one hundred and forty years, and saw his children, and his children's children, four generations. [17]And Job died, old and full of days.

Excerpts from Texts Referring to the Maccabean Revolt of 165 BCE*

1 Maccabees 1:41-64

(original language = Greek; 1 Maccabees is part of the Catholic and Greek Orthodox canons, but is not in the Protestant or Jewish canons)

[41]Then the king [i.e., Antiochus IV Epiphanes] wrote to his whole kingdom that all should be one people, [42]and that all should give up their particular customs. [43]All the Gentiles accepted the command of the king. Many even from Israel gladly adopted his religion; they sacrificed to idols and profaned the sabbath. [44]And the king sent letters by messengers to Jerusalem and the towns of Judah; he directed them to follow customs strange to the land, [45]to forbid burnt offerings and sacrifices and drink offerings in the sanctuary, to profane sabbaths and festivals, [46]to defile the sanctuary and the priests, [47]to build altars and sacred precincts and shrines for idols, to sacrifice swine and other unclean animals, [48]and to leave their sons uncircumcised. They were to make themselves abominable by everything unclean and profane, [49]so that they would forget the law and change all the ordinances. [50]He added, "And whoever does not obey the command of the king shall die."

[51]In such words he wrote to his whole kingdom. He appointed inspectors over all the people and commanded the towns of Judah to offer sacrifice, town by town. [52]Many of the people, everyone who forsook the law, joined them, and they did evil in the land; [53]they drove Israel into hiding in every place of refuge they had.

[54]Now on the fifteenth day of Chislev, in the one hundred forty-fifth year [ca. 167 BCE], they erected a desolating sacrilege on the altar of burnt offering. They also built altars in the surrounding towns of Judah, [55]and offered incense at the doors of the houses and in the streets. [56]The books of the law that they found they tore to pieces and burned with fire. [57]Anyone found possessing the book of the covenant, or anyone who adhered to the law, was condemned to death by decree of the king. [58]They kept using violence against Israel, against those who were found month after month in the towns. [59]On the twenty-fifth day of the month they offered sacrifice on the altar that was on top of the altar of burnt offering. [60]According to the decree, they put to death the women who had their children circumcised, [61]and their families and those who circumcised them; and they hung the infants from their mothers' necks.

[62]But many in Israel stood firm and were resolved in their hearts not to eat unclean food. [63]They chose to die rather than to be defiled by food or to profane the holy covenant; and they did die. [64]Very great wrath came upon Israel.

2 Maccabees 7

(original language = Greek; 2 Maccabees is part of the Catholic and Greek Orthodox canons, but is not in the Protestant or Jewish canons)

The martyrdom of seven brothers and their mother

[7]It happened also that seven brothers and their mother were arrested and were being compelled by the king [i.e., Antiochus IV Epiphanes], under torture with whips and thongs, to partake of unlawful swine's flesh. [2]One of them, acting as their spokesman, said, "What do you intend to ask and learn from us? For we are ready to die rather than transgress the laws of our ancestors."

[3]The king fell into a rage, and gave orders to have pans and caldrons heated. [4]These were heated immediately, and he commanded that the tongue of their spokesman be cut out and that they scalp him and cut off his hands and feet, while the rest of the brothers and the mother looked on. [5]When he was utterly helpless, the king ordered them to take him to the fire, still breathing, and to fry him in a pan. The smoke from the pan

spread widely, but the brothers and their mother encouraged one another to die nobly, saying, [6]"The Lord God is watching over us and in truth has compassion on us, as Moses declared in his song that bore witness against the people to their faces, when he said, 'And he will have compassion on his servants.'"

[7]After the first brother had died in this way, they brought forward the second for their sport. They tore off the skin of his head with the hair, and asked him, "Will you eat rather than have your body punished limb by limb?" [8]He replied in the language of his ancestors and said to them, "No." Therefore he in turn underwent tortures as the first brother had done. [9]And when he was at his last breath, he said, "You accursed wretch, you dismiss us from this present life, but the King of the universe will raise us up to an everlasting renewal of life, because we have died for his laws."

[10]After him, the third was the victim of their sport. When it was demanded, he quickly put out his tongue and courageously stretched forth his hands, [11]and said nobly, "I got these from Heaven, and because of his laws I disdain them, and from him I hope to get them back again." [12]As a result the king himself and those with him were astonished at the young man's spirit, for he regarded his sufferings as nothing.

[13]After he too had died, they maltreated and tortured the fourth in the same way. [14]When he was near death, he said, "One cannot but choose to die at the hands of mortals and to cherish the hope God gives of being raised again by him. But for you there will be no resurrection to life!"

[15]Next they brought forward the fifth and maltreated him. [16]But he looked at the king, and said, "Because you have authority among mortals, though you also are mortal, you do what you please. But do not think that God has forsaken our people. [17]Keep on, and see how his mighty power will torture you and your descendants!"

[18]After him they brought forward the sixth. And when he was about to die, he said, "Do not deceive yourself in vain. For we are suffering these things on our own account, because of our sins against our own God. Therefore astounding things have happened. [19]But do not think that you will go unpunished for having tried to fight against God!"

[20]The mother was especially admirable and worthy of honorable memory. Although she saw her seven sons perish within a single day, she bore it with good courage because of her hope in the Lord. [21]She encouraged each of them in the language of their ancestors. Filled with a noble spirit, she reinforced her woman's reasoning with a man's courage, and said to them, [22]"I do not know how you came into being in my womb. It was not I who gave you life and breath, nor I who set in order the elements within each of you. [23]Therefore the Creator of the world, who shaped the beginning of humankind and devised the origin of all things, will in his mercy give life and breath back to you again, since you now forget yourselves for the sake of his laws."

[24]Antiochus felt that he was being treated with contempt, and he was suspicious of her reproachful tone. The youngest brother being still alive, Antiochus not only appealed to him in words, but promised with oaths that he would make him rich and enviable if he would turn from the ways of his ancestors, and that he would take him for his Friend and entrust him with public affairs. [25]Since the young man would not listen to him at all, the king called the mother to him and urged her to advise the youth to save himself. [26]After much urging on his part, she undertook to persuade her son. [27]But, leaning close to him, she spoke in their native language as follows, deriding the cruel tyrant: "My son, have pity on me. I carried you nine months in my womb, and nursed you for three years, and have reared you and brought you up to this point in your life, and have taken care of you. [28]I beg you, my child, to look at the heaven and the earth and see everything that is in them, and recognize that God made them out of things that did not exist. And in the same way the human race came into being. [29]Do not fear this butcher, but prove worthy of your brothers. Accept death, so that in God's mercy I may get you back again along with your brothers."

[30]While she was still speaking, the young man said, "What are you waiting for? I will not obey the king's command, but I obey the command of the law that was given to our ancestors through Moses. [31]But you, who have contrived all sorts of evil against the Hebrews, will certainly not escape the hands of God. [32]For we are suffering because of our own sins. [33]And if our living Lord is angry for a little while, to rebuke and discipline us, he will again be reconciled with his own servants. [34]But you, unholy wretch, you most defiled of all mortals, do not be elated in vain and puffed up by uncertain hopes, when you raise your hand against the children of heaven. [35]You have not yet escaped the judgment of the almighty, all-seeing God. [36]For our brothers after enduring a brief suffering have drunk of ever-flowing life, under God's covenant; but you, by the judgment of God, will receive just punishment for your arrogance. [37]I, like my brothers, give up body and life for the laws of our ancestors, appealing to God to show mercy soon to our nation and by trials and plagues to make you confess that he alone is God, [38]and through me and my brothers to bring to an end the wrath of the Almighty that has justly fallen on our whole nation."

³⁹The king fell into a rage, and handled him worse than the others, being exasperated at his scorn. ⁴⁰So he died in his integrity, putting his whole trust in the Lord.

⁴¹Last of all, the mother died, after her sons.

⁴²Let this be enough, then, about the eating of sacrifices and the extreme tortures.

2 Maccabees 8:1-7

Judas Maccabee leads the Maccabean Revolt

⁸Meanwhile Judas, who was also called Maccabeus, and his companions secretly entered the villages and summoned their kindred and enlisted those who had continued in the Jewish faith, and so they gathered about six thousand. ²They implored the Lord to look upon the people who were oppressed by all; and to have pity on the temple that had been profaned by the godless; ³to have mercy on the city that was being destroyed and about to be leveled to the ground; to hearken to the blood that cried out to him; ⁴to remember also the lawless destruction of the innocent babies and the blasphemies committed against his name; and to show his hatred of evil.

⁵As soon as Maccabeus got his army organized, the Gentiles could not withstand him, for the wrath of the Lord had turned to mercy. ⁶Coming without warning, he would set fire to towns and villages. He captured strategic positions and put to flight not a few of the enemy. ⁷He found the nights most advantageous for such attacks. And talk of his valor spread everywhere.

2 Maccabees 9 (*an excerpt*)

The Lord strikes down Antiochus IV Ephiphanes

⁹About that time, as it happened, Antiochus had retreated in disorder from the region of Persia. ²He had entered the city called Persepolis and attempted to rob the temples and control the city. Therefore the people rushed to the rescue with arms, and Antiochus and his army were defeated, with the result that Antiochus was put to flight by the inhabitants and beat a shameful retreat. ³While he was in Ecbatana, news came to him of what had happened to Nicanor and the forces of Timothy. ⁴Transported with rage, he conceived the idea of turning upon the Jews the injury done by those who had put him to flight; so he ordered his charioteer to drive without stopping until he completed the journey. But the judgment of heaven rode with him! For in his arrogance he said, "When I get there I will make Jerusalem a cemetery of Jews."

⁵But the all-seeing Lord, the God of Israel, struck him with an incurable and invisible blow. As soon as he stopped speaking he was seized with a pain in his bowels, for which there was no relief, and with sharp internal tortures— ⁶and that very justly, for he had tortured the bowels of others with many and strange inflictions. ⁷Yet he did not in any way stop his insolence, but was even more filled with arrogance, breathing fire in his rage against the Jews, and giving orders to drive even faster. And so it came about that he fell out of his chariot as it was rushing along, and the fall was so hard as to torture every limb of his body. ⁸Thus he who only a little while before had thought in his superhuman arrogance that he could command the waves of the sea, and had imagined that he could weigh the high mountains in a balance, was brought down to earth and carried in a litter, making the power of God manifest to all. ⁹And so the ungodly man's body swarmed with worms, and while he was still living in anguish and pain, his flesh rotted away, and because of the stench the whole army felt revulsion at his decay. ¹⁰Because of his intolerable stench no one was able to carry the man who a little while before had thought that he could touch the stars of heaven. ¹¹Then it was that, broken in spirit, he began to lose much of his arrogance and to come to his senses under the scourge of God, for he was tortured with pain every moment. ¹²And when he could not endure his own stench, he uttered these words, "It is right to be subject to God; mortals should not think that they are equal to God."

¹³Then the abominable fellow made a vow to the Lord, who would no longer have mercy on him, stating ¹⁴that the holy city, which he was hurrying to level to the ground and to make a cemetery, he was now declaring to be free; ¹⁵and the Jews, whom he had not considered worth burying but had planned to throw out with their children for the wild animals and for the birds to eat, he would make, all of them, equal to citizens of Athens;

[16]and the holy sanctuary, which he had formerly plundered, he would adorn with the finest offerings; and all the holy vessels he would give back, many times over; and the expenses incurred for the sacrifices he would provide from his own revenues; [17]and in addition to all this he also would become a Jew and would visit every inhabited place to proclaim the power of God. [18]But when his sufferings did not in any way abate, for the judgment of God had justly come upon him, he gave up all hope for himself . . .

[28]So the murderer and blasphemer, having endured the more intense suffering, such as he had inflicted on others, came to the end of his life by a most pitiable fate, among the mountains in a strange land. [29]And Philip, one of his courtiers, took his body home; then, fearing the son of Antiochus, he withdrew to Ptolemy Philometor in Egypt.

2 Maccabees 10:1-8

Judas Maccabee retakes and purifies the temple and celebrates the first Hannukah

[10]Now Maccabeus and his followers, the Lord leading them on, recovered the temple and the city; [2]they tore down the altars that had been built in the public square by the foreigners, and also destroyed the sacred precincts. [3]They purified the sanctuary, and made another altar of sacrifice; then, striking fire out of flint, they offered sacrifices, after a lapse of two years, and they offered incense and lighted lamps and set out the bread of the Presence. [4]When they had done this, they fell prostrate and implored the Lord that they might never again fall into such misfortunes, but that, if they should ever sin, they might be disciplined by him with forbearance and not be handed over to blasphemous and barbarous nations. [5]It happened that on the same day on which the sanctuary had been profaned by the foreigners, the purification of the sanctuary took place, that is, on the twenty-fifth day of the same month, which was Chislev. [6]They celebrated it for eight days with rejoicing, in the manner of the festival of booths, remembering how not long before, during the festival of booths, they had been wandering in the mountains and caves like wild animals. [7]Therefore, carrying ivy-wreathed wands and beautiful branches and also fronds of palm, they offered hymns of thanksgiving to him who had given success to the purifying of his own holy place. [8]They decreed by public edict, ratified by vote, that the whole nation of the Jews should observe these days every year.

Daniel 12:1-3 *167 and 164 BCE*

(original language = Hebrew; this passage is in the Jewish and all the Christian canons)

[1]At that time Michael, the great prince, the protector of your people, shall arise. There shall be a time of anguish, such as has never occurred since nations first came into existence. But at that time your people shall be delivered, everyone who is found written in the book. [2]Many of those who sleep in the dust of the earth shall awake, some to everlasting life, and some to shame and everlasting contempt. [3]Those who are wise shall shine like the brightness of the dome [of the sky or heaven], and those who lead many to righteousness, like the stars for ever and ever. *↳ 7 Stars.*

Excerpts from the Ancient Jewish Historian Josephus on the Beliefs of the Essenes, the Pharisees and the Sadducees Regarding the Afterlife in the First Century CE
(Translations are mine and those of the Loeb edition)

The Essenes believe "that bodies are corruptible and that the matter of which they are composed is impermanent; but that souls are immortal and endure forever. Emanating from the finest ether, souls become entangled, as it were, in the prison house of the body, to which they are dragged down by a sort of physical spell; but when they are released from the bonds of the flesh, then, as though liberated from long servitude, they rejoice and are borne aloft. Sharing the beliefs of the children of Greece, the Essenes maintain that for virtuous souls there is reserved an abode beyond the ocean, a place that is not oppressed by rain or snow or heat, but is refreshed by the ever gentle breath of the west wind coming in from the ocean; while they relegate wicked souls to a murky and tempestuous dungeon, full of never-ending punishments. . . . Their aim was first to establish the eternal nature of souls, and secondly to promote virtue and to deter from vice; for the good are made better in their lifetime by the hope of a reward after death, and the passions of the wicked are restrained by the fear that, even if they escape detection while alive, they will undergo never-ending punishment after their death" (*Jewish War* 2.154–2.158).

The Pharisees, "who are considered to be the most accurate interpreters of the laws, and hold the position of the leading sect," believe that "every soul is imperishable, but only the soul of the good passes into a different body, whereas the souls of the wicked are chastised with an eternal punishment" (*Jewish War* 2.163).

The Pharisees believe "that souls possess an immortal vigor" and that "for the wicked souls there is foreordained eternal imprisonment, while for the good souls there is an easy passage to living again" (*Antiquities* 18.14–18.15).

"The Sadducees, the second of the orders,...do away with the permanence of the soul as well as punishments and rewards in the underworld"(*Jewish War* 2.164–2.165).

"For the Sadducees, reason dictates that souls disappear together with their bodies. They accept no observance whatsoever as binding that differs in any way from the [written] laws" (*Antiquities* 18.16).

Jesus on the Afterlife in the Gospels,

in Kurt Aland, Editor, *Synopsis of the Four Gospels*

(New York: United Bible Societies, 1997)

The Question about the Resurrection

Matt. 22. 23-33

23 The same day Sadducees came to him, who say that there is no resurrection; and they asked him a question, 24saying, "Teacher, Moses said,   'If a man dies, having no children, his brother must marry the widow, and raise up children for his brother.'   25Now there were seven brothers among us; the first married,   and died, and having no children left his wife to his brother. 26So too the second

and third, down to the seventh. 27After them all, the woman   died. 28In the resurrection, therefore,   to which of the seven will she be wife? For they all had her." 29But Jesus answered them,   "You are wrong, because you know neither the scriptures nor the power of God.

30For in the resurrection they neither marry nor are given in marriage, but are like angels in heaven.

31And as for the resurrection of the dead, have you not read what was said to you by God, 32'I am the God of Abraham, and the God of Isaac, and the God of Jacob'? He is not God of the dead, but of the living." 33And when the crowd heard it, they were astonished at his teaching.

Mark 12.18-27

18And Sadducees came to him, who say that there is no resurrection; and they asked him a question, saying, 19"Teacher, Moses wrote for us that if a man's brother dies and leaves a wife, but leaves no child, the man must take the wife, and raise up children for his brother. 20There were seven brothers;   the first took a wife, and when he died left no children; 21and the second took her, and died, leaving no children; and the third likewise; 22and the seven left no children.   Last of all the woman also died. 23In the resurrection whose wife will she be? For the seven had her as wife." 24Jesus said to them,   "Is not this why you are wrong, that you know neither the scriptures nor the power of God?

25For when they rise from the dead, they neither marry nor are given in marriage, but are like angels in heaven.

26And as for the dead being raised, have you not read in the book of Moses, in the passage about the bush, how God said to him, 'I am the God of Abraham, and the God of Isaac, and the God of Jacob'? 27He is not God of the dead, but of the living; you are quite wrong."

Luke 20.27-40

27There came to him some Sadducees, those who say that there is no resurrection, 28 and they asked him a question, saying, "Teacher, Moses wrote for us that if a man's brother dies, having a wife but no children, the man must take the wife and raise up children for his brother.   29Now there were seven brothers;   the first took a wife, and died without children; 30and the second

31and the third took her, and likewise all seven left no children and died. 32Afterward the woman also died. 33In the resurrection, therefore, whose wife will the woman be? For the seven had her as wife." 34And Jesus said to them,

"The sons of this age marry and are given in marriage; 35but those who are accounted worthy to attain to that age and to the resurrection from the dead neither marry nor are given in marriage, 36for they cannot die any more, because they are equal to angels and are sons of God, being sons of the resurrection.   37But that the dead are raised, even Moses showed, in the passage about the bush, where he calls the Lord the God of Abraham and the God of Isaac and the God of Jacob. 38Now he is not God of the dead, but of the living; for all live to him." 39And some of the scribes answered, "Teacher, you have spoken well."

Warnings Concerning Temptations

Matt. 18.6-9   **Mark 9.42-50**   **Luke 17.1-2**

[1]And he said to his disciples,
"Temptations to sin are sure to
come; but woe to him by whom they comel

[6]"But whoever causes one of these little ones who believe in me to sin, it would be better for him to have a great millstone fastened round his neck and to be drowned in the depth of the sea. [7]Woe to the world for temptations to sin! For it is necessary that temptations come, but woe to the man by whom the temptation comes! [8]And if your hand or your foot causes you to sin, cut it off and throw it away; it is better for you to enter life maimed or lame than with two hands or two feet to be thrown into the eternal fire.

[42]"Whoever causes one of these little ones who believe in me to sin, it would be better for him if a great millstone were hung round his neck and he were thrown into the sea.

[2]It would be better for him if a millstone were hung round his neck and he were cast into the sea, than that he should cause one of these little ones to sin.

[43]And if your hand causes you to sin, cut it off; it is better for you to enter life maimed than with two hands to go to hell, to the unquenchable fire. [45]And if your foot causes you to sin, cut it off; it is better for you to enter life lame than with two feet to be thrown into hell. [47]And if your eye causes you to sin, pluck it out;

[9]And if your eye causes you to sin, pluck it out and throw it away; it is better for you to enter life with one eye than with two eyes to be thrown into the hell of fire.

it is better for you to enter the kingdom of God with one eye than with two eyes to be thrown into hell, [48]where their worm does not die, and the fire is not quenched.

eternal burning

Early Christians on the Afterlife

1. The Apostle Paul (1 Corinthians 15)
(Sharon Lea Mattila's rather literal translation of the Greek)

[1]Now I would make known to you, brothers, the good news that I announced to you, which you in turn received, in which you also stand, [2]through which you also are being saved if you hold fast to that word of good news which I announced to you, unless you came to believe frivolously.

[3]For I handed on to you in the first place what I in turn had received:

that Christ died for our sins in accordance with the scriptures, [4]and that he was buried, and that he was raised on the third day in accordance with the scriptures, [5]and that he appeared to Cephas [i.e., Peter], then to the twelve. [6]Then he appeared to more than five hundred brothers at one time, most of whom remain [alive] until now, although some have fallen asleep. [7]Then he appeared to James [the brother of Jesus], then to all the apostles.

[8]Last of all, as to one abnormally born, he appeared also to me. [9]For I am the least of the apostles, who myself am not worthy to be called an apostle, because I persecuted the church of God. [10]It is by the grace of God that I am what I am, and his grace toward me has not proven to be empty, but I toiled more abundantly than all of them, although not I, but the grace of God that is with me.

[11]Whether I or they, therefore, this is what we proclaim and this is what you have believed.

[12]Now if Christ is proclaimed as having been raised from the dead, how are some among you saying that there is no resurrection of the dead?

[13]If there is no resurrection of the dead, then neither has Christ been raised; [14]and if Christ has not been raised, then empty is our proclamation, empty also your faith. [15]And we are even found to be false witnesses of God, because we testified about God that he raised Christ—whom he did not raise if in fact the dead are not raised. [16]For if the dead are not raised, then neither has Christ been raised. [17]If Christ has not been raised, futile is your faith and you are still in your sins. [18]In that case also those who have fallen asleep in Christ have perished. [19]If in this life only we have hoped in Christ, we are of all people the most to be pitied.

[20]But in fact Christ has been raised from the dead, the first fruits of those who have fallen asleep. [21]For since death came through a human being, the resurrection of the dead also comes through a human being; [22]for as all die in Adam, so all will be made alive in Christ. [23]But each in his own proper order: Christ the first fruits, then at his coming those who are Christ's. [24]Then comes the end, when he hands over the kingdom to God the Father, after he has destroyed every ruler and every authority and power. [25]For he must reign until he has put all his enemies under his feet. [26]The last enemy to be destroyed is death. [27]For "he has put all things in subjection under his feet." But when he has said, "All things have been put in subjection," it is plain that this does not include the one who put all things in subjection under him. [28]When all things are subjected to him, then the Son himself will also be subjected to the one who put all things in subjection under him, so that God may be all things in all things.

[29]Otherwise, what will those people do who are being baptized on behalf of the dead? If the dead are not raised at all, why are they being baptized on their behalf?

[30]And why are we putting ourselves in danger every hour? [31]I am dying day after day. I swear by my boasting of you, which I have in Christ Jesus our Lord. [32]If according to human [hope] I fought with wild beasts in Ephesus, what advantage was it to me? If the dead are not raised,

"Let us eat and drink,
        for tomorrow we die."

[33]Do not be led astray:

"Evil company ruins good morals."

[34]Become sober as righteousness demands and do not continue to sin; for some [of you] are ignorant of God. I say this to your shame.

[35]But someone will say, "How are the dead raised? With what kind of body do they come?"

PAUL IS not a Platonist

[36]Fool! You yourself sow a thing that is not made alive unless it dies; [37]indeed, the thing that you sow, it is not the body that is to be that you sow, but a naked grain, whether it happens to be of wheat or of one of the rest of the types of grain. [38]But God gives it a body just as he has willed, and to each one of the seeds its own body.

[39]Not all flesh is the same flesh, but there is one of human beings, another flesh of animals, another flesh of birds, and another of fish. [40]And there are heavenly bodies and earthly bodies; but on the one hand the glory of the heavenly bodies is different, and on the other hand that of the earthly bodies is different. [41]There is one glory of the sun, and another glory of the moon, and another glory of the stars; for even star differs from star in glory.

[42]Thus also is the resurrection of the dead. It is sown is perishability, it is raised in imperishability. [43]It is sown in dishonor, it is raised in glory. It is sown in weakness, it is raised in power. [44]It is sown an ensouled (or animate) body, it is raised a spiritual body. If there is an ensouled (or animate) body, there is also a spiritual body. [45]Thus it has also been written, "The first human being, Adam, became a living soul; the last Adam became a spirit that makes alive. [46]But it is not the spiritual body that is first, but the ensouled (or animate) one, and then the spiritual one. [47]The first human being was made of dust from the earth; the second human being is from heaven. [48]As was the one of dust, so are those who are of dust; and as is the one of heaven, so are those who are of heaven. [49]Just as we have borne the image of the one of dust, so we will also bear the image of the one of heaven.

[50]This is what I am saying, brothers: flesh and blood cannot inherit the kingdom of God, nor does the perishable inherit the imperishable.

[51]Behold, I am telling you a mystery! We will not all fall asleep, but we will all be transformed, [52]in an indivisible moment of time, in the blinking of an eye, at the last trumpet. For he will sound the trumpet and the dead will be raised imperishable, and we ourselves will be transformed. [53]For this perishable body must be clothed with imperishability, and this mortal body must be clothed with immortality. [54]When this perishable body is clothed with imperishability, and this mortal body is clothed with immortality, then the saying that has been written will come to pass:

"Death has been swallowed up into victory."

[55]"Where, O death, is your victory?

Where, O death, is your sting?"

[56]The sting of death is sin, and the power of sin is the law. [57]But thanks be to God, who gives us the victory through our Lord Jesus Christ.

[58]Therefore, my beloved brothers, be steadfast, immovable, always abounding in the work of the Lord, knowing that your toil is not empty in the Lord.

2. Revelation 20:6-22:7*

New Revised Standard Version (NRSV)

[6]Blessed and holy are those who share in the first resurrection. Over these the second death has no power, but they will be priests of God and of Christ, and they will reign with him a thousand years.

[7]When the thousand years are ended, Satan will be released from his prison [8]and will come out to deceive the nations at the four corners of the earth, Gog and Magog, in order to gather them for battle; they are as numerous as the sands of the sea. [9]They marched up over the breadth of the earth and surrounded the camp of the saints and the beloved city. And fire came down from heaven and consumed them. [10]And the devil who had deceived them was thrown into the lake of fire and sulfur, where the beast and the false prophet were, and they will be tormented day and night forever and ever.

The Dead Are Judged

[11]Then I saw a great white throne and the one who sat on it; the earth and the heaven fled from his presence, and no place was found for them. [12]And I saw the dead, great and small, standing before the throne, and books were opened. Also another book was opened, the book of life. And the dead were judged according to their works, as recorded in the books. [13]And the sea gave up the dead that were in it, Death and Hades gave

up the dead that were in them, and all were judged according to what they had done. [14]Then Death and Hades were thrown into the lake of fire. This is the second death, the lake of fire; [15]and anyone whose name was not found written in the book of life was thrown into the lake of fire.

[21]Then I saw a new heaven and a new earth; for the first heaven and the first earth had passed away, and the sea was no more. [2]And I saw the holy city, the new Jerusalem, coming down out of heaven from God, prepared as a bride adorned for her husband. [3]And I heard a loud voice from the throne saying,

"See, the tabernacle of God is among mortals.
He will tabernacle with them;
they will be his peoples,
and God himself will be with them;
[4]he will wipe every tear from their eyes.
Death will be no more;
mourning and crying and pain will be no more,
for the first things have passed away."

[5]And the one who was seated on the throne said, "See, I am making all things new." Also he said, "Write this, for these words are trustworthy and true." [6]Then he said to me, "It is done! I am the Alpha and the Omega, the beginning and the end. To the thirsty I will give water as a gift from the spring of the water of life. [7]Those who conquer will inherit these things, and I will be their God and they will be my children. [8]But as for the cowardly, the unbelieving, the polluted, the murderers, the fornicators, the sorcerers, the idolaters, and all liars, their place will be in the lake that burns with fire and sulfur, which is the second death."

[9]Then one of the seven angels who had the seven bowls full of the seven last plagues came and said to me, "Come, I will show you the bride, the wife of the Lamb." [10]And in the spirit he carried me away to a great, high mountain and showed me the holy city Jerusalem coming down out of heaven from God. [11]It has the glory of God and a radiance like a very rare jewel, like jasper, clear as crystal. [12]It has a great, high wall with twelve gates, and at the gates twelve angels, and on the gates are inscribed the names of the twelve tribes of the Israelites; [13]on the east three gates, on the north three gates, on the south three gates, and on the west three gates. [14]And the wall of the city has twelve foundations, and on them are the twelve names of the twelve apostles of the Lamb.

[15]He who talked to me had a measuring rod of gold to measure the city and its gates and walls. [16]The city lies foursquare, its length the same as its width; and he measured the city with his rod, fifteen hundred miles [Greek, twelve thousand stadia]; its length and width and height are equal. [17]He also measured its wall, almost seventy five yards [Greek, one-hundred and forty-four cubits] by human measurement, which the angel was using. [18]The wall is built of jasper, while the city is pure gold, clear as glass. [19]The foundations of the wall of the city are adorned with every jewel; the first was jasper, the second sapphire, the third agate, the fourth emerald, [20]the fifth onyx, the sixth carnelian, the seventh chrysolite, the eighth beryl, the ninth topaz, the tenth chrysoprase, the eleventh jacinth, the twelfth amethyst. [21]And the twelve gates are twelve pearls, each of the gates is a single pearl, and the street of the city is pure gold, transparent as glass.

[22]I saw no temple in the city, for its temple is the Lord God the Almighty and the Lamb. [23]And the city has no need of sun or moon to shine on it, for the glory of God is its light, and its lamp is the Lamb. [24]The nations will walk by its light, and the kings of the earth will bring their glory into it. [25]Its gates will never be shut by day—and there will be no night there. [26]People will bring into it the glory and the honor of the nations. [27]But nothing unclean will enter it, nor anyone who practices abomination or falsehood, but only those who are written in the Lamb's book of life.

[22]Then he showed me the river of the water of life, bright as crystal, flowing from the throne of God and of the Lamb [2]through the middle of the street of the city. On either side of the river is the tree of life with its twelve kinds of fruit, producing its fruit each month; and the leaves of the tree are for the healing of the nations. [3]Nothing accursed will be found there any more. But the throne of God and of the Lamb will be in it, and his slaves will worship him; [4]they will see his face, and his name will be on their foreheads. [5]And there will be no more night; they need no light of lamp or sun, for the Lord God will be their light, and they will reign forever and ever.

[6]And he said to me, "These words are trustworthy and true, for the Lord, the God of the spirits of the prophets, has sent his angel to show his slaves what must soon take place."

[7]"See, I am coming soon! Blessed is the one who keeps the words of the prophecy of this book."

Excerpts from Dante's Divine Comedy
(1308-1321 CE) Middle ages

The Inferno

Journey through the universe.

Canto III*

THROUGH ME THE WAY INTO THE DOLEFUL CITY,
 THROUGH ME THE WAY INTO ETERNAL GRIEF,
 THROUGH ME THE WAY AMONG A RACE FORSAKEN.

JUSTICE MOVED MY HEAVENLY CONSTRUCTOR;
 DIVINE OMNIPOTENCE CREATED ME,
 AND HIGHEST WISDOM JOINED WITH PRIMAL LOVE.

BEFORE ME NOTHING BUT ETERNAL THINGS
 WERE MADE, AND I SHALL LAST ETERNALLY.
 ABANDON HOPE, FOREVER, YOU WHO ENTER.

I saw these words spelled out in somber colors
 inscribed along the ledge above a gate;
 "Master," I said, "these words I see are cruel."

He answered me, speaking with experience:
 "Now here you must leave all distrust behind;
 let all your cowardice die on this spot.

We are at the place where earlier I said
 you could expect to see the suffering race
 of souls who lost the good of intellect."

Placing his hand on mine, smiling at me
 in such a way that I was reassured,
 he led me in, into those mysteries.

Here sighs and cries and shrieks of lamentation
 echoed throughout the starless air of Hell;
 at first these sounds resounding made me weep:

tongues confused, a language strained in anguish
 with cadences of anger, shrill outcries
 and raucous groans in time to slapping hands,

Canto XI

We reached the curving brink of a steep bank
   constructed of enormous broken rocks;
   below us was a crueler den of pain.

And the disgusting overflow of stench
   the deep abyss was vomiting, forced us
   back from the edge. Crouched underneath the lid

of some great tomb, I saw it was inscribed:
   "Within lies Anastasius, the Pope
   Photinus lured away from the straight path."[1]

"Our descent will have to be delayed somewhat
   so that our sense of smell may grow accustomed
   to these vile fumes; then we will not mind them,"

my master said. And I: "You will have to find
   some way to keep our time from being wasted."[2]
   "That is precisely what I had in mind,"

he said, and then began the lesson: "My son,
   within these boulders' bounds are three more circles,
   concentrically arranged like those above,

all tightly packed with souls; and so that, later,
   the sight of them alone will be enough,
   I'll tell you how and why they are imprisoned.

All malice has injustice as its end,
   an end achieved by violence or by fraud;[3]
   while both are sins that earn the hate of Heaven,

since fraud belongs exclusively to man,
   God hates it more and, therefore, far below,
   the fraudulent are placed and suffer most.

In the first of the circles below are all the violent;
   since violence can be used against three persons,
   into three concentric rounds it is divided:

violence can be done to God, to self,
   or to one's neighbor—to him or to his goods,
   as my reasoned explanation will make clear.

By violent means a man can kill his neighbor
   or wound him grievously; he can violate
   his goods by arson, theft and devastation;

so, homicides and those who strike with malice,
    those who destroy and plunder, are all punished
    in the first round, but all in different groups.

Man can raise violent hands against himself
    and his own goods; so in the second round,
    paying the debt that never can be paid,

are suicides, self-robbers of your world,
    or those who gamble all their wealth away
    and weep up there when they should have rejoiced.

One can use violence against the deity
    by heartfelt disbelief and cursing Him,
    or by despising Nature and God's bounty;

therefore, the smallest round stamps with its seal
    both Sodom and Cahors and all those souls[4]
    who hate God in their hearts and curse His name.

Fraud, that gnaws the conscience of its servants,
    can be used on one who puts his trust in you
    or else on one who has no trust invested.

This latter sort seems only to destroy
    the bond of love that Nature gives to man;
    so in the second circle there are nests

of hypocrites, flatterers, dabblers in sorcery,
    falsifiers, thieves and simonists,
    panders, seducers, grafters and like filth.

The former kind of fraud both disregards
    the love Nature enjoys and that extra bond
    between men which creates a special trust;

thus, it is in the smallest of the circles,
    at the earth's center, around the throne of Dis,[5]
    that traitors suffer their eternal pain."

And I, "Master, your reasoning runs smooth,
    and your explanation certainly makes clear
    the nature of this pit and of its inmates,[6]

but what about those in the slimy swamp,
    those driven by the wind, those beat by rain,
    and those who come to blows with harsh refrains?

Why are they, too, not punished here inside
    the city of flame, if they have earned God's wrath?
    If they have not, why are they suffering?"[7]

And he to me, "Why do you let your thoughts
   stray from the path they are accustomed to?
   Or have I missed the point you have in mind?

Have you forgotten how your *Ethics* reads,
   those terms it explicates in such detail:
   the three conditions that the heavens hate,

incontinence, malice and bestiality?
   Do you not remember how incontinence
   offends God least, and merits the least blame?[8]

If you will reconsider well this doctrine
   and then recall to mind who those souls were
   suffering pain above, outside the walls,

you will clearly see why they are separated
   from these malicious ones, and why God's vengeance
   beats down upon their souls less heavily."

Notes

[1.] *Within lies Anastasius, the Pope:* Anastasius II, Pope from 496 to 498, was popularly believed for many centuries to be a heretic because, supposedly, he allowed Photinus, a deacon of Thessalonica who followed the heresy of Acacius, to take communion. This heresy denied Christ's divine birth, asserting that He was begotten by a mortal man; thus Anastasius II supposedly revealed his belief in the heretical doctrine. It has been proved, however, that this Pope was confused with the Byzantine Emperor Anastasius I (491–518) by Dante's probable sources. Emperor Anastasius was convinced by Photinus to accept the heretical doctrine.

[2.] *to keep our time from being wasted:* Note how the Pilgrim has become a student eager to learn. The *Inferno* consists to a great extent of action; Church doctrine is usually revealed first by the realistic panorama that confronts the student-pilgrim. But as he learns more and more by example (i.e. by action), a method any new student must use at first, he begins to hear more and more philosophical and theological doctrine from his teachers (Virgil, Beatrice, St. Bernard chiefly). The preponderance of doctrine increases in the *Purgatory* and grows even greater in the *Paradise*.

[3.] *by violence or by fraud:* The distinction between Violence and Fraud is taken from Cicero's *De Officiis* I, 13.

[4.] *both Sodom and Cahors:* Sodom is, of course, the Biblical city (Genesis 18–19) destroyed by God for its vicious sexual offenses. Cahors is a city in the south of France which was widely known in the Middle Ages as a thriving seat of usury. So notorious was Cahors for this sin that *Caorsino* came to be synonymous with "usurer" in medieval times. Dante uses the city names to indicate the Sodomites and Usurers who are punished in the smallest round of Circle VII.

[5.] *at the earth's center, around the throne of Dis:* Here the name refers to Lucifer. See Canto VIII, 68.

[6.] *the nature of this pit and of its inmates:* Virgil's explanation of the *Inferno* can be reduced to the following outline:

DIVISION OF HELL	INNER DIVISIONS	CIRCLE	CANTO
Limbo		I	IV
INCONTINENCE [sins of the She-Wolf]			
Lustful		II	V
Gluttonous		III	VI
Hoarders & Wasters		IV	VII
Wrathful & Slothful		V	VII–VIII
[City of Dis]			VIII–IX
Heretics		VI	IX–XI

VIOLENCE

[sins of the Lion]

Violent	1) Against Neighbors (murderers, destroyers)	VII	XII
	2) Against Self (suicides, self-robbers)		XIII
	3) Against God, Nature, Art (blasphemers, perverts, usurers)		XIV–XVII

FRAUD

[sins of the Leopard]

	The Malebolge		
	1) Panders and Seducers	VIII	XVIII
	2) Flatterers		XVIII
Against those who have no special faith in the deceiver	3) Simonists		XIX
	4) Sorcerers (Soothsayers)		XX
	5) Grafters (Barrators)		XXI–XXIII
	6) Hypocrites		XXIII–XXIV
	7) Thieves		XXIV–XXVI
	8) Like filth (Deceivers)		XXVI–XXVII
	9) Like filth (Sowers of Discord)		XXVIII–XXIX
	10) Falsifiers and counterfeiters		XXIX–XXX
			XXXI
Against those who have faith in the deceiver: Traitors	Caina: Traitors to kindred	IX	XXXII
	Antenora: Traitors to country		XXXII–XXXIII
	Ptolomea: Traitors to guests and hosts		XXXIII
	Judecca: Traitors against benefactors		XXXIV

[7.] *but what about those in the slimy swamp:* The sinners about whom Dante questions Virgil are those guilty of Incontinence. Virgil's answer (76–90) is that the Incontinent suffer a lighter punishment because their sins, being without malice, are less offensive to God.

[8.] *Have you forgotten how your* Ethics *reads?:* Virgil says "your *Ethics* in referring to Aristotle's *Ethica Nicomachea* because he realizes how thoroughly the Pilgrim studied this work (note his reference to "your *Physics*" in line 101).

While the distinction here offered between Incontinence and Malice is based on Aristotle (Book VII, Ch. 8) it should be clear that the overall classification of sins in the *Inferno* is not. Dante's is a twofold system, the main divisions of which may be illustrated as follows:

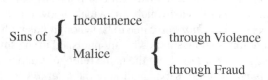

Aristotle, however, has a threefold classification: Incontinence, Malice and Bestiality (Book VII, Ch. 1), the third category having no correspondence with the outline offered by Virgil, in spite of many scholars' attempts to identify this with one of the subdivisions mentioned by him. Virgil's mention of the three sins treated by Aristotle is merely a device to introduce the work of the Greek philosopher and to indicate the exact book from which he will quote his distinction between Incontinence and Malice. For the threefold reference is found in the first sentence of Book VII of the *Nicomachean Ethics*.

It should be noted that Virgil makes no reference to the sinners in ante-Inferno, in Limbo and in the Sixth Circle; nor is it possible to fit their sins into the system presented in this canto: the Pusillanimous, the Unbaptized and the Heretics are guilty neither of Incontinence nor of Malice. With the last two groups we have to do with wrong beliefs rather than sinful acts; and with the first group it is the failure to act that is being punished. And Dante has indicated the tangential nature of their place within his moral system by the geographical location he has assigned them. The first two groups are not in Hell proper; the Heretics are within a kind of No-Man's-Land, between the sins of Incontinence and those of Malice, within the Gates of Dis but at the top of its abyss.

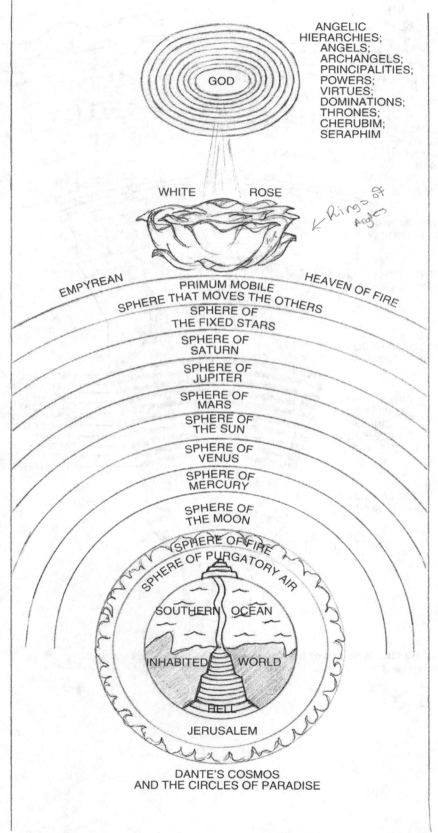

ANGELIC
HIERARCHIES;
ANGELS;
ARCHANGELS;
PRINCIPALITIES;
POWERS;
VIRTUES;
DOMINATIONS;
THRONES;
CHERUBIM;
SERAPHIM

GOD

WHITE ROSE

← Rings of Angles

EMPYREAN HEAVEN OF FIRE

PRIMUM MOBILE
SPHERE THAT MOVES THE OTHERS

SPHERE OF
THE FIXED STARS

SPHERE OF
SATURN

SPHERE OF
JUPITER

SPHERE OF
MARS

SPHERE OF
THE SUN

SPHERE OF
VENUS

SPHERE OF
MERCURY

SPHERE OF
THE MOON

SPHERE OF FIRE

SPHERE OF PURGATORY AIR

SOUTHERN OCEAN

INHABITED WORLD

HELL

JERUSALEM

DANTE'S COSMOS
AND THE CIRCLES OF PARADISE

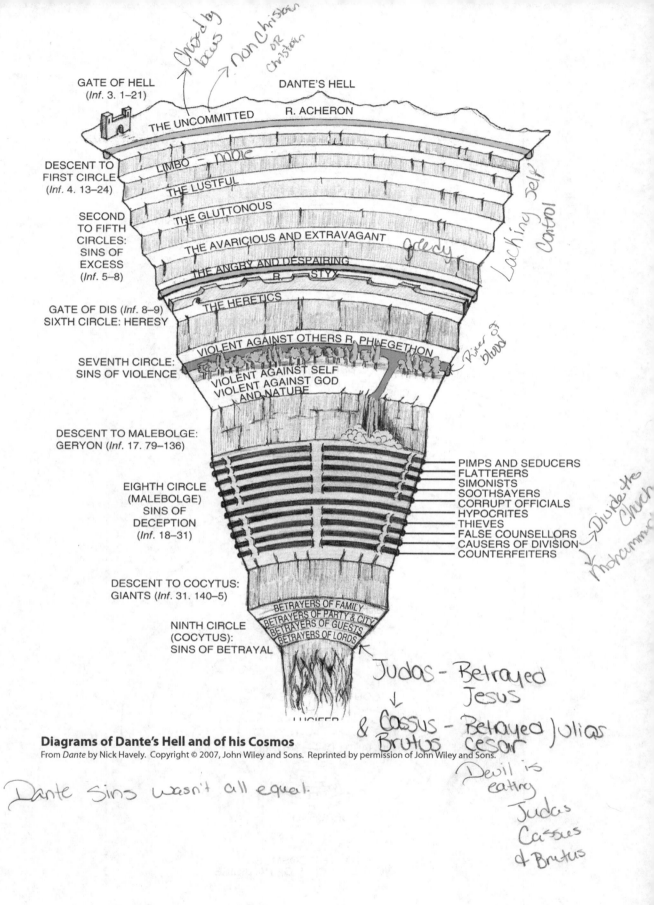

Diagrams of Dante's Hell and of his Cosmos
From *Dante* by Nick Havely. Copyright © 2007, John Wiley and Sons. Reprinted by permission of John Wiley and Sons.

Dante sins wasn't all equal.

Not a place of punishment

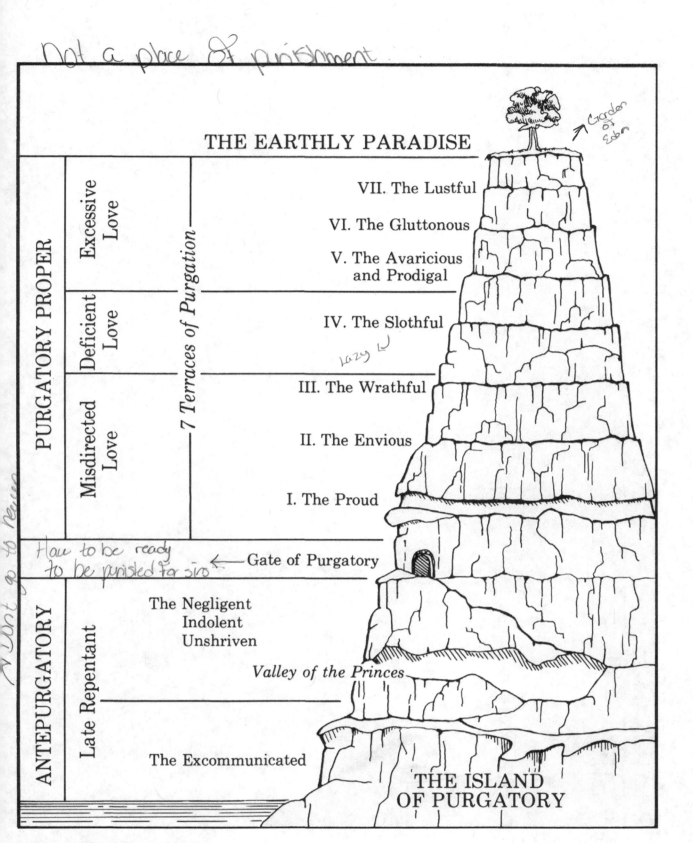

THE EARTHLY PARADISE

Garden of Eden

PURGATORY PROPER

Excessive Love

VII. The Lustful

VI. The Gluttonous

V. The Avaricious and Prodigal

Deficient Love

IV. The Slothful

Lazy w

7 Terraces of Purgation

III. The Wrathful

Misdirected Love

II. The Envious

I. The Proud

How to be ready to be punished for sin ← Gate of Purgatory

I dont go to heaven

ANTEPURGATORY

Late Repentant

The Negligent
Indolent
Unshriven

Valley of the Princes

The Excommunicated

THE ISLAND OF PURGATORY

Diagram of Dante's Purgatory

From *Dante's Purgatory* by Mark Musa (Translator and Editor). Copyright © 1981 by Indiana University Press. Reprinted by permission.

Section Five
Division and Further Division
The Split between Judaism and Christianity and the Church's Three-Way Split

Study Guide/Section Five

(Questions with an * can be answered on the basis of the readings; others must be answered using your class notes.)

1. *The first split of the early Church from Judaism*:
   a. List the most important differences between Jesus' ministry and Paul's ministry.
   b. *According to both the book of Acts and Paul himself in his letter to the Galatians, what was the main point of contention for the earliest Christians regarding what was necessary to be saved?
   c. Explain the relationship between the Jewish "Oral Torah," the Pharisees, the Sadducees, Jesus, the Rabbis, the Mishnah, and the two Talmuds.
   d. *Which teaching of Jesus does Hillel's teaching, recorded in the Babylonian Talmud, remind you of? ⤷a pharsie rabe. ⤷live before Jesus
   e. *According to the Mishnah, why did God create the first human being alone, as recorded in the Yahwist account of creation?
   f. *According to the great medieval Jewish teacher, Maimonides, who was responsible for Christians breaking away from obedience to the Jewish law? How does your reading of the excerpts from Acts and Paul's letter to the Galatians show that Maimonides was mistaken?
   g. *Summarize Maimonides' opinions about Jesus as he presents them in the excerpt from his writings in this sourcebook.

2. *The split between the Orthodox and Catholic Churches*:
   a. *What is the "filioque clause" and why did the Orthodox Church object so strongly to its addition into the original Nicene Creed by the Catholics?
   b. What were the two other main causes of the Catholic vs. Orthodox split?
   c. What did the "Franks" (i.e., the Crusaders) do to the Great Church of Hagia Sophia ("Holy Wisdom") in Constantinople after sacking the city?

3. *The Protestant Reformation*:
   a. What was Martin Luther before he initiated the Reformation? Monk
   b. What Catholic teachings and abuses in particular did Luther seek to reform? endulgences catledies of preist.

4. *Disputes among Protestants: An Example—Calvin versus Arminius on the Issues of Human Nature, Free Will, and Predestination, in Turn Contrasted with a Traditional Jewish View (Maimonides)*:
   a. *Compare and contrast the views of Calvin, Arminius, and Maimonides on these three topics.
   b. *How do they each describe human nature and divine predestination vs. human free will?
   c. *Explain the very different way that Maimonides interprets the Yahwist story of when the first woman and man ate from the tree of knowledge of good and evil, in contrast to how both Protestant thinkers interpret this story.

HISTORICAL TIME-LINE / SECTION FIVE

30s CE

The ministry of **Jesus of Nazareth**, which is **predominantly to his fellow Jews** living in Palestine. His contacts with Gentiles are rare, and never is he recorded as eating with Gentiles or saying that circumcision is no longer necessary.

Late 30s to 60s CE

The ministry of **the apostle Paul** who has fierce **Jewish Christian opponents** who insist that **one must follow Torah** in order to be saved. The **Jerusalem Council** decides that **Gentiles do not need to keep Torah**; but Paul later has a **major fight with Peter**, Barnabas, and people from James over the issue of Jews eating with Gentiles.

70 CE

[handwritten: Split between Judaism & Christianity]

The **Jerusalem Temple is destroyed. Pauline Christians, mostly Gentiles**, outnumber Jewish Christians, so **Christianity now becomes a new religion**. Most of the priestly Sadducees and the Essenes die out, so **Rabbinic Judaism**, based in **synagogues**, comes to the fore.

325 CE

[handwritten: monotheists]

Constantine the Great **makes Christianity the official religion** of the Roman Empire, shifts his capital to **Constantinople**, and convenes the Council of Nicea, which composes the **Nicene Creed**.

581 CE

The Council of Toledo in Spain, the **Latin western part** of the Empire, **adds the *filioque* clause** to the **Nicene Creed**, which is **rejected by the eastern Orthodox church to this day**.

1054 CE

The **Great Schism** takes place between the western **Latin, Catholic church** on the one hand, and the **eastern Greek Orthodox (= Byzantine)** church on the other. The issues included the *filioque* clause, the status of the Pope, and the language difference.

1100s CE

The great **Jewish philosopher, Maimonides**, thrives in Muslim occupied southern Spain.

1204 CE

The **Sack of Constantinople** by the **Catholic Crusaders** and the pillaging of Orthodox churches consolidates the breach between the eastern and western churches.

1517 CE

The Catholic monk, **Martin Luther**, posts his 95 theses against abuses in the Catholic Church, leading to the **Protestant Reformation**.

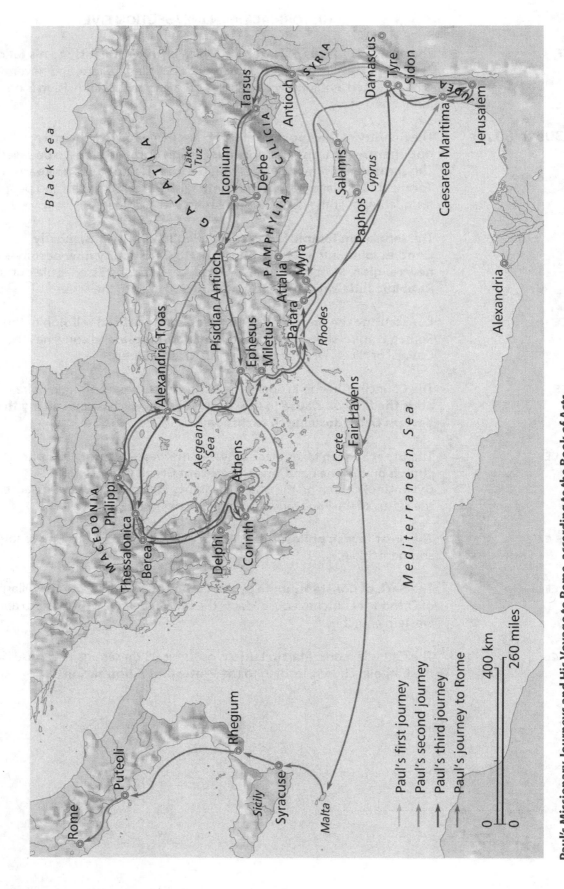

Paul's Missionary Journeys and His Voyage to Rome, according to the Book of Acts

Map taken from *The Archaeology of the Bible* by James K Hoffmeier, published by Lion Hudson plc, 2008. Copyright © 2008 Lion Hudson plc. Used with permission of Lion Hudson plc.

Black Sea

SYRIA

Damascus

Tyre
Sidon

Tarsus

Antioch

CILICIA

JUDEA

Jerusalem

GALATIA

Lake
Tuz

Iconium

Derbe

Salamis

Cyprus

Paphos

Caesarea Maritima

Pisidian Antioch

PAMPHYLIA

Attalia

Myra

Alexandria Troas

Ephesus
Miletus

Patara

Rhodes

Alexandria

Aegean
Sea

Athens

Crete

Fair Havens

Mediterranean Sea

MACEDONIA

Philippi
Thessalonica
Berea

Delphi

Corinth

Rhegium

Puteoli

Rome

Sicily

Syracuse

Malta

Paul's first journey
Paul's second journey
Paul's third journey
Paul's journey to Rome

400 km
260 miles

0
0

The Apostle Paul's Letter to the Galatians
1:11 to 2:14

(Sharon Lea Mattila's Translation)

written earlier than Acts.

Paul Describes His Conversion, His Prior Life, and Early Years of Ministry with Barnabas

[11]For I want you to know, brothers, that the good news proclaimed by me is not of human origin; [12]for I neither received it from any human being, nor was I taught it, but I received it through a revelation of Jesus Christ.

[13]For you heard of my former manner of life in Judaism, that I was persecuting the church of God beyond measure and was trying to destroy it. [14]I advanced in Judaism beyond many [Jews] of the same age, having been more abundantly zealous for the traditions of my ancestors. [15]But when God, who set me apart from my mother's womb and called me through his grace, considered it fit [16]to reveal his Son in me, in order that I might proclaim the good news concerning him among the [Gentile] peoples, immediately afterwards I neither conferred with flesh and blood, [17]nor did I go up into Jerusalem to those who were apostles before me, but I departed into Arabia and [then] returned back to Damascus.

[18]Then after three years I went up into Jerusalem in order to visit Cephas [Peter's Aramaic name] and remained with him fifteen days; [19]but I did not see any other apostle except James the brother of the Lord. [20]Concerning these matters that I am writing to you, behold, before God, I am not lying! [21]Then I went into the regions of Syria and of Cilicia, [22]but I continued to be unknown by face to the churches of Judea that are in Christ. [23]They were only hearing that "The one who formerly was persecuting us is now proclaiming the good news concerning the faith he formerly sought to destroy." [24]And they glorified God [who is] in me.

The Jerusalem Council According to Paul

2.[1]Then after fourteen years I went back up into Jerusalem with Barnabas, taking Titus also along with me; [2]but I went up according to a revelation; and I set before them the good news that I am announcing among the [Gentile] peoples, although privately to those considered to be of repute, [so as to ensure that] somehow I am not running, or had not run, into emptiness [or, in vain]. [3]But not even Titus, who was with me, although he is a Greek, was compelled to be circumcised; [4]on account of the false brothers who were privately admitted [into the meeting]. These men slipped in to spy on the freedom we have in Christ Jesus, in order that they might enslave us. [5]To them we did not succumb in submission for any period of time, so that the truth of the gospel might remain with you. [6]But from those who are considered to be something [of repute]—whatever they were makes no difference to me; God does not accept people according to their face [i.e., according to appearances]—those considered to be of repute added nothing to me. [7]But on the contrary, when they saw that I have been entrusted with the good news of the uncircumcision, just as Peter [the good news] of the circumcision—[8]for he who worked in Peter making him into an apostle of the circumcision also worked in me toward the [Gentile] peoples—[9]and when they came to know the grace which was given to me, James and Cephas [Peter's Aramaic name] and John, the ones considered to be pillars, gave to Barnabas and me the right hand of fellowship, in order that we [should go] to the [Gentile] peoples and they to the [people of the] circumcision; [10]the only thing they insisted is that we remember the poor, the very thing that I myself was eager to do.

Paul Rebukes Peter at Antioch

[11]But when Cephas came into Antioch, I opposed him to his face, for he was condemned. [12]For before certain people from James came, he used to eat with the [Gentile] peoples. But when they came, he withdrew and kept himself separate, fearing those of the circumcision. [13]And the rest of the Jews played the hypocrite along with him, so that even Barnabas was led astray by their hypocrisy. [14]But when I saw that they were not walking correctly with regard to the truth of the good news, I said to Cephas in front of all of them, "If you yourself, being a Jew, live like the [Gentile] peoples and not like a Jew, how can you compel the [Gentile] peoples to live like Jews?"

The Council at Jerusalem according to *The Book of Acts**

○Coming from Jerusalem

15.1 Then certain individuals came down from Judea and were teaching the brothers, "Unless you are circumcised according to the custom of Moses, you cannot be saved." [2]And after Paul and Barnabas had no small dissension and debate with them, Paul and Barnabas and some of the others were appointed to go up to Jerusalem to discuss this question with the apostles and the elders. [3]So they were sent on their way by the church, and as they passed through both Phoenicia and Samaria, they reported the conversion of the Gentiles, and brought great joy to all the believers. [4]When they came to Jerusalem, they were welcomed by the church and the apostles and the elders, and they reported all that God had done with them. [5]But some believers who belonged to the sect of the Pharisees stood up and said, "It is necessary for them to be circumcised and ordered to keep the Law of Moses." *—you have to keep Froth to be Saued —Paul argued this*

[6]The apostles and the elders met together to consider this matter. [7]After there had been much debate, Peter stood up and said to them, "My brothers, you know that in the early days God made a choice among you, that I should be the one through whom the Gentiles would hear the message of the good news and become believers. [8]And God, who knows the human heart, testified to them by giving them the Holy Spirit, just as he did to us; [9]and in cleansing their hearts by faith he has made no distinction between them and us. [10]Now therefore why are you putting God to the test by placing on the neck of the disciples a yoke that neither our ancestors nor we have been able to bear? [11]On the contrary, we believe that we will be saved through the grace of the Lord Jesus, just as they will."

[12]The whole assembly kept silence, and listened to Barnabas and Paul as they told of all the signs and wonders that God had done through them among the Gentiles. [13]After they finished speaking, James replied, "My brothers, listen to me. [14]Simeon has related how God first looked favorably on the Gentiles, to take from among them a people for his name. [15]This agrees with the words of the prophets, as it is written,

[16]'After this I will return,
and I will rebuild the dwelling of David, which has fallen;
from its ruins I will rebuild it,
and I will set it up,
[17]so that all other peoples may seek the Lord—
even all the Gentiles over whom my name has been called.
Thus says the Lord, who has been making these things [18]known from long ago.'

[19]Therefore, I have reached the decision that we should not trouble those Gentiles who are turning to God, [20]but we should write to them to abstain only from things polluted by idols and from fornication and from whatever has been strangled and from blood. [21]For in every city, for generations past, Moses has had those who proclaim him, for he has been read aloud every Sabbath in the synagogues."

The Council's Letter to Gentile Believers

[22]Then the apostles and the elders, with the consent of the whole church, decided to choose men from among their members and to send them to Antioch with Paul and Barnabas. They sent Judas called Barsabbas, and Silas, leaders among the brothers, [23]with the following letter: "The brothers, both the apostles and the elders, to the believers of Gentile origin in Antioch and Syria and Cilicia, greetings. [24]Since we have heard that certain persons who have gone out from us, though with no instructions from us, have said things to disturb you and have unsettled your minds, [25]we have decided unanimously to choose representatives and send them

to you, along with our beloved Barnabas and Paul, [26]who have risked their lives for the sake of our Lord Jesus Christ. [27]We have therefore sent Judas and Silas, who themselves will tell you the same things by word of mouth. [28]For it has seemed good to the Holy Spirit and to us to impose on you no further burden than these essentials: [29]that you abstain from what has been sacrificed to idols and from blood and from what is strangled and from fornication. If you keep yourselves from these, you will do well. Farewell."

[30]So they were sent off and went down to Antioch. When they gathered the congregation together, they delivered the letter. [31]When its members read it, they rejoiced at the exhortation. [32]Judas and Silas, who were themselves prophets, said much to encourage and strengthen the believers. [33]After they had been there for some time, they were sent off in peace by the believers to those who had sent them. [35]But Paul and Barnabas remained in Antioch, and there, with many others, they taught and proclaimed the word of the Lord.

Paul and Barnabas Separate

[36]After some days Paul said to Barnabas, "Come, let us return and visit the believers in every city where we proclaimed the word of the Lord and see how they are doing." [37]Barnabas wanted to take with them John called Mark. [38]But Paul decided not to take with them one who had deserted them in Pamphylia and had not accompanied them in the work. [39]The disagreement became so sharp that they parted company; Barnabas took Mark with him and sailed away to Cyprus. [40]But Paul chose Silas and set out, the believers commending him to the grace of the Lord. [41]He went through Syria and Cilicia, strengthening the churches.

Excerpts from Rabbinic Texts*

Excerpt from the Mishnah, Tractate Sanhedrin 4:5, as Translated by Herbert Danby (Oxford University Press, 1933), with a Few Modifications

"Therefore, only a single man was created in the world, to teach that if any man has caused a single soul to perish, Scripture imputes it to him as though he had caused a whole world to perish; and if any man saves alive a single soul, Scripture imputes it to him as though he had saved alive a whole world. Again [only a single man was created] for the sake of peace among humankind, that none should say to his fellow, 'My father was greater than your father.'... Again [only a single man was created] to proclaim the greatness of the Holy One, Blessed be He, for humankind stamps many coins from one mold, they are all like one another, but the King of Kings, the Holy One, Blessed be He, has stamped every human being with the mold of the first one, and yet not one of them is like his [or her] fellow. Therefore, everyone must say, 'The world was created for my sake.'"

Excerpt from the Babylonian Talmud's Gemara (Commentary) on the Mishnah Tractate Shabbat 2:5/31A, from Jacob Neusner and Naom M. M. Neusner, eds, *The Book of Jewish Wisdom: The Talmud of the Well-Considered Life* (New York: Continuum, 1996), with a Few Modifications

"There was a case of a gentile who came before Shammai. He said to him, 'Convert me on condition that you teach me the entire Torah while I am standing on one foot.' [Shammai] drove him off with the building cubit that he had in his hand. [The gentile] came before Hillel: 'Convert me' [on the same condition]. [Hillel] said to him, 'What is hateful to you, to your fellow don't do. That's the entirety of Torah; everything else is commentary. So go, study."

※ Torah ↳ what you don't want done to you don't do to others.

Jesus time ↓ Golden Rule!

Many Jewish Sects (most die out):

Essenes   Sadducees   **Pharisees**

Zealots and Sicarri

Christians (Pauline and Jewish)

THE DESTRUCTION OF THE SECOND TEMPLE (70 CE)

Mostly Pauline Christianity (with a few Jewish Christians surviving)

Rabbinic Judaism

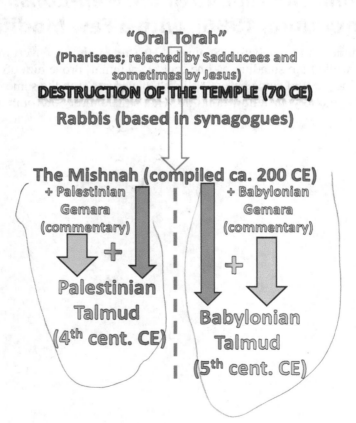

"Oral Torah"
(Pharisees; rejected by Sadducees and sometimes by Jesus)
DESTRUCTION OF THE TEMPLE (70 CE)
Rabbis (based in synagogues)

The Mishnah (compiled ca. 200 CE)

+ Palestinian Gemara (commentary)

+ Babylonian Gemara (commentary)

Palestinian Talmud (4th cent. CE)

Babylonian Talmud (5th cent. CE)

The Medieval Jewish Philosopher, Maimonides (1135-1204 CE), on Jesus of Nazareth*

After that there arose a new sect which combined the two methods, namely, conquest and controversy, into one, because it believed that this procedure would be more effective in wiping out every trace of the Jewish nation and religion. It, therefore, resolved to lay claim to prophecy and to found a new faith, contrary to our divine religion, and to contend that it was equally God-given. Thereby it hoped to raise doubts and to create confusion, since one is opposed to the other and both supposedly emanate from a divine source, which would lead to the destruction of both religions. For such is the remarkable plan contrived by a man who is envious and querulous. He will strive to kill his enemy and to save his own life, but when he finds it impossible to attain his objective, he will devise a scheme whereby they both will be slain.

The first one to have adopted this plan was Jesus the Nazarene, may his bones be ground to dust. He was a Jew because his mother was a Jewess although his father was a Gentile. For in accordance with the principles of our law, a child born of a Jewess and a Gentile, or of a Jewess and a slave, is legitimate (Yevamot 45a). Jesus is only figuratively termed an illegitimate child. He impelled people to believe that he was a prophet sent by God to clarify perplexities in the Torah, and that he was the Messiah that was predicted by each and every seer. He interpreted the Torah and its precepts in such a fashion as to lead to their total annulment, to the abolition of all its commandments and to the violation of its prohibitions. The sages, of blessed memory, having become aware of his plans before his reputation spread among our people, meted out fitting punishment to him.

Daniel had already alluded to him when he presaged the downfall of a wicked one and a heretic among the Jews who would endeavor to destroy the Law, claim prophecy for himself, make pretenses to miracles, and allege that he is the Messiah, as it is written, "Also the children of the impudent among your people shall make bold to claim prophecy, but they shall fall" (Dan. 11:14).

- Maimonides doesn't believe that Jesus was raised from the dead.
- Doesn't believe that Jesus was the Son of God nor Joseph. but of a Roman soldier.
- Was a legit Jew because his mother was a jew. Father was a Gentile.
- Doesn't believe that Jesus was Messiah nor was he performing miricals

The Nicene Creed*

The Nicene Creed was initially composed during the early church period and adopted in revised form at the Council at Nicea in 325 CE. It was further modified at the Council of Constantinople in 381 CE, although some scholars believe it took its penultimate form at the Council at Chalcedon in 451 CE. At the local Council of Toledo in 589 CE, the sentence "I believe in the Holy Ghost . . . who proceeds from the father" was expanded to read "who proceeds from the father and the son (filioque)." The issue involves whether the Holy Ghost originated from the father alone, or both the father and the son. Known as the filioque clause, its inclusion provoked discord with the Eastern Orthodox churches, and became their rallying cry in the Great Schism of 1054. The filioque clause was definitively added to the creed by the Catholics at the Second Council of Lyons in 1274. Today, the Nicene Creed remains the most popular confession of faith in Catholic, Orthodox, and most Protestant liturgies, although Orthodox churches omit the filioque clause.

I believe in one God the father almighty, maker of heaven and earth, and of all things visible and invisible. And in one lord Jesus Christ, the only begotten son of God, begotten of his father before all worlds, God of God, light of light, true God of true God, begotten, not made, being of one substance with the father, by whom all things were made. Who for us men, and for our salvation came down from heaven, and was incarnate by the Holy Ghost of the Virgin Mary, and was made man, and was crucified also for us under Pontius Pilate. He suffered and was buried, and the third day he rose again according to the scriptures, and ascended into heaven, and sits on the right hand of the father. And he shall come again with glory to judge both the quick and the dead: whose kingdom shall have no end. And I believe in the Holy Ghost, the lord and giver of life, who proceeds from the father and the son, who with the father and the son together is worshipped and glorified, who spoke by the prophets. And I believe in one catholic and apostolic church. I acknowledge one baptism for the remission of sins, and I look for the resurrection of the dead, and the life of the world to come. Amen.

The Sack of Constantinople by the Crusaders in 1204 CE
Palazzo Ducale, Venice, Italy/Bridgeman Images

Calvin, Arminius, and Maimonides on Human Nature, Divine Predestination, and Free Will

Calvin on Original Sin and Total Depravity*

As it was the spiritual life of Adam to remain united and bound to his Maker, so estrangement from him was the death of his soul. Nor is it any wonder that he consigned his race to ruin by his rebellion when he perverted the whole order of nature in heaven and on earth. . . . Therefore, after the heavenly image was obliterated in him, he was not the only one to suffer this punishment—that, in place of wisdom, virtue, holiness, truth, and justice, with which adornments he had been clad, there came forth the most filthy plagues, blindness, impotence, impurity, vanity, and injustice—but he also entangled and immersed his offspring in the same miseries.

This is the inherited corruption, which the church fathers termed "original sin," meaning by the word "sin" the depravation of a nature previously good and pure. . . .

Therefore all of us, who have descended from impure seed, are born infected with the contagion of sin. In fact, before we saw the light of this life we were soiled and spotted in God's sight. . . . Hence, rotten branches came forth from a rotten root, which transmitted their rottenness to the other twigs sprouting from them. For thus were the children corrupted in the parent, so that they brought disease upon their children's children. That is, the beginning of corruption in Adam was such that it was conveyed in a perpetual stream from the ancestors into their descendants. . . .

So that these remarks may not be made concerning an uncertain and unknown matter, let us define original sin. It is not my intention to investigate the several definitions proposed by various writers, but simply to bring forward the one that appears to me most in accordance with truth. Original sin, therefore, seems to be a hereditary depravity and corruption of our nature, diffused into all parts of the soul, which first makes us liable to God's wrath, then also brings forth in us those works which Scripture calls "works of the flesh" (Gal. 5:19). . . . For, since it is said that we became subject to God's judgment through Adam's sin, we are to understand it not as if we, guiltless and undeserving, bore the guilt of his offense but in the sense that, since we through his transgression have become entangled in the curse, he is said to have made us guilty. . . .

In every age there have been persons who, guided by nature, have striven toward virtue throughout life. I have nothing to say against them even if many lapses can be noted in their moral conduct. For they have by the very zeal of their honesty given proof that there was some purity in their nature. . . . These examples, accordingly, seem to warn us against adjudging man's nature wholly corrupted, because some men have by its prompting not only excelled in remarkable deeds, but conducted themselves most honorably throughout life. But here it ought to occur to us that amid this corruption of nature there is some place for God's grace; not such grace as to cleanse it, but to restrain it inwardly. For if the Lord gave loose rein to the mind of each man to run riot in his lusts, there would doubtless be no one who would not show that, in fact, every evil thing for which Paul condemns all nature is most truly to be met in himself (Ps. 14:3; Rom. 3:12).

What then? Do you count yourself exempt from the number of those whose "feet are swift to shed blood" (Rom. 3:15), whose hands are fouled with robberies and murders, "whose throats are like open graves, whose tongues deceive, whose lips are envenomed" (Rom. 3:13); whose works are useless, wicked, rotten, deadly; whose hearts are without God; whose inmost parts, depravities; whose eyes are set upon stratagems; whose minds are eager to revile—to sum up, whose every part stands ready to commit infinite wickedness (Rom. 3:10-18)? . . .

Therefore let us hold this as an undoubted truth which no siege engines can shake: the mind of man has been so completely estranged from God's righteousness that it conceives, desires, and undertakes, only that which is impious, perverted, foul, impure, and infamous. The heart is so steeped in the poison of sin, that it can breathe out nothing but a loathsome stench. But if some men occasionally make a show of good, their minds nevertheless ever remain enveloped in hypocrisy and deceitful craft, and their hearts bound by inner perversity.

Calvin on Election and Predestination*

If it is plain that it comes to pass by God's bidding that salvation is freely offered to some while others are barred from access to it, at once great and difficult questions spring up, explicable only when reverent minds regard as settled what they may suitably hold concerning election and predestination. A baffling question this seems to many. For they think nothing more inconsistent than that out of the common multitude of men some should be predestined to salvation, others to destruction. . . .

But before I enter into the matter itself, I need to mention by way of preface two kinds of men. Human curiosity renders the discussion of predestination, already somewhat difficult of itself, very confusing and even dangerous. No restraints can hold it back from wandering in forbidden bypaths and thrusting upward to the heights. If allowed, it will leave no secret to God that it will not search out and unravel. . . . Let this, therefore, first of all be before our eyes: to seek any other knowledge of predestination than what the Word of God discloses is not less insane than if one should purpose to walk in a pathless waste (cf. Job 12:24), or to see in darkness. And let us not be ashamed to be ignorant of something in this matter, wherein there is a certain learned ignorance. . . .

There are others who, wishing to cure this evil, all but require that every mention of predestination be buried; indeed, they teach us to avoid any question of it as we would a reef. . . . Therefore, to hold to a proper limit in this regard also, we shall have to turn back to the Word of the Lord, in which we have a sure rule for the understanding. For Scripture is the school of the Holy Spirit, in which, as nothing is omitted that is both necessary and useful to know, so nothing is taught but what is expedient to know. Therefore we must guard against depriving believers of anything disclosed about predestination in Scripture, lest we seem either wickedly to defraud them of the blessing of their God or to accuse and scoff at the Holy Spirit for having published what it is in any way profitable to suppress. . . .

As Scripture, then, clearly shows, we say that God once established by his eternal and unchangeable plan those whom he long before determined once for all to receive into salvation, and those whom, on the other hand, he would devote to destruction. We assert that, with respect to the elect, this plan was founded upon his freely given mercy, without regard to human worth; but by his just and irreprehensible but incomprehensible judgment he has barred the door of life to those whom he has given over to damnation. Now among the elect we regard the call as a testimony of election. Then we hold justification another sign of its manifestation, until they come into the glory in which the fulfillment of that election lies. But as the Lord seals his elect by call and justification, so, by shutting off the reprobate from knowledge of his name or from the sanctification of his Spirit, he, as it were, reveals by these marks what sort of judgment awaits them. . . .

Although the voice of the gospel addresses all in general, yet the gift of faith is rare. . . . For seed to fall among thorns (Matt. 13:7) or on rocky ground (Matt. 13:5) is nothing new, not only because the greater part indeed show themselves obstinately disobedient to God, but because not all have been supplied with eyes and ears. . . .

Now a word concerning the reprobate. . . . If, then, we cannot determine a reason why he vouchsafes mercy to his own, except that it so pleases him, neither shall we have any reason for rejecting others, other than his will. For when it is said that God hardens or shows mercy to whom he wills, men are warned by this to seek no cause outside his will. . . .

If we seek God's fatherly mercy and kindly heart, we should turn our eyes to Christ, on whom alone God's Spirit rests (cf. Matt. 3:17). If we seek salvation, life, and the immortality of the Heavenly Kingdom, then there is no other to whom we may flee, seeing that he alone is the fountain of life, the anchor of salvation, and the heir of the Kingdom of Heaven. Now what is the purpose of election but that we, adopted as sons by our Heavenly Father, may obtain salvation and immortality by his favor? . . . Christ, then, is the mirror wherein we must, and without self-deception may, contemplate our own election. . . .

* From *Calvin: Institutes of the Christian Religion* by John T. McNeill. Copyright © 1960 by Westminster John Knox Press. Reprinted by permission.

Therefore, if we desire to know whether God cares for our salvation, let us inquire whether he has entrusted us to Christ, whom he has established as the sole Savior of all his people. If we still doubt whether we have been received by Christ into his care and protection, he meets that doubt when he willingly offers himself as shepherd, and declares that we shall be numbered among his flock if we hear his voice (John 10:3). Let us therefore embrace Christ, who is graciously offered to us, and comes to meet us. He will reckon us in his flock and enclose us within his fold.

What Is an Arminian?*

To say, "This man is an Arminian," has the same effect on many hearers, as to say, "This is a mad dog." It puts them into a fright at once: They run away from him with all speed and diligence; and will hardly stop, unless it be to throw a stone at the dreadful and mischievous animal.

The more unintelligible the word is, the better it answers the purpose. Those on whom it is fixed know not what to do: Not understanding what it means, they cannot tell what defence to make, or how to clear themselves from the charge. And it is not easy to remove the prejudice which others have imbibed, who know no more of it, than that it is "something *very* bad," if not *"all* that is bad!"

To clear the meaning, therefore, of this ambiguous term, may be of use to many: To those who so freely pin this name upon others, that they may not say what they do not understand; to those that hear them, that they may be no longer abused by men saying they know not what; and to those upon whom the name is fixed, that they may know how to answer for themselves. . . .

The rise of the word was this: James Harmens, in Latin, *Jacobus Arminius,* was first one of the Ministers of Amsterdam, and afterwards Professor of Divinity at Leyden. He was educated at Geneva; but in the year 1591 began to doubt of the principles which he had till then received. And being more and more convinced that they were wrong, when he was vested with the Professorship, he publicly taught what he believed the truth, till, in the year 1609, he died in peace. But a few years after his death, some zealous men with the Prince of Orange at their head, furiously assaulted all that held what were called his opinions; and having procured them to be solemnly condemned, in the famous Synod of Dort, (not so numerous or learned, but full as impartial, as the Council or Synod of Trent,) some were put to death, some banished, some imprisoned for life, all turned out of their employments, and made incapable of holding any office, either in Church or State.   ↙ Calvinists

The errors charged upon these (usually termed *Arminians*) by their opponents, are five: (1.) That they deny original sin; (2.) That they deny justification by faith; (3.) That they deny absolute predestination; (4.) That they deny the grace of God to be irresistible; and, (5.) That they affirm, a believer may fall from grace.

With regard to the two first of these charges, they plead, Not Guilty. They are entirely false. No man that ever lived, not John Calvin himself, ever asserted either original sin, or justification by faith, in more strong, more clear and express terms, than Arminius has done. These two points, therefore, are to be set out of the question: In these both parties agree. In this respect, there is not a hair's breadth difference between Mr. Wesley and Mr. Whitefield.

But there is an undeniable difference between the Calvinists and Arminians, with regard to the three other questions. Here they divide; the former believe absolute, the latter only conditional, predestination. The Calvinists hold, God has absolutely decreed, from all eternity, to save such and such persons, and no others; and that Christ died for these, and none else. The Arminians hold, God has decreed, from all eternity, touching all that have the written word, "He that believeth shall be saved: He that believeth not, shall be condemned:" And in order to this, "Christ died for all, all that were dead in trespasses and sins;" that is, for every child of Adam, since "in Adam all died."

The Calvinists hold, Secondly, that the saving grace of God is absolutely irresistible; that no man is any more able to resist it, than to resist the stroke of lightning. The Arminians hold, that although there may be some moments wherein the grace of God acts irresistibly, yet, in general, any man may resist, and that to his eternal ruin, the grace whereby it was the will of God he should have been eternally saved.

* *The Works of John Wesley*, X, 358–60.

The Calvinists hold, Thirdly, that a true believer in Christ cannot possibly fall from grace. The Arminians hold, that a true believer may "make shipwreck of faith and a good conscience;" that he may fall, not only foully, but finally, so as to perish for ever.

The Jewish Philosopher, Maimonides, on Human Nature, Free will, and Divine Providence*

Chapter 5

[1]Free will is bestowed on every human being. If one desires to turn toward the good way and be righteous, he has the power to do so. If one wishes to turn toward the evil way and be wicked, he is at liberty to do so. And thus it is written in the Torah, "Behold, the man is become as one of us, to know good and evil" (Gen. 3:22)—which means that the human species had become unique in the world—there being no other species like it in the following respect, namely, that man, of himself and by the exercise of his own intelligence and reason, knows what is good and what is evil, and there is none who can prevent him from doing that which is good or that which is evil. And since this is so there is reason to fear "lest he put forth his hand . . ." (*ibid.*).

[2]Let not the notion, expressed by foolish Gentiles and most of the senseless folk among Israelites, pass through your mind that at the beginning of a person's existence the Almighty decrees that he is to be either righteous or wicked. This is not so. Every human being may become righteous like Moses our Teacher, or wicked like Jeroboam; wise or foolish, merciful or cruel, niggardly or generous, and so with all other qualities. There is no one that coerces him or decrees what he is to do, or draws him to either of the two ways; but every person turns to the way which he desires, spontaneously and of his own volition. Thus Jeremiah said, "Out of the mouth of the Most High proceeds not evil and good?" (Lam, 3:38); that is to say, the Creator does not decree either that a man shall be good or that he shall be wicked. Accordingly it follows that it is the sinner who has inflicted injury on himself; and he should, therefore, weep for and bewail what he has done to his soul—how he has mistreated it. This is expressed in the next verse, "Wherefore does a living man complain, a strong man, because of his sins" (*ibid.* 3:39). The prophet continues: since liberty of action is in our hands and we have, of our free will, committed all these evils, it behooves us to return in a spirit of repentance, and forsake our wickedness, for we have the power to do so. This thought is expressed in the next verse, "Let us search and try our ways, and return to the Lord" (*ibid.* 3:40).

[3]This doctrine is an important principle, the pillar of the Law and the commandment, as it is said, "See, I set before you this day life and good, and death and evil" (Deut. 30:15); and again it is written, "Behold, I set before you this day a blessing and a curse" (*ibid.* 11:26). This means that the power is in your hands, and whatever a man desires to do among the things that human beings do, he can do, whether they are good or evil; and, because of this faculty, it is said, "O that they had such a heart as this always" (*ibid.* 5:26), which implies that the Creator neither puts compulsion on the children of men nor decrees that they should do either good or evil, but it is all left to their discretion.

[4]If God had decreed that a person should be either righteous or wicked, or if there were some force inherent in his nature which irresistibly drew him to a particular course, or to a special branch of knowledge, to special views or activities, as the foolish astrologers out of their own fancy pretend, how could the Almighty have charged us through the prophets: "Do this and do not do that, improve your ways, do not follow your wicked impulses," when, from the beginning of his existence his destiny had already been decreed, or his innate constitution irresistibly drew him to that from which he could not set himself free? What room would there be for the whole of the Torah? By what right or justice could God punish the wicked or reward the righteous? "Shall not the Judge of all the earth act justly?" (Gen. 1.8:25).

Section Six
Islam
Descendants of Abraham's Eldest Son, Ishmael

Study Guide on Islam/Section Six

(These questions can be answered on the basis of the readings, the glossary, and the films to be shown in class, *Empire of Islam, Part 1*, and *Inside Mecca*).

1. *Short-Answer Questions*:
   a. Who was Muhammad's first convert, and what was her name?
   b. What was the *hijrah*, and why does it mark the beginning of the Muslim calendar?
   c. Why is Muhammad's face usually veiled when he is represented in Muslim art?
   d. From where did Muhammad ascend toward the highest of the Seven Heavens, according to Muslim tradition?
   e. In what physical state did Jesus ascend, according to Muslim tradition? *Ascended to heaven whole.*
   f. What branches of mathematics were invented by Arab mathematicians?
   g. What are the numerals that we use called, and why?
   h. What do the words "Islam" and "Muslim," mean?
   i. What does the honorific title "Muhammad," mean?
   j. Who was Ali, and what was his relationship to Muhammad?
   k. What is the main difference between Sunni and Shi'ite Muslims?
   l. How are the *surahs* in the Qur'an traditionally arranged?
   m. What does the word Qur'an mean?
   n. What are the *Hadith*?
   o. What does the Arabic word *jihād* mean?
   p. What is the "steep road," according to the Qur'an?
   q. Why do Muslims pray toward Mecca? What is present there?
   r. Does the Qur'an stipulate that women wear the *hijab*? Why do many Muslim women wear it?
   s. What is the "black stone" and where is it presently located?

2. What were the main events in the life of Muhammad?

3. Was Mary a virgin when Jesus was born, according to the Qur'an? Explain how the Qur'anic tradition of how Jesus was born differs from Christian tradition, as expressed in the Nicene Creed.

4. According to the Qur'an, what are the objections that both Allah and Jesus himself make against the Christian doctrine of the Trinity?

5. According to the Qur'an, what was the cause of Satan's (Iblis') fall?

6. How does the Qur'an interpret the Yahwist account of creation in the Bible?

7. What are the five "pillars" of Islam?

8. Why do many Muslim men and women "fast walk" between two hills prior to engaging on the rituals of the Hajj? What is this commemorating?

9. What are the various rituals practiced during the Hajj?

10. Why do Muslims circle seven times around the Ka'bah?

11. Why does the Hajj close with a ritual sacrifice? What is this commemorating?

12. What is the state of *Ihram*, and how does it differ for men and for women?

13. Who were the three main pilgrims discussed in the film, *Inside Mecca*, and what were their most important challenges during the *Hajj*?

HISTORICAL TIME-LINE/SECTION SIX/THE LIFE OF MUHAMMAD
AND FOUNDATION OF ISLAM

570 CE   **Muhammad** is born in **Mecca, Saudi Arabia.** At the time he is born, Mecca is a great center of trade, and the **Ka'bah** houses **multitudinous statues of various deities**. His parents die while he is still a young boy and he is raised by his uncle. He becomes a caravan merchant.

→ He was 25.

595 CE   At 25, Muhammad marries **Khadija**, a wealthy widow of almost 40. She bore him a number of children, one of whom was Fatima, who became the wife of **his cousin, Ali.**

610 CE   At 40, Muhammad has a life-changing vision, and many other visions follow, in which are revealed to him the words of Allah, above all the message **that Allah is the only God**. Khadijah becomes his first convert. Muhammad's message is well received by a small group of followers, but most of the Meccans reject the claim that their gods are no gods. Hostilities increase after the death of his wife and uncle.

622 CE   The *hijrah* **(Arabic, flight)** of Muhammad and around 100 of his followers from Mecca to Yathrib, where he had been invited to arbitrate disputes. This **marks the beginning of the Muslim calendar** because this is when the Muslims could first worship freely at the **first mosque** in Muhammad's home. Yathrib is later called **Medina**, "City of the Prophet." The Meccans later attack the city various times, but fail to eradicate the Muslims. Muhammad's following grows. He receives a vision that Muslims must pray towards the Ka'bah, even though it is still full of idols.

630 CE   Muhammad and his followers **take Mecca**, with little bloodshed. They **circle the Ka'bah seven times and then enter and smash all its idols to dust**. From then on the Ka'bah is devoted to the One God, Allah. Muhammad **dies in Medina** some time later.

661 CE   The fourth caliph, Muhammad's **son-in-law and cousin, Ali**, is assassinated by Mu'awiyah, the founder of the Ummayad Caliphate, and Islam is divided into **Shi'ites loyal to Ali** and who do not recognize the first three caliphs, and **Sunnis, who recognize all the caliphs and form the majority group**.

THE NIGHT JOURNEY OF MUHAMMAD

ASCENT THROUGH THE HEAVENS

The second part of the prophet's night journey is represented here, during which he ascends to the highest of the seven heavens from a rock on the Temple Mount in Jerusalem.

FROM MECCA TO JERUSALEM
In the first part of the journey, Muhammad is miraculously carried from Mecca to Jerusalem, as recorded in the Qur'an: "Glorified be He who carried His Servant from the Holy Mosque [the Ka'aba in Mecca] to the Far-Distant Mosque [traditionally interpreted to be the al-Aqsa Mosque near the Dome of the Rock in Jerusalem]" (*Sura 17:1*).

THE ANGEL GABRIEL
Along with other angels, the Angel Gabriel, chief of God's angelic servants, accompanies Muhammad on his journey, and serves as his guide. Gabriel's halo of fire is not as great as that of Muhammad, perhaps indicating humanity's superior status over the angels, whom Allah commanded to bow prostrate before Adam (*Sura 2:34*).

MUHAMMAD MEETS EARLIER PROPHETS
This is not represented in this illustration, but according to the traditional story, Muhammad met earlier prophets, such as Abraham, Moses, and others on the Temple Mount and led them in prayer before ascending. He again encountered these prophets while journeying up through the seven heavens.

MUHAMMAD INSTITUTES PRAYER FIVE TIMES A DAY
It was during his night journey that Muhammad received the injunction from God that Muslims should pray five times a day.

MUHAMMAD'S DEATH
Muhammad did not remain in the heavens but was returned to Jerusalem after his journey and then back to Mecca. Unlike Jesus, who was taken whole up to heaven, but like all of the other prophets besides Jesus, Muhammad died. He was buried in Medina.

MUHAMMAD'S FACE VEILED
Many depictions of events in the life of the prophet cover his face with a white veil. This is to show him reverence, but it is also because Islam conventionally prohibits representations of Muhammad.

THE BURAQ
Muhammad was carried on his night journey and then through the heavens on the back of a white steed with a female head, called *al-buraq*, meaning "lightning."

THE ROCK
The rock on the Temple Mount, from which Muhammad ascended towards the highest of the seven heavens. The Dome of the Rock was built in 691 CE around this rock, which bears the prophet's footprint. The Dome of the Rock, together with the al-Aqsa Mosque also located on the Temple Mount, is the third holiest site of Islam, after Mecca and Medina.

SCIENCE IN THE MUSLIM WORLD

MUSLIM SCHOLARS AT WORK IN AN OBSERVATORY

This illustration is from an Ottoman manuscript of the late sixteenth century CE. The observatory was built in the 1500s in Istanbul for the astronomer Taqi al-Din. The scholars are shown working with various scientific instruments.

MATHEMATICAL SOPHISTICATION

It was Muslim mathematicians who adopted, and then passed down to the Western world, the Indian number system, which we thus call "Arabic numerals" (as opposed to the more cumbersome Roman numerals that had been in use in the West before). It was Arab mathematicians who invented algebra, logarithms, and algorithms.

PLOTTING PLANETARY MOVEMENTS

These two scholars are using an instrument to plot the movements of the planets, while a third scholar writes down the results.

TRANSLATION OF EARLIER SCIENTIFIC WORKS

Muslim scholars translated into Arabic the Persian, Indian, and Greek classics, which permitted them to build on earlier knowledge. Muslim astronomy was greatly influenced by the Greek natural philosopher, Ptolemy, whose model of the cosmos and explanation of the planetary movements were also very influential on Medieval Western astronomy.

THE ASTROLABE

Two Muslim scholars examine an astrolabe, an instrument invented by the Greeks. The rotating parts simulate the apparent daily rotations of the sun, moon, planets, and stars, as seen from a specific latitude on earth, as these change during the course of a year. This device accordingly had many useful functions.

THE OBSERVATORY LIBRARY

The shelves are well stocked with scientific works, and a caretaker stands in front of these, ready to bring them to the scholars when needed for consultation.

THE QUADRANT

This device had various forms and uses: It could be used to measure the precise time of day on the basis of the position of the sun in the sky. This was important for determining the precise times for the five daily payers. Another form of this device could be used to determine the latitudes of the stars. Many of the major stars visible to the naked eye are still called by their Arabic names.

THE GLOBE

A scholar turns a globe of the earth so that Istanbul and the Ottoman domains are at the front. For its time, this globe was impressive, and probably was the result of many measurements and caculations.

Istanbul University Library, Istanbul, Turkey/Bridgeman Images

Islam*

Islam's basic tenets are expressed in its most holy creed: "There is no God but Allah, and Muhammad is his messenger." *Islam* means surrender, and adherents to the religion are called *Muslims*, meaning those who surrender. Staunchly monotheistic, Islam sees Allah as the omnipotent creator God who, through a series of prophets, has called people to obedience. At the end of time, Allah will resurrect the dead, condemn the wicked to hell, and entrust believers to eternal peace in his garden. Following prophets such as Moses and Jesus, Muhammad is the final and greatest prophet, who delivered the definitive expression of Allah's voice in the Qur'an, Islam's most holy book. Drawing on Jewish narratives, Muslims trace their religious heritage from Adam, to Noah, to Abraham, and finally, to Ishmael, Abraham's first son. Muslim faith is embodied not only in religious practice but in a social order governed by Islamic law.

History of Islam

Time of Ingratitude

The cradle of Islam was the Arabian Peninsula, during a period which Muslims contemptuously refer to as the *time of ingratitude (al-jahiliyyah)*, that is, ingratitude toward God. Economically, desert conditions of the peninsula disallowed for widespread agriculture, so inhabitants depended on trade with the surrounding empires. When the Arabs later lost their spice monopoly, trading cities such as Petra died. As a convenient stopping place on well-traveled trade routes, though, Mecca survived as the prosperous center of trading in the Arab world. Politically, Mecca was plagued by warring factions involving their two main tribes, the Quraysh and the Khuza'a, each with divisive clans.

Religiously, inhabitants believed in a range of spiritual forces and deities. Belief in polydemonism prevailed, involving supernatural *jinn,* sprites, and demons, some good and others evil, which inhabited special objects or locations. Tapping into their ancient Semitic heritage, they set up shrines to various nature gods and goddesses. Hubal, god of the moon, was the principal deity of the Meccans, and before his idol people would cast lots and divining arrows. Three chief goddesses of Mecca, Al-Lat, Al-Manat, and Al-Uzza, were worshiped. There was widespread belief in a creator deity, named Allah, who was high god of the regional pantheon. Sacred shrines with carved and uncarved stones were thought to be the dwelling places of these spirits and deities, and they became the focus of offerings and prayers. There was also a significant Jewish and Christian monotheistic presence. Large numbers of Diaspora Jews, fleeing enemies for over a thousand years, settled in Arabia's desert. The Jews interacted well with their new neighbors, and many Arabs converted to Judaism. Hermit Christian monks settled in the desert regions, along with heretical Christian sects escaping the authority of the Roman church. Muslim tradition also notes the presence of pre-Islamic monotheists, known as *Hanif,* who carried the torch of Abraham's religion through the time of ingratitude.

Festivals and pilgrimages dominated the religious activities of the Meccans. Annual festivals lasting weeks drew inhabitants from throughout the peninsula to the two cities of Mina and Ukaz. With its 365 shrines, one for each day of the year, Mecca was a constant attraction to pilgrims. Meccan religious activity centered on the Ka'bah, an austere cubical structure housing idols, murals of the gods, and the Black Stone. The stone, believed to have fallen from heaven, was the object of a special ritual in which naked pilgrims would circle it seven times and then kiss it. Muslim tradition maintains that the Ka'bah was originally built by Abraham.

Early Years of Muhammad

Even a brief survey of world religions indicates that the lives of the religious founders are shrouded in legend, often to the point that their historical lives can no longer be recovered. Although many accounts of Muhammad are also legendary, Islam has the advantage of early written sources, not just by early Muslims, but by Muhammad himself.

Born about 570 CE, Muhammad was from the Hashimite family clan of Mecca, part of the Quraysh tribe. The clan's founder, from whom Muhammad descended, traced his lineage back to Ishmael, Abraham's first son according to Jewish legend. Muhammad's birth name is unknown, although his honorific title, *Muhammad,* means "highly praised." Tragedy marked his infant and childhood years. His father died before he was born, and as a minor under pre-Islamic law he was unable to acquire inheritance. He was entrusted to his grandfather who, according to one tradition, had him raised by a Bedouin foster mother. His natural mother died when he was six, and his grandfather two years later. Under the care of his uncle, he became involved with caravans. A story relates that the 12-year-old Muhammad accompanied his uncle to Syria on a caravan, where he met a Christian monk who recognized him as the future great prophet. Because of his reputation for honesty, Muhammad was soon entrusted with the leadership of caravans. A pivotal moment in his life arrived when, at 25, he led a caravan for a wealthy widow named Khadija. Although she was 15 years his senior, the two married, and for years she became an important source of encouragement for Muhammad. She bore him four daughters and three sons who died in infancy. Fatima, the most well known daughter, later married his cousin Ali.

According to his tribal custom, during one month of every year Muhammad retreated for religious reflection. He reflected on the good fortune given him by Allah, in view of his family and successful caravan career. He also thought about Jews and Christians who had a *book,* the Bible, by virtue of which they were prospering more than his own people. This moved him toward monotheism. Islam was born on the *Night of Power* (Laylat al-Qadr) when, on retreat in a cave outside of Mecca, the 40-year-old Muhammad had a life-changing vision. In a voice like reverberating bells, the angel Gabriel approached him, commanding him to recite a phrase: "And the Lord is most Generous, who by the pen has taught mankind things they knew not." He went through a period of doubt for a few months, even contemplating suicide, fearing he was an ecstatic visionary, an occupation not held in high esteem in his society. He also considered that he might be mad, or that he had heard the voice of a *jinn.* Eventually his doubts dispersed and his wife became his first convert, believing that he was a prophet.

Visions and revelations of this kind continued throughout his life. They were recorded or memorized by others as they occurred, and then compiled into the text of the Qur'an. The moments of revelation began with Muhammad becoming entranced while shaking and sweating. Then, in rhymed prose, rhapsodies in Arabic flowed from his mouth. During his early prophetic career, the main points of his message were that Allah is the only God, that the dead will resurrect, and that Allah will judge all. After his wife, his next converts included his cousin Ali and a merchant named Abu Bakr, both of whom assumed leadership positions after Muhammad's death. As his following grew, the first Muslims experienced verbal attacks, threats, and later physical violence. The opposition was in part economically motivated by those whose livelihoods depended on religious pilgrimages to the Ka'bah; Muhammad's message of a single God, they assumed, threatened this. Many Meccan merchants assumed that a single god would draw fewer pilgrims than the many idols housed in their city.

For protection, Muhammad first sent a band of his followers to Ethiopia, where they were warmly received by local Christians. He and about 50 followers were then placed under siege in their Meccan neighborhood in an attempt to starve them into submission. Under pressure, Muhammad strangely reported a new revelation: Along with Allah, the three key Meccan goddesses were acknowledged. The siege was then lifted, and the exiles returned from Ethiopia. Later Muhammad announced that the new revelation was inspired by the devil, and the relevant passages were removed from his record of revelations. Hostility increased when his wife and uncle died. He tried to establish himself in an oasis town named Taif, about 60 miles southeast of Mecca, but failed.

Later Years of Muhammad

The turning point in Muhammad's mission occurred during a pilgrimage festival. He met residents of the northern city Yathrib who suggested that their people would be more receptive to him, in part because the city had many Jews who were awaiting the arrival of a prophet. The city was in political turmoil, and the residents believed that they could benefit from Muhammad's administrative skills. A period of negotiations followed. It was agreed that Muhammad would be the final arbiter of all disputes and that the various religious groups, including the Jews and Muslims, would be autonomous. The migration to Yathrib, called the *hijrah* (flight) began with around 100 of his followers' families. In 622 CE, at age 52, Muhammad joined them, fleeing Meccan authorities as he made the journey. This migration is so momentous for Islam that it marks the starting point of the Muslim calendar.

Muhammad quickly became a successful administrator and statesman, an accomplishment with which even his enemies agreed. He renamed the city *Medina,* city of the prophet. Living unpretentiously in a clay house and milking goats, he was ever available for consultation. He punished the guilty, but was merciful toward his personal enemies. Of his several diplomatic marriages, his primary wife, A'isha, daughter of Abu Bakr, had particular influence over him, and is the source of many of the traditions later ascribed to him.

Although successful in Medina, hostilities with Mecca continued. Believing that he had a responsibility to provide for the Meccan emigrant followers living in Medina, Muhammad intercepted a caravan to Mecca for its booty. Attempting this a second time, his band of 300 encountered an army of 1,000 Meccans at a site called Badr. The ensuing battle was a victory for Muhammad. Not dissuaded, a few years later the Meccans launched a military offensive against Muhammad's army. Known as the Battle of Uhud, the Muslims were badly outnumbered, forced to retreat, and Muhammad himself was slightly wounded. Even so, the battle was a moral victory since the Meccans failed to eradicate Muhammad. Two years later the Meccans attacked Medina directly with a confederate army of surrounding cities and nomads. By recommendation of a Persian soldier in his camp, Muhammad ordered a trench dug around the entire city, a strategy that resulted in victory.

With each military victory (and moral victories like Uhud), his converts increased, and his control over Medina became more firm. The Jewish population, which attracted him to the city, ironically failed to accept him as God's prophet. Some even aided the Meccans in their attack. Now with increased authority, Muhammad drove them out. His disappointment with the Jews had theological consequences as well. The Jewish and Christian elements of his religion were suppressed, and the traditional Arab elements were emphasized. No longer would Muslims pray facing Jerusalem, but towards Mecca. Qur'anic passages of this period enjoined Muslims to make pilgrimages to Mecca, which included circumambulation of the Ka'bah and kissing its Black Stone. Friday became the official day of rest, not Saturday or Sunday. During his rule in Medina, other central Muslim doctrines were established, such as fasting, alms giving, and ritual prayer. Social laws involving marriage, divorce, inheritance, and treatment of slaves and prisoners were also formalized.

In the fifth year of the migration, Muhammad and his followers approached Mecca with the intention of making a pilgrimage, but were met with resistance from the city leaders. The two sides reached a face-saving compromise, in which Muhammad and his followers withdrew, with the understanding that the next year they would return and the city would be open to them for a pilgrimage. However, in the intervening year a Meccan broke the truce, and Muhammad responded by marching on the city. Realizing that they were unable to resist his force, the leaders of the city surrendered and bloodshed was avoided. Riding into the Ka'bah on his camel, with his own hands he smashed its 360 idols, declaring, "Truth has come and falsehood has vanished." Thus, he reclaimed the shrine for God. All of Mecca converted, giving no resistance. The territory around the Ka'bah was declared sacred (*haram*), and non-Muslims were prohibited from entering the area. Muhammad then returned to Medina.

In the tenth year after his migration, he made a final announcement at the Ka'bah: "Today I have completed my religion for you and I have fulfilled the extent of my favor towards you. It is my will that Islam be your religion. I have completed my mission. I have left you the Book of Allah and clear commandments. If you keep them you will never go wrong." Shortly thereafter, reporting severe headaches, he died while in A'isha's house and was buried on that spot.

The Caliphate

Muhammad founded both a new religion and a new social order. Although he believed that his mission as a religious prophet was complete at the time of his death, plans for a larger Muslim social community (*umma*) were not as yet realized. He had planned to conquer Syria and Iraq, but died too soon. Upon his death, key political decisions were made by Muhammad's early companions (*Sahaba*), many of whom were his first converts. Their first task was to appoint a successor, or Caliph, who would fill Muhammad's political leadership role, but not his prophetic role. From the start, however, there was political dissent. To the consternation of Ali,

Muhammad's cousin who expected to step into the leadership role, the early companions selected Abu Bakr as the first Caliph. For the sake of unity, Ali deferred to his rival. Plans were drawn for military expansion, but the aged Caliph died only two years into his rule.

For the next ten years, the newly appointed Caliph Umar expanded Muslim territory far into the Persian and Byzantine empires. Non-Arab converts were denied equal political rights, and it would be almost a hundred years until a unified Muslim political order would emerge. Umar was stabbed to death by a Persian slave, and Uthman became the third Caliph. According to legend, trouble started for Uthman when he lost Muhammad's seal ring in a well. He prompted further negative reaction by favoring his family clan, the Umayyads, which originally opposed Muhammad in Mecca. A small rebellion erupted in Medina, in which a disaffected faction (which later became the Kharajites) laid siege to his house. Civil war broke later and, 12 years into his rule, Uthman was assassinated by rebel Muslim troops from Egypt. The early companions finally elected Ali as the fourth Caliph, but he was immediately opposed by Syrian governor Mu'awiyah, who sought to avenge the death of Uthman, his cousin. War broke out between Ali and Mu'awiyah and, on the eve of the decisive battle, Ali was killed by a soldier from a rebel group that had split with him as a result of disagreement with his policies. The Caliphate fell to Ali's son, Husan, but he quickly ceded it to Mu'awiyah.

Under the first wave of Muslim expansion by the first four Caliphs, all of Arabia, Persia, and North Africa were conquered. For the next 90 years the Caliphate was held by the secular Umayyad Dynasty (661–750), established by Mu'awiyah. After Mu'awiyah's death, the Caliphate was passed to his unpopular son Yazid. In 680 an insurrection against Yazid was launched by Ali's son, Husayn. Husayn and his followers were massacred in what is now the Iraqi city of Kerbala (a tragedy which became the rallying cry of the Shi'i Muslims). Centered in Damascus, the Umayyads continued to push Muslim boundaries. Moving across north Africa and into Spain, expansion into Europe halted at the French borders in the Battle of Tours in 732. The Caliphate was next held by the Abbasid Dynasty (750–1285), centered in Baghdad, and then by the Ottoman Empire (1300–1922), centered in Istanbul. In 1924 the Caliphate was abolished by the Turkish National Assembly, inheritors of the Ottoman Empire. To justify this controversial decision the Assembly maintained that "The idea of a single caliph, exercising supreme religious authority over all the peoples of Islam, is an idea taken from fiction, not from reality."

Sunni and Shi'a

Just as political factions divided early Islam, so did theological differences, the key issue being whether Ali and his successors had a special spiritual status. Islam today is divided into two main groups over this issue. The Sunni, or Sunnite, attribute no special function to Ali, whereas the Shi'a, or Shi'ite, do. Sunnis make up approximately 90 percent of Muslims worldwide. Their full name is *Ahl al-Sunnah wa 'l-Hadith*, that is, followers of the path laid out by the prophet in his sayings. In addition to rejecting the special spiritual status of Ali, Sunnis recognize the first four Caliphs as political successors to Muhammad and acknowledge the political authority of the Caliphate in general. Sunnis must also follow one of the four schools of Islamic law (*madhahib*), developed in the eighth and ninth centuries.

Prior to the emergence of the four Sunni schools of law, Muslims used several guides to determine proper conduct. After the Qur'an was consulted for guidance, appeals were made to practices of Muhammad (*sunna*) as compiled by scholars into texts called *Hadith*. When these avenues failed, decisions were made in one of three ways: analogical deductions from existing laws (*qiyas*), consensus of the Muslim community or its leading scholars (*ijma*), and independent decisions of a single jurist (*ijtihad*).

The four schools of Islamic law not only systematized the above appeal routes, but developed their own codes of behavior from these. The methodological differences between the four schools are subtle, although their geographical domains are more distinct. The *Hanafite* school, which provides the greatest scope of reasoning, predominates in former Turkish empire areas (Turkey, Palestine, Egypt), and India. The *Malikite* school, which focuses more on the traditions of Muhammad's companions rather than Muhammad, is dominant in west Africa. The *Shafi'ite* school, which developed the standard hierarchy of appeals, is most prominent in Indonesia. Finally, the *Hanbalite* school, the most literalist in adhering to the letter of the Qur'an, is found in Saudi Arabia and Qatar.

Shi'a Muslims, consisting of 10 percent of the Muslim population, are located primarily in Iran. Shi'a origins are difficult to trace because of negative Sunni chronologies and biased reports by later Shi'as. However, with the assassination of Ali and the creation of the Umayyad Caliphate in 661, a faction loyal to the memory of Ali emerged. Devotion to Ali and his selected descendants became the test for true faith. Early Shi'as were in continual opposition to the ruling Caliph, some groups advocating armed resistance.

About 40 factions of Shi'as have emerged over the years. The most numerous are the Twelvers (*Ithna 'Asha-Riyyah*), who comprise about 80 percent of their number. The central Twelver doctrine is that of the Imam, or leader. Twelvers believe that Muhammad's spiritual abilities (*wilaya*) were passed on to a series of Imams, beginning with Ali. Twelver theology holds that human beings require inspired leadership in order to adhere faithfully to the dictates of Islam and that successive Imams are clearly designated by predecessors (*nass*). Imams are also thought to be guided by Allah and to be infallible (*isma*). Eleven Imams have appeared so far, and they await the appearance of the 12th and final, named Mahdi, who is alive but hidden from view. More precisely, the Mahdi is in a state called *occultation,* in which he can see others, but others cannot see him; at age four, Allah placed him in that state for protection after the death of his father, the 11th Imam, in 873 CE. It is believed that the Mahdi made four representations (*wakils*) between 873–940, a period called the *lesser occultation.* He will return at the end of time, take vengeance on unbelievers, and initiate an era of peace. Until then, leaders called the *Mujtahid* make decisions of canon law on behalf of the hidden Imam. In this century, the Ayatollahs have this function.

Two other Shi'a factions deserve mentioning. The Fivers (*Zaydis*) split from Twelver tradition by recognizing Zaydis as the fifth Imam (as opposed to Muhammad al-Baqir). Concentrated in Yemen, they do not assert the necessity of Imams and accept some of the early Caliphs. The Seveners (*Isma'ili*) split from Twelver tradition by recognizing Isma'il as the seventh Imam (rather than Musa-l-Kazim). They see Isma'il as the final Imam, Mahdi, who will return for the day of judgment.

Muslim Scriptures

The sacred literature of Islam falls into three categories. First and foremost is the Qur'an, its most holy scripture. Next, at a deuterocanonical level, are the *Hadith* canons. Finally, there are sectarian texts that are revered by Sunni, Shi'i, and Sufi practitioners.

The Qur'an

The Qur'an is the collected revelations of Muhammad written during the last 23 years of his life. It is the primary sacred text for all sects of Islam. The text is divided into 114 sections called *surahs,* in lengths varying from three verses to almost 300 verses. The term "Qur'an" means "to recite," in the sense that Muhammad is verbally delivering Allah's message to the people. The traditional arrangement of the *surahs* is neither chronological nor topical, but according to length, beginning with the longest and ending with the shortest. *Surah* titles are derived from a prominent or recurring word, such as Cow, Abraham, Mary, Angels, Muhammad, Divorce, Infidels. Every *surah* (save one[1]) begins with the phrase, "In the name of God, the Merciful, the Compassionate," which was probably the original indicator of the *surah* divisions.

The exact chronology of the *surahs* was forgotten even during Muhammad's life, and many short revelations from different periods were joined together to form longer *surahs.* Modern scholars have offered several chronological schemes for organizing the *surahs,* although traditional Muslims believe that such attempts compromise the inherent beauty of the nonhistorical arrangement. Nevertheless, each *surah* is associated with either the Meccan or Medinan periods of Muhammad's life. The Meccan *surahs* are the earliest and reflect Muhammad's struggle to persuade his skeptical Meccan listeners to abandon polytheism and idolatry. They are shorter and more poetic than the Medinan sections, and they are characterized by vivid imagery. Meccan *surahs* describe the world's cataclysmic end and emphasize Allah's omnipotence and active role in history.

Within the Meccan period itself the style and content of the *surahs* developed. The earliest use short sentences, particularly powerful imagery and are the most lyrical. The later ones, by contrast, are longer, more direct and sermonizing, and less heated. Stories of the early prophets become more developed. When Muhammad and his followers migrated to Medina, political circumstances were considerably more favorable, and the *surahs* reflect the confident voice of a lawgiver concerned with social and political issues. These are the longest *surahs* in the Qur'an, and deal with the giving of the law.

Stylistically, most of the Qur'an is written in first, second, and third person, with Allah addressing believers, unbelievers, or Muhammad. The first person is used when God describes his divine attributes, and the second when describing actions in which humans participate. Passages not in the voice of Allah are prefaced by the word "say," indicating that they are to be recited by believers. Most of the Qur'an is written in rhymed prose, as opposed to poetry with meter. The latter approach was typical of poets who were thought to be guided by *jinn,* an association which Muhammad strongly resisted. Phrases are repetitive and well-suited for reciting; indeed, several traditional Qur'anic division schemes break the text into sections for daily reading. Muslims believe that the literary quality of the Qur'an itself validates Muhammad's claims of prophet-hood. For, although illiterate, he produced a literary work of great merit.

The initial compilation of the Qur'an is a remarkable story. After each of Muhammad's revelations, efforts were made to record their content, either through writing or memorization by specially assigned reciters. Although Muhammad may have done some editing of the earlier *surahs* when in Medina, no definitive "book" existed at the time of his death. A year after Muhammad's death, many of the original reciters were killed in battle. Fearing that the Qur'an's contents would be lost through time, the first Caliph, Abu Bakr, ordered the compilation of the first complete text of the Qur'an. The task was assigned to Zayd ibn Thabit, an aide of Muhammad, who pieced the text together from oral and written sources in Medina. Variant Qur'an fragments continued to circulate for 24 more years, until the third Caliph, Uthman, ordered the creation of a definitive text. Again Zayd supervised the compilation. He gathered all existing manuscript fragments and met with the original reciters accompanying Muhammad who had the complete contents memorized. When the compilation was complete, all previous written versions were destroyed, assuring that only one version of the Qur'an would remain. Although variant editions appeared later, the definitive text of the Qur'an we have today is the work of Zayd. Diacritical marks were later introduced to fix proper vocalization for recitation.

The content of the Qur'an covers a variety of subjects. Many stories parallel accounts in the Old Testament, and some from the New Testament, especially those of Adam, Noah, Abraham, Joseph, and Jesus. It is unlikely that Muhammad had access to Arabic translations of Jewish or Christian texts, but instead relied on oral traditions of the local Jewish and Christian populace. Other narratives are of Arabian origin.[2] Large sections of the Qur'an provide legislation for the newly formed Muslim community in Medina.

For Muslims, the Qur'an records more than the words of Muhammad; it is Allah's eternal speech; the Torah and Bible are earlier and incomplete revelations of Allah. Most Muslims believe that the Qur'an is uncreated, existing from eternity, with an original engraved tablet of the Qur'an in heaven. This eternal Qur'an is written in the Arabic language, and so authentic copies of the Qur'an will also only be in Arabic. The first unofficial translation appeared in 1141 in Latin, which was loathed by Muslims for its disparaging renderings. The physical book itself is sacred, and copies of the Qur'an are touched only after ceremonial cleansing of the handler.

Hadith Canons

After the Qur'an, the second most authoritative group of texts in Islam are the *Hadith* canons. The term *Hadith* means talk or speech, and it refers to collected narratives reporting actions and sayings of Muhammad recounted by his companions. These monumental collections are the principal basis for interpreting the Qur'an and were used to develop early Islamic legal systems.

While Muhammad was alive, his companions took note of his life events and his sayings. Within the first hundred years after Muhammad's death, individual sayings were transmitted both orally and in written form from teachers of *Hadith* to their students. Within the second hundred years, booklets of *Hadith* appeared on single topics, and later on several topics. The number of *Hadith* grew to about three quarters of a million, most being duplicates with only slight variations as generated by the continually growing number of teachers and students of *Hadith.* Finally, they were systematically compiled in the 9th and 10th centuries into no less than 12 multivolume collections.

The Sunnis have nine collections, six of which are particularly revered. The most widely accepted of these are referred to as the *Two Sahih* (authentic): *Sahih al-Bukhari* and *Sahih Muslim.* The first of these, compiled by al-Bukhari (d. 875), is the most important. A prominent teacher of *Hadith,* al-Bukhari examined 600,000 sayings, the majority being duplicate versions, and sifted them down to 7,275 authentic ones. Of these, about 2,700 are nonrepetitious. Limited by space constraints, he remarks that he left out other sayings that he believed were authentic. The sayings are topically categorized in 97 books, with some longer sayings split and categorized into two distinct topical divisions. The second most revered collection is that by Muslim ibn al-Hajjaj (d. 875), who examined 300,000 traditions and reduced them to 4,000. A student of al-Bukhari, al-Hajjaj is thought to have been more critical in deeming a saying "authentic" and, unlike his teacher, presents the longer sayings in their integrated form. The remaining four collections (or *Sunan*) were compiled by Abu Dawud (d. 886), at-Tirmidhi (d. 892), an-Nasa'i (d. 915), and Ibn Majah (d. 886).[3] Of the six *Hadith* collections, those by al-Bukhari, Muslim al-Hajjaj and Dawud have been made available in English translation. Three Shi'a collections, called *akhbar* (as opposed to *Hadith*) are traditionally thought to originate with Ali and the Imams (Ja'far al-Sadiq in particular). Larger than the Sunni collections, they were compiled by al-Kafi of al-Kulini (d. 939) (whose collection is the most widely respected), al-Qummi (d. 991), and al-Tusi (d. 1067).

Hadith sayings are in two parts. First is the story itself (*matn*), and second is a list of names constituting the chain of sources which establish the story's authenticity (*isnad*). The stories themselves are of two types. The first, called sacred *Hadith* (*Hadith qudsi*), contain divine revelations similar to those in the Qur'an. The second, called noble *Hadith* (*Hadith sharif*), relate to Muhammad's personal life and nonprophetic utterances. For *Hadith* compilers, a story's authenticity rested on the integrity of each person mentioned in the chain of sources. A discipline emerged that critically scrutinized the lives of the transmitters. According to the norms of this field of study, even an otherwise authentic statement that bears a faulty chain of transmitters should be regarded as inauthentic. Muslims agree that many of the *Hadith* were invented in the early days of Islam to answer questions of law, support religious factions, or serve political needs in struggles for power. Thousands were rejected early on for this very reason. An early *Hadith* scholar was even executed for confessing he fabricated 4,000 sayings for financial gain. Critical *Hadith* scholarship is still in its infancy, however, and judgment regarding the extent of their authenticity must be postponed.

Sectarian Writings

Muslim sectarian writings are voluminous, and the lines distinguishing sacred texts from works of mere theology are often blurred. Writings from the various schools of Islamic law are particularly respected. Foundational works in the *Hanafite* school are *The Book of Roots* by Muhammad ibn al-Hasan al-Shaybani (d. 805) and the *Hidaya* by Burhan al-Din al-Marghinani (d. 1197). From the Malikite school there is the *Muwatta* by Malik ibn Anas (712–795), the school's founder. From the Shafi'ite tradition there is the *Rasala* by al-Shafi'i (767–820), founder of the school. Finally, from the Hanbalite school there is the *Musnad* by founder ibn Hanbal (780–855), and the *Kitab -al-'Umada* by Ibn Qudama (1146–1223).

There are also a number of important writings by Sufis, that is, Islamic mystics whose writings emphasize mystical union with Allah. Key writers among the Sufis include: Rabi'a al-'Adawiya (717–801), a freed slave girl whose writings stress the intense love of Allah; al-Ghazali (1058–1111), a scholar of Islamic Law; and ibn-al-Arabi (1165–1240), a Spanish-born metaphysician. The most widely influential Sufi writer is Jalal ad-Din ar-Rumi (1207-1273). Rumi's six book *Masnawi*, sometimes refereed to as the "Qur'an in Persian," is a compendium of lyric poetry and stories allegorizing Sufi doctrine.

The Five Pillars Of Islam

Islam has five primary obligations, or pillars of faith, that each Muslim must fulfill in his or her lifetime. They are as follows:

The Five Pillars of Islam:

1. The Muslim declaration of faith, which is very simple: "There is no God but God; and Muhammad is the messenger of God." This declaration emphases the Oneness of God, and that Muhammad is the final prophet of God. Muslims will recite it regularly, in order to help focus on God alone. *there is no God*

2. Prayer five times a day towards the Ka'aba in Mecca: at daybreak, at noon, in the afternoon, at sunset, and before going to bed. One does not need to be in a mosque or in the company of Muslims when one prays, but can do so anywhere. Nevertheless, it is considered especially meritorious to pray with others in a mosque.

3. Zakah, or giving charity to the poor and needy, usually at least one-fortieth (2.5%) of one's income. Social responsibility is considered an essential part of one's service to God. *- act of charity*

4. Fasting (abstaining from food, drink, and sex) during the daylight hours (from sunrise to sunset) throughout the ninth month in the Islamic lunar calendar, called Ramadan. Pregnant women, young children, and those who are ill are not expected to fast. *- 1 month of fasting every yr. (Daylight)*

5. The Hajj, or the pilgrimage to Mecca in the last month of the Islamic calendar, which every Muslim who is physically and financially able to do so is expected to make at least once in his or her lifetime.

Excerpts from the Qur'an

The Cow*

(177)

It is not righteous
that you turn your faces
east and west:
but they are righteous
who believe in God
and the last day,
and the angels and the Book,
and the prophets;
and who donate goods and money
for love of God
to relatives and orphans,
and to the poor and the wayfarer,
and to the needy,
and for freeing slaves;
and who are constant in prayer
and give alms for welfare,
and those who fulfill their promises
when they make them,
and who are patient
in suffering, adversity, and hard times.
They are the truthful ones,
and they are the conscientious.

(254)

Faithful believers,
spend of what We have provided for you,
before there comes a day
on which there is no barter
and no friendship
and no mediation.
And it is the ungrateful
who abuse and oppress.

(255)

God!
There is no God but The One,
the Living, the Self-subsistent:
drowsiness does not overtake God,

---

* Excerpts from "The Cow" [pp. 14-15], "The City [pp. 142-3] from THE ESSENTIAL KORAN by THOMAS CLEARY. Copyright
© 1994 by Thomas Cleary. Reprinted by permission of HarperCollins Publishers.

nor sleep.
To God belongs
what is in the heavens and the earth:
who could there be
who can intercede with God
except by leave of God?
God knows what is in front of them,
and what is behind them;
but they do not comprehend
anything of God's knowledge
except as God wills.
The throne of God
extends over the heavens and the earth,
and the preservation of them both
is not oppressive to God,
for God is most exalted, most sublime.

(256)

There is to be no compulsion in religion.
True direction is in fact distinct from error:
so whoever disbelieves in idols
and believes in God
has taken hold
of the most reliable handle,
which does not break.
For God is all-hearing and all-knowing.

The City

In the name of god, the compassionate, the merciful

(1–20)

I swear by this city
—and you are a free dweller in this city—
and by the begetter and the begotten;
surely We have created humanity in difficulty.
Do they think no one has power over them?
They say they have spent much wealth;
do they think no one sees them?
Have we not given them two eyes,
and a tongue, and two lips?
And We showed them the two highways.
But they have not embarked upon the steep road.
And what will convey to you what the steep road is?
Emancipating a slave,
or feeding on a day of hunger
an orphaned relative
or a pauper in misery.
Then one will be of those who believe,
and enjoin patience on one another,
and exhort each other to kindness:
they are the company on the Right Hand.

But those who repudiate our signs,
they are the company on the Left Hand:
over them will be a vault of fire.

Surah 3

42. Behold! the angels said: "O Mary! Allah has chosen you and purified you - chosen you above the women of all nations.

43. "O Mary! worship your Lord devoutly: prostrate yourself, and bow down (in prayer) with those who bow down."

44. This is part of the tidings of the things unseen, which We reveal unto you (O Messenger!) by inspiration: you were not with them when they cast lots with arrows, as to which of them should be charged with the care of Mary: nor were you with them when they disputed (the point).

45. Behold! the angels said: "O Mary! Allah gives you glad tidings of a Word from Him: his name will be Christ Jesus, the son of Mary, held in honor in this world and the Hereafter and of (the company of) those nearest to Allah;

46. "He shall speak to the people in childhood and in maturity. And he shall be (of the company) of the righteous."

47. She said: "O my Lord! how shall I have a son when no man has touched me?" He said: "Even so: Allah creates what He wills: when He has decreed a Plan, He but says to it, 'Be,' and it is!

48. "And Allah will teach him the Book and Wisdom, the Law and the Gospel,

49. "And (appoint him) a Messenger to the Children of Israel, (with this message): "'I have come to you, with a Sign from your Lord, in that I make for you out of clay, as it were, the figure of a bird, and breathe into it, and it becomes a bird by Allah's leave: and I heal those born blind, and the lepers, and I quicken the dead, by Allah's leave; and I declare to you what you eat, and what you store in your houses. Surely therein is a Sign for you if you did believe;

50. "'(I have come to you), to attest the Law which was before me. And to make lawful to you part of what was (before) forbidden to you; I have come to you with a Sign from your Lord. So fear Allah, and obey me.

51. "'It is Allah Who is my Lord and your Lord; then worship Him. This is a Way that is straight.'"

52. When Jesus found unbelief on their part, he said: "Who will be my helpers to (the work of) Allah?" Said the Disciples: "We are Allah's helpers: we believe in Allah, and you bear witness that we are Muslims.

53. "Our Lord! we believe in what You have revealed, and we follow the Messenger; then write us down among those who bear witness."

54. And (the unbelievers) plotted and planned, and Allah too planned, and the best of planners is Allah.

55. Behold! Allah said: "O Jesus! I will take you and raise you to Myself and clear you (of the falsehoods) of those who blaspheme; I will make those who follow you superior to those who reject faith, to the Day of Resurrection: then you shall all return to me, and I will judge between you of the matters wherein you dispute.

56. "As to those who reject faith, I will punish them with terrible agony in this world and in the Hereafter, nor will they have anyone to help.

57. "As to those who believe and work righteousness, Allah will pay them (in full) their reward; but Allah does not love those who do wrong.

58. "This is what We rehearse to you of the Signs and the Message of Wisdom."

59. The similitude of Jesus before Allah is as that of Adam; He created him from dust, then said to him: "Be": and he was.

60. The Truth (comes) from Allah alone; so be not of those who doubt.

61. If any one disputes in this matter with you, now after (full) knowledge has come to you, say: "Come! let us gather together, - our sons and your sons, our women and your women, ourselves and yourselves: then let us earnestly pray, and invoke the curse of Allah on those who lie!"

62. This is the true account: there is no god except Allah; and Allah - He is indeed the Exalted in Power, the Wise.

63. But if they turn back, Allah has full knowledge of those who do mischief.

64. Say: "O People of the Book! come to common terms as between us and you: that we worship none but Allah; that we associate no partners with Him; that we do not erect, from among ourselves, lords and patrons other than Allah." If then they turn back, you say: "Bear witness that we (at least) are Muslims (bowing to Allah's Will)."

65. You People of the Book! why do you dispute about Abraham, when the Law and the Gospel were not revealed till after him? Have you no understanding?

66. Ah! You are those who fell to disputing (even) in matters of which you had some knowledge! But why do you dispute in matters of which you have no knowledge? It is Allah Who knows, and you who do not know!

67. Abraham was not a Jew nor yet a Christian; but he was true in Faith, and bowed his will to Allah's, (which is Islam), and he did not join gods with Allah.

Surah 4

153. The People of the Book ask you to cause a book to descend to them from heaven: indeed they asked Moses for an even greater (miracle), for they said: "Show us Allah in public," but they were dazed for their presumption, with thunder and lightning. Yet they worshipped the calf even after Clear Signs had come to them; even so We forgave them; and gave Moses manifest proofs of authority.

154. And for their Covenant We raised over them (the towering height) of Mount (Sinai); and (on another occasion) We said: "Enter the gate with humility"; and (once again) We commanded them: "Do not transgress in the matter of the Sabbath." And We took from them a solemn Covenant.

155. (They have incurred divine displeasure): in that they broke their Covenant; that they rejected the Signs of Allah; that they slew the Messengers in defiance of right; that they said, "Our hearts are the wrappings (which preserve Allah's Word; we need no more)"; - nay, Allah has set the seal on their hearts for their blasphemy, and little is it they believe; -

156. That they rejected Faith; that they uttered against Mary a grave false charge;

157. That they said (in boast), "We killed Christ Jesus the son of Mary, the Messenger of Allah"; - but they did not kill him, nor crucified him, but so it was made to appear to them, and those who differ therein are full of doubts, with no (certain) knowledge, but only conjecture to follow, for of a surety they did not kill him: -

158. Nay, Allah raised him up unto Himself; and Allah is Exalted in Power, Wise; -

159. And there is none of the People of the Book but must believe in Him before his death; and on the Day of Judgment He will be a witness against them; -

160. For the iniquity of the Jews We made unlawful for them certain (foods) good and wholesome which had been lawful for them; - in that they hindered many from Allah's Way; -

161. That they took usury, though they were forbidden; and that they devoured men's substance wrongfully; - We have prepared for those among them who reject Faith a grievous punishment.

162. But those among them who are well-grounded in knowledge, and the Believers, believe in what has been revealed to you and what was revealed before you: and (especially) those who establish regular prayer and practise regular charity and believe in Allah and in the Last Day: to them shall We soon give a great reward.

163. We have sent you inspiration, as We sent it to Noah and the Messengers after him: We sent inspiration to Abraham, Ismail, Isaac, Jacob and the Tribes, to Jesus, Job, Jonah, Aaron, and Solomon, and to David We gave the Psalms.

164. Of some Messengers We have already told you the story; of others we have not; - and to Moses Allah spoke direct; -

165. Messengers who gave good news as well as warning, that mankind, after (the coming) of the Messengers, should have no plea against Allah: for Allah is Exalted in Power, Wise.

166. But Allah bears witness that what He has sent to you He has sent from His (own) knowledge, and the angels bear witness: but enough is Allah for a Witness.

167. Those who reject Faith and keep off (men) from the Way of Allah, have verily strayed far, far away from the Path.

168. Those who reject Faith and do wrong, - Allah will not forgive them nor guide them to any way -

169. Except the way of Hell, to dwell therein for ever. And this to Allah is easy.

170. O mankind! the Messenger has come to you in truth from Allah: believe in him: it is best for you. But if you reject Faith, to Allah belong all things in the heavens and on earth: and Allah is All-knowing, All-wise.

171. O People of the Book! commit no excesses in your religion: nor say of Allah anything but the truth. Christ Jesus the son of Mary was (no more than) a Messenger of Allah, and His Word, which He bestowed on Mary, and a Spirit proceeding from Him: so believe in Allah and His Messengers. Do not say "Trinity": desist: it will be better for you: for Allah is One God: glory be to Him: (far Exalted is He) above having a son. To Him belong all things in the heavens and on earth. And enough is Allah as a Disposer of affairs.

172. Christ does not disdain to serve and worship Allah, nor do the angels, those nearest (to Allah): those who disdain His worship and are arrogant, - He will gather them all together unto Himself to (answer).

173. But to those who believe and do deeds of righteousness, He will give their (due) rewards, - and more, out of His bounty: but those who are disdainful and arrogant, He will punish with a grievous penalty; nor will they find, besides Allah, any to protect or help them.

174. O mankind! Verily there has come to you a convincing proof from your Lord: for We have sent to you a light (that is) manifest.

Surah 5

69. Those who believe (in the Qur'an), those who follow the Jewish (scriptures), and the Sabians and the Christians, - any who believe in Allah and the Last Day, and work righteousness, - on them shall be no fear, nor shall they grieve.

70. We took the Covenant of the Children of Israel and sent them Messengers. Every time there came to them a Messenger with what they themselves did not desire - some (of these) they called impostors, and some they (go so far as to) slay.

71. They thought there would be no trial (or punishment); so they became blind and deaf; yet Allah (in mercy) turned to them; yet again many of them became blind and deaf. But Allah sees well all that they do.

72. They do blaspheme who say: "God is Christ the son of Mary." But Christ said: "O Children of Israel! worship God, my Lord and your Lord." Whoever joins other gods with Allah, - Allah will forbid him the Garden, and the Fire will be his abode. There will for the wrong-doers be no one to help.

73. They do blaspheme who say: God is one of three in a Trinity: for there is no god except one God (Allah). If they do not desist from their word (of blasphemy), verily a grievous penalty will befall the blasphemers among them.

74. Why do they not turn to Allah, and seek His forgiveness? For Allah is Oft-forgiving, Most Merciful:

75. Christ the son of Mary was no more than a Messenger; many were the Messengers that passed away before him. His mother was a woman of truth. They had both to eat their (daily) food. See how Allah makes His Signs clear to them; yet see in what ways they are deluded away from the truth!

76. Say: "Will you worship, besides Allah, something which has no power either to harm or benefit you? But Allah, - He it is that hears and knows all things."

77. Say: "O People of the Book! exceed not in your religion the bounds (of what is proper), trespassing beyond the truth, nor follow the vain desires of people who went wrong in times gone by, - who misled many, and strayed (themselves) from the even Way.

78. Curses were pronounced on those among the Children of Israel who rejected Faith, by the tongue of David and of Jesus the son of Mary: because they disobeyed and persisted in Excesses.

110. Then will Allah say: "O Jesus the son of Mary! recount My favor to you and to your mother. Behold! I strengthened you with the holy spirit, so that you spoke to the people in childhood and in maturity. Behold! I taught you the Book and Wisdom, the Law and the Gospel. And behold! you made out of clay, as it were, the figure of a bird, by My leave, and you breathed into it, and it became a bird by My leave, and you healed those born blind, and the lepers, by My leave. And behold! you brought forth the dead by My leave. And behold! I did restrain the Children of Israel from (violence to) you when you showed them the Clear Signs, and the unbelievers among them said: 'This is nothing but evident magic.'

111. "And behold! I inspired the Disciples to have faith in Me and Mine Messenger: they said, 'We have faith, and you bear witness that we bow to Allah as Muslims.'"

112. Behold! the Disciples said: "O Jesus the son of Mary! can your Lord send down to us a Table set (with viands) from heaven?" Jesus said: "Fear Allah, if you have faith."

113. They said: "We only wish to eat thereof and satisfy our hearts, and to know that you have indeed told us the truth; and that we ourselves may be witnesses to the miracle."

114. Jesus the son of Mary said; "O Allah our Lord! send us from heaven a Table set (with viands), that there may be for us - for the first and the last of us - a solemn festival and a Sign from You; and provide for our sustenance, for You are the best Sustainer (of our needs)."

115. Allah said: "I will send it down to you: but if any of you after that resists faith, I will punish him with a penalty such as I have not inflicted on any one among all the peoples."

116. And behold! Allah, will say: "O Jesus the son of Mary! Did you say to men, worship me and my mother as gods in derogation of Allah'?" He will say: "Glory to You! Never could I say what I had no right (to say). Had I said such a thing, You would indeed have known it. You know what is in my heart, though I do not know what is in Yours. For You know in full all that is hidden.

117. "Never said I to them anything except what You commanded me to say, to wit, 'Worship Allah, my Lord and your Lord'; And I was a witness over them whilst I dwelt amongst them; when You took me up, You were the Watcher over them, and You are a Witness to all things.

118. "If You punish them, they are Your servants: if You forgive them, You are the Exalted in power, the Wise."

Surah 7

3. Follow (O men!) the revelation given to you from your Lord, and follow not, as friends or protectors, other than Him. Little it is you remember of admonition.

4. How many towns have We destroyed (for their sins)? Our punishment took them on a sudden by night or while they slept for their afternoon rest.

5. When (thus) Our punishment took them, no cry did they utter but this: "Indeed we did wrong."

6. Then shall We question those to whom Our Message was sent and those by whom We sent it.

7. And verily We shall recount their whole story with knowledge, for We were never absent (at any time or place).

8. The balance that day will be true (to a nicety): those whose scale (of good) will be heavy, will prosper:

9. Those whose scale will be light, will find their souls in perdition, for that they wrongfully treated Our Signs.

10. It is We Who have placed you with authority on earth, and provided you therein with means for the fulfilment of your life: small are the thanks that you give!

11. It is We Who created you and gave you shape; then We bade the angels bow down to Adam, and they bowed down; not so Iblis [i.e., Satan]; he refused to be of those who bow down.

12. (Allah) said: "What prevented you from bowing down when I commanded you?" He said: "I am better than he: You created me from fire, and him from clay."

13. (Allah) said: "Get you down from this: it is not for you to be arrogant here: get out, for you are of the meanest (of creatures)."

14. He said: "Give me respite till the day they are raised up."

15. (Allah) said: "Be you among those who have respite."

16. He said: "Because You have thrown me out of the Way, lo! I will lie in wait for them on Your Straight Way:

17. "Then I will assault them from before them and behind them, from their right and their left: nor will You find gratitude in most of them (for Your mercies)."

18. (Allah) said: "Get out from this, disgraced and expelled. If any of them follow you, I will fill Hell with you all.

19. "O Adam! you and your wife dwell in the Garden, and enjoy (its good things) as you wish: but do not approach this tree, or you run into harm and transgression."

20. Then began Satan to whisper suggestions to them, bringing openly before their minds all their shame that was hidden from them (before): he said: "Your Lord only forbade you this tree, lest you should become angels or such beings as live for ever."

21. And he swore to them both, that he was their sincere adviser.

22. So by deceit he brought about their fall: when they tasted of the tree, their shame became manifest to them, and they began to sew together the leaves of the Garden over their bodies. And their Lord called to them: "Did I not forbid you that tree, and tell you that Satan was an avowed enemy to you?"

23. They said: "Our Lord! we have wronged our own souls: if You do not forgive us and do not bestow upon us Your Mercy, we shall certainly be lost."

24. (Allah) said: "Get you down, with enmity between yourselves. On earth will be your dwelling-place and your means of livelihood, - for a time."

25. He said: "Therein you shall live, and therein you shall die; but from it you shall be taken out (at last)." ← *Said they will be raised on the last day.*

26. O you Children of Adam! We have bestowed raiment upon you to cover your shame, as well as to be an adornment to you. But the raiment of righteousness, - that is the best. Such are among the Signs of Allah, that they may receive admonition!

27. O you Children of Adam! let not Satan seduce you, in the same manner as he got your parents out of the Garden, stripping them of their raiment, to expose their shame: for he and his tribe watch you from a position where you cannot see them: We made the Evil Ones friends (only) to those without Faith.

28. When they do anything that is shameful, they say: "We found our fathers doing so"; and "Allah commanded us thus": Say: "Nay, Allah never commands what is shameful: do you say of Allah what you do not know?"

29. Say: "My Lord has commanded justice; and that you set your whole selves (to Him) at every time and place of prayer, and call upon Him, making your devotion sincere as in His sight: such as He created you in the beginning, so shall you return."

30. Some He has guided: others have (by their choice) deserved the loss of their way; in that they took the Evil Ones, in preference to Allah, for their friends and protectors, and think that they receive guidance.

31. O Children of Adam! wear your beautiful apparel at every time and place of prayer: eat and drink: but do not waste by excess, for Allah does not love the wasters.

Surah 17

The Israelites

Bani Isra-il, or the Children of Israel

In the name of Allah, Most Gracious, Most Merciful

1. Glory to (Allah) Who took His Servant for a Journey by night from the Sacred Mosque to the Farthest Mosque, whose precincts We did bless, - in order that We might show him some of Our Signs: for He is the One Who hears and sees (all things).

2. We gave Moses the Book, and made it a Guide to the Children of Israel, (commanding): "Do not take other than Me as Disposer of (your) affairs."

3. O you that are sprung from those whom We carried (in the Ark) with Noah! Verily he was a devotee most grateful.

4. And We gave (clear) warning to the Children of Israel in the Book, that twice would they do mischief on the earth and be elated with mighty arrogance (and twice would they be punished)!

5. When the first of the warnings came to pass, We sent against you Our servants given to terrible warfare: they entered the very inmost parts of your homes; and it was a warning (completely) fulfilled.

6. Then We granted you the Return as against them: We gave you increase in resources and sons, and made you the more numerous in man-power.

7. If you did well, you did well for yourselves; if you did evil, (you did it) against yourselves. So when the second of the warnings came to pass, (We permitted your enemies) to disfigure your faces, and to enter your Temple as they had entered it before, and to visit with destruction all that fell into their power.

8. It may be that your Lord may (yet) show Mercy to you; but if you revert (to your sins), We shall revert (to Our punishments): and We have made Hell a prison for those who reject (all Faith).

9. Verily this Qur'an guides to that which is most right (or stable), and gives the glad tidings to the Believers who work deeds of righteousness, that they shall have a magnificent reward.

Struggle (Jihād)*:

The Arabic word *jihād* is one of the most misunderstood terms of Islam. Literally, it means exerting oneself or struggling. Qur'ānic passages suggest that it is a struggle for Allah, but not always with a sword as a Holy War. Here, it has the sense of mission to establish Islam. We have already seen in the famous passage from Sūra 2:256 that 'there is no compulsion in religion', a doctrine which underscores the peaceful aspect of *jihād*. However, there is the defensive struggle with arms when Islam is endangered.

Section Seven
Hinduism
An Umbrella Term for a Rich Diversity of Beliefs

Study Guide on Hinduism/Section Seven

In order to answer the questions below, you will need to refer to the illustrations and readings for Section Seven. You will also need to refer to your notes from in-class lectures. In particular, the answers to questions #4 to 5 and 15 to 18 are not found in the readings, but will be explained in class, as well as answered in the films for this section, *The Soul of India* and *The Elephant God*.

1. *Explain* how some Hindus are monotheists, while others are polytheists.

2. *Pantheism* stems from the Greek word *pan*, meaning "everything," and *theos,* meaning "God"—i.e., God is everything and everything is God. It is a belief that God and the universe essentially are one and the same thing. The Stoic philosophers of the ancient Greek world were pantheists. Explain how some Hindus are pantheists.

3. *Explain* how some Hindus are atheists and agnostics, and why this does not lead to their excommunication, or rejection as Hindus.

4. Who were the Aryans?

5. What are the Vedas?

6. What kind of Hindu god is Shiva? Describe the basic iconic features usually associated with his image.

7. What goddess lies nested in the god Shiva's deadlocks? Why is she considered to be a goddess of fertility?

8. What is Shiva's third eye, and how did it appear?

9. Who is Ganesh's father?

10. According to the most common legend, how did Ganesh end up with the head of an elephant?

11. What does the demon Ravana do that induces Prince Rama to attack him and defeat him?

12. What kind of god is Hanuman and what kind of army does he lead in support of Prince Rama's victory over Ravana?

13. Study the excerpt from the *Rig Veda* on the "Creation of the Universe" in combination with the excerpts from the Laws of Manu ("Duties of the Four Social Classes [i.e., castes]"). On the basis of these readings, name each of the four main castes of Hinduism and describe their function in society and the prescribed duties of each one. Also, explain how, during the creation of the universe, each of these castes was formed. Be sure to be complete in your answers.

14. According the Hindu Laws of Manu, what are the four stages of life for men of the three upper castes? Be sure to include the length of each stage and the ages when they take place (these differ slightly from caste to caste).

15. Define and explain the following Hindu concepts: (1) samsara, (2) Karma, (3) the Atman, (4) the Brahman, (5) moksha. How do these concepts interrelate in Hindu cosmology?

16. What is the goal of Hindu meditation? Be sure to include the terms, moksha, samsara, the Atman, and the Brahman in your answer.

17. Explain the difference between monistic Hindus and dualistic Hindus.

18. Who was Mahatma Gandhi and what did he accomplish for the Indian people?

Hinduism*

Defining "Hinduism"

Contemporary Hindus commonly refer to their tradition as the "universal truth" (*sanatana-dharma*), implying that it is a meta-tradition which is able to embrace the truths of all other systems of thought while transcending them through its expansive ability to embrace truth in multiple manifestations. Hinduism is the dominant religious tradition of the Indian subcontinent, and currently over 700 million people consider themselves to be Hindus.

Hinduism is, however, a difficult tradition to define. Its dominant feature is diversity, and its adherents are not required to accept any doctrine or set of doctrines, to perform any particular practices, or to accept any text or system as uniquely authoritative. Many Hindus, for example, are monotheists and believe that there is only one God, despite the proliferation of gods in Hinduism. They assert that God has many manifestations, and that God may appear differently to different people and different cultures.

Other Hindus are polytheists who believe that the various gods they worship are distinct entities, while pantheistic Hindus perceive the divine in the world around them, as a principle that manifests in natural phenomena, particular places, flora and fauna, or other humans. Some Hindus consider themselves to be agnostic, contending that God is in principle unknown and unknowable. Other Hindus are atheists who do not believe in the existence of any gods, but this position does not lead to their excommunication by their fellow Hindus. Even more confusingly, in daily practice it is common to see one person or community sequentially manifesting combinations of these attitudes in different circumstances.

Hinduism has a plethora of doctrines and systems, but there is no collection of tenets that could constitute a universally binding Hindu creed, nor is there any core belief that is so fundamental that it would be accepted by all Hindus. Hinduism has produced a vast collection of sacred texts, but no one has the authority of the Christian Bible, the Jewish Torah, or the Muslim Qur'an. Perhaps the most widely revered sacred texts are the Vedas ("Wisdom Texts"), most of which were written over 2,000 years ago, but despite their generally accepted authoritativeness, few Hindus today are even able to read them, and the *brahmins* (priests) whose sacred task is to memorize and recite them generally are unable to explain what they mean.

In searching for a way to define the boundaries of Hinduism, the term "Hindu" may provide some help. It was originally coined by Persians who used it to refer to the people they encountered in northern India. Thus, the term "Hindu" originally referred to the inhabitants of a geographical area, and in later centuries it was adopted by people of India who identified themselves with the dominant religious tradition of the subcontinent.

Contemporary Hinduism is still delimited more by geography than by belief or practice: A Hindu is someone who lives on the Indian subcontinent or is descended from people of the region, who considers himself or herself to be a Hindu, and who is accepted as such by other Hindus. There are no distinctive doctrines whose acceptance would serve as a litmus test of orthodoxy, no ecclesiastical authority that is able to declare some to be Hindus in good standing or label others as heretics, and no ceremony whose performance would serve as a definitive rite of passage into the tradition. There is no founder of the tradition, it has no dominant system of theology or a single moral code. Contemporary Hinduism embraces groups whose respective faiths and practices have virtually nothing in common with each other.

This is not to say, however, that Hinduism lacks distinctive doctrines, practices, or scriptures; in fact, the exact opposite is the case. Hinduism has developed a plethora of philosophical schools, rituals, and sacred texts, and its adherents commonly assert a belief in a shared heritage, historical continuity, and family relationships between the multiple manifestations of their tradition. The selections given below represent only a small sampling of the vast corpus of Hindu religious literature. In addition, it should be noted that this literature represents only a tiny part of the Hindu tradition, and primarily reflects the views and practices of a small intellectual elite. The vast majority of Hindus have been—and continue to be—primarily illiterate agricultural workers with little if any knowledge of the sacred scriptures. Their practices are generally derived from local cults and beliefs that often have little in common with the religion and philosophy of the authors of the scriptures. Furthermore, these texts do not form a coherent system, but are as diverse as Hinduism itself. They were written over the course of millennia and reflect shifting paradigms and political, religious, and social agendas, geographical differences, and varying ideas about how people should worship, think, live, and interact.

History of Hinduism and Hindu Scriptures

Hinduism may be compared to a complex symphony in which new themes are introduced as the piece develops, while old ones continue to be woven into its texture. Nothing is ever truly lost, and elements of the distant past often return to prominence at unexpected times, although often in forms that are altered in accordance with the intellectual and religious currents of a particular time and place. The scriptures of Hinduism reflect its diversity and its complex history. They include ancient hymns to anthropomorphic gods and liturgical texts detailing how priests should prepare sacrifices, mystical texts that speculate on the nature of ultimate reality, devotional literature to a variety of deities, philosophical texts of great subtlety and insight, and combinations of these and related themes.

Creation of the Universe*

The following selections are taken from the Rig Veda, *and are hymns and ritual texts devoted to the worship of the Vedic gods. These verses describe the attributes of the gods, recount the mythos of each god and his or her particular sacrificial functions and associations. The first hymn depicts the creation of the universe as beginning with the sacrifice of Purusha ("Man"), a giant god whose body formed the raw material for the formation of the stars, the planets, and for living things. According to the story, the four social classes* (varna) *of Hinduism were also created through this sacrifice, thus providing a scriptural justification for the stratification of Indian society.*

1. The Man had a thousand heads, a thousand eyes, a thousand feet. He pervaded the earth on all sides and extended beyond it as far as ten fingers.

2. It is the Man who is all this, whatever has been and what ever is to be. He is the ruler of immortality, when he grows beyond everything through food.

3. Such is his greatness, and the Man is yet more than this. All creatures are a quarter of him; three quarters are what is immortal in heaven.

4. With three quarters the Man rose upwards, and one quarter of him still remains here. From this he spread out in all directions, into that which eats and that which does not eat. . . .

6. When the gods spread the sacrifice with the Man as the offering, spring was the clarified butter, summer the fuel, autumn the oblation.

7. They anointed the Man, the sacrifice born at the beginning, upon the sacred grass. With him the gods, Sadhyas, and sages sacrificed.

8. From that sacrifice in which everything was offered, the melted fat was collected, and he made it into those beasts who live in the air, in the forest, and in villages.

9. From that sacrifice in which everything was offered, the verses and chants were born, the metres were born from it, and from it the formulas were born.

10. Horses were born from it, and those other animals that have two rows of teeth; cows were born from it, and from it goats and sheep were born.

11. When they divided the Man, into how many parts did they apportion him? What do they call his mouth, his two arms and thighs and feet?

12. His mouth became the Brahmin; his arms were made into the Warrior (*kshatriya*), his thighs the People (*vaishya*), and from his feet the Servants (*shudra*) were born. . . .

15. The moon was born from his mind; from his eye the sun was born. Indra and Agni came from his mouth, and from his vital breath the Wind was born.

14. From his navel the middle realm of space arose; from his head the sky evolved. From his two feet came the earth, and the quarters of the sky from his ear. Thus they set the worlds in order. . . .

16. With the sacrifice the gods sacrificed to the sacrifice. These were the first ritual laws (*dharma*). These very powers reached the dome of the sky where dwell the Sadhyas, the ancient gods.

[*Rig Veda* 10.90: *Purusha-Sukta*]

* From *Scriptures of the World's Religions* by J. Fieser and S. Powers. Copyright © 1998 McGraw-Hill Education. Reprinted by permission.

Shiva, the Destroyer

A RING OF FIRE
The fire represents the destructive nature of Shiva's dance, and the fact that the universe is not eternal but is always in the process of being destroyed; however the ring also indicates that there is never destruction without recreation. The fire is therefore not just destructive but also purifying, destroying the old only to give birth to the new.

FLAME OF DESTRUCTION
In one hand, Shiva holds the flame of destruction, showing his control over the destruction of the universe. In his opposite hand, however, is the double-sided drum of recreation, indicating that the universe is always recreated after it has been destroyed.

THIRD EYE
Shiva's third eye arose when his wife, Parvati, in sport, playfully put her hands over his two eyes, threatening to plunge the universe into darkness. The appearance of Shiva's third eye prevented this from happening. This eye represents Shiva's higher conciousness, and his ability to zap his enemies with fire.

GESTURE OF FEARLESSNESS
This open palm with its strong attached symbol indicates the lack of fear of the god, and thus the lack of fear that should be felt by his devotees.

KING OF THE DANCERS
In this image Shiva is represented in a dancing posture. His cosmic dance is called the Dance of Bliss, and represents the cycle of creation and destruction, as well as the daily cycle of death and rebirth.

THE GODDESS OF THE GANGES RIVER
Ganga emerges from Shiva's matted hair, sometimes represented as a water spout. She is the goddess of fertility, because she provides water for the land.

THE DOUBLE-SIDED DRUM OF CREATION
The beat of this drum summons up a new creation and is held in Shiva's hand directly opposite to the flame of destruction.

THE SNAKE
The image of Shiva is almost always accompanied by an image of a snake coiled around his body. There are multiple explanations for why this is so.

THE SACRED THREAD
Shiva wears across his torso the sacred thread of upper-caste Hindu males.

PROTECTION FOR THE DEVOTEE
This hand points downwards, indicating protecion for the worshipper of Shiva.

THE DEMON SLAYER
Shiva dances on the back of the dwarf demon of ignorance and illusion.

Ganesh, the Elephant God

GOD OF GOOD FORTUNE, OF NEW BEGINNINGS, AND OF WISDOM AND LEARNING Ganesh is one of the most popular gods in india.

HOW GANESH CAME TO HAVE AN ELEPHANT'S HEAD
Various legends exist regarding how this happened, but the most common one is that Shiva's wife, Parvati, was about to take a bath and created a small boy from the dirt of her body to stand guard in order to ensure her privacy. Shiva arrived and wanted to see his wife, but the young boy did not know he was her husband, and so audaciously tried to prevent him. Enraged, Shiva beheaded the boy with his trident. When Parvati emerged from her bath and discovered that the son she had created was dead, she insisted that Shiva bring him back to life. So Shiva instructed his servants to bring back the first creature they encountered in the forest, which was an elephant, and he replaced the boy's head with the elephant's head.

ELEPHANT GOAD
In one hand, Ganesh holds an elephant goad, a sharp stick used to drive elephants.

GANESH'S WIFE OR CONSORT
Sometimes called Riddhi (wealth or prosperity) and sometimes called Siddhi (intellectual or spiritual powers). In this image, she carries in her hand a lotus blossom.

SACRED THREAD / COBRA
In this image of Ganesh's sacred thread (worn by all devout upper-caste Hindu males), the thread is simultaneously a cobra, associating him with his father god, Shiva.

GOD OF LEARNING
In one hand, Ganesh holds his broken tusk, which he himself broke off in order to to use it as a pen in the interests of promoting wisdom and learning.

ROYAL POSTURE
Ganesh's seated posture, with one leg raised, is a royal one.

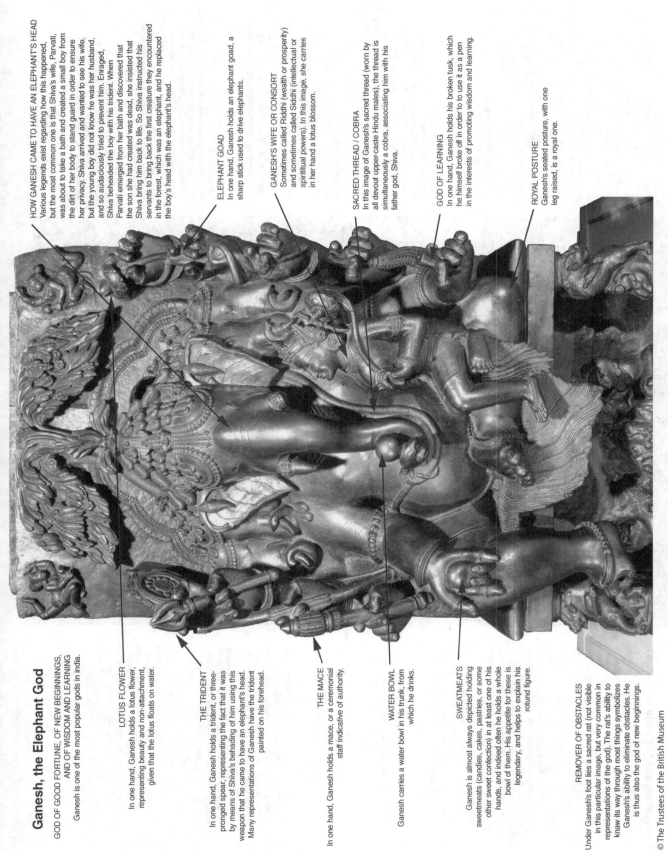

LOTUS FLOWER
In one hand, Ganesh holds a lotus flower, representing beauty and non-attachment, given that the lotus floats on water.

THE TRIDENT
In one hand, Ganesh holds a trident, or three-pronged spear, representing the fact that it was by means of Shiva's behading of him using this weapon that he came to have an elephant's head. Many representations of Ganesh have the trident painted on his forehead.

THE MACE
In one hand, Ganesh holds a mace, or a ceremonial staff indicative of authority.

WATER BOWL
Ganesh carries a water bowl in his trunk, from which he drinks.

SWEATMEATS
Ganesh is almost always depicted holding sweetmeats (candies, cakes, pastries, or some other sweet confection) in at least one of his hands, and indeed often he holds a whole bowl of them. His appetite for these is legendary, and helps to explain his rotund figure.

REMOVER OF OBSTACLES
Under Ganesh's foot lies a sacred rat (not visible in this particular image, but very common in representations of the god). The rat's ability to knaw its way through most things symbolizes Ganesh's ability to eliminate obstacles. He is thus also the god of new beginnings.

123

The Ramayana (Voyage of Rama)

A FAMOUS HINDU EPIC POEM
Written in Sanskrit and containing 24,000 verses, the poem tells the story of Prince Rama, an avatar of the Hindu god, Vishnu, and how he rescued his wife, Sita, from the demon king, Ravana, who had abducted her in revenge for Rama's rejection of the demon's sister.

SITA IMPRISONED IN RAVANA'S CASTLE
Sita was the embodiment of chastity and wifely devotion because she voluntarily accompanied her husband into exile and because she remained steadfast in her faithfulness to her husband during her imprisonment. After rescuing her, at first Rama was hesitant to take her back because after a year in captivity her purity was uncertain. In distress, Sita ordered a pyre to be lit and entered it, praying to the god of fire, Agni, to demonstrate her purity by protecting her from the heat of the flames. After emerging from the fire unharmed, her purity now publicly proven, Rama took her back as his wife.

RAVANA'S DEMON HORDES
Ravana's army consists of hideously ugly demons, who can fly faster than the wind.

THE DEFEAT OF RAVANA
This is the moment of the epic illustrated here. Every year Hindus celebrate this moment by burning a massive effigy of the demon king.

THE DEMON RAVANA
The king of the demons of the island of Lanka (probably Sri Lanka) has ten heads and twenty arms. This demon king is invincible to attacks by gods or goddesses, and can only be killed by a human being. If one of his heads or arms is chopped off, another one instantly grows in its stead. The god Vishnu decided to take on human form in order to defeat Ravana because he was oppressing the gods and goddesses and wreaking havoc on the earth.

THE ISLAND OF SRI LANKA
Traditionally the location of Ravana's city of Lanka. Hanuman had to cross the ocean to find Sita, and the monkey army had to build a floating bridge to this island in order to enable Rama and his armies to cross over to engage Ravana and his demons in battle.

PRINCE RAMA'S EXILE
Rama was the eldest son of his father, Dasharatha, king of Ayodhya, capital of an ancient kingdom located in the region of the Ganges River. He was meant to accede to the throne, but the the king had promised to grant his second wife, Rama's stepmother, two wishes. Urged on by her wicked maid-servant, she wished that her own son, Bharata, should instead rule after the king's death and that Rama should be banished for fourteen years. As a dutiful son, Rama willingly went into exile in order to help his father keep his word. Baratha himself disagreed with his mother and placed Rama's sandals on the throne, agreeing to rule only in Rama's name and no longer than the ascribed fourteen years.

THE GOLD CITY OF LANKA
Lanka is traditionally believed to have been on the Island of Sri Lanka. It was here that the demon king of Lanka, Ravana, lived, together with his demon hordes.

HANUMAN, THE MONKEY GOD
General of the monkey army and son of the wind god. He is able to fly and to change shape. It was Hanuman who first discovered where the kidnapped Sita was located, by expanding to an enormous size and leaping across the ocean to the Island of Lanka, and then taking on a tiny form to find her while remaining undetected. He gives Sita Rama's ring and reassures her that she will be rescued. After being captured, his tail is lit on fire, but he flies away, first lighting on fire the city of Lanka and then putting out the fire on his tail in the ocean. He then commands his army to build a bridge to the Island of Lanka and leads his army to assist Rama in Sita's rescue. Hanuman is the epitome of the selfless and loyal servant.

PRINCE RAMA, SEVENTH AVATAR OF VISHNU
Prince Rama's blue skin indicates that he is an avatar, or incarnation, if the Hindu god, Vishnu.

THE BRAHMASTRA
Represented here as a bow and arrow, the brahmastra was in fact a divine weapon, given to Rama by the creator god, Brahma. It never missed its mark, and utterly annihilated whatever it struck. Its immense destructive power is sometimes compared with that of a modern nuclear warhead. It is only with this weapon, after a prolonged battle, that Rama was finally able to destroy Ravana.

LAKSHMANA, HALF-BROTHER OF RAMA
Lakshmana, Rama's half-brother, also accompanied Rama into exile, as did Sita, Rama's wife. He also participated in the defeat of the demon, Ravana.

Key Hindu Concepts

Samsara = The phenomenal world, or the circle of life, death, rebirth, life, death, rebirth, life, death, etc.

Atman = From Sanskrit, *ātman*, meaning "breath," or "spirit"; in Hinduism, the individual self, or soul. The Atman is immortal and is the part of sentient beings that is reborn after death, albeit in a different physical form. The Atman thus undergoes repeated birth and death within samsara.

Karma = A law of the universe, wherein every action produces a reaction or consequence, whether immediately or in the future, in this life or in a future life.

Brahman = The supreme existence or ultimate reality, the spiritual source of the finite world or samsara; for dualistic Hindus, it is also located beyond samsara.

For monistic Hindus, the Brahman is *all there is*. Hence, samsara is an illusion, the product of maya.

Dualistic versus Monistic Hindus

Dualistic Hindus

The Atman ≠ the Brahman

For dualistic Hindus, the Atman and the Brahman are distinct. Everyone has an individual Atman, and the goal is to lose that individuality and be absorbed into the ultimate reality or Brahman, something like an individual drop of rain water being absorbed into the ocean. This is the majority position.

For dualistic Hindus, **moksha** = liberation, or the release of the Atman from samsara and its absorption into the Brahman. It is the goal of Hindu meditation.

Monistic Hindus

The Atman = the Brahman

For monistic Hindus, the notion that the Atman is distinct from the Brahman is an illusion, the product of maya, a term meaning literally "magic," or "illusion." By eliminating this illusion and acquiring the true knowledge of the identity of the Atman with the Brahman, a person can be liberated from reincarnation after death, and merge back into the Brahman. This true knowledge is intuitive, not logical. Hence, for monistic Hindus, **moksha** is achieved through coming to a full understanding that the Brahman and the Atman are one.

Maya*

Maya *plays a central role in Shankara's interpretation of the Upanishads. The term literally means "magic" or "illusion," and he claims that it is the power by which the Brahman hides the truth from ordinary beings. It is a creative power that causes the apparent phenomena of cyclic existence to be superimposed on the unitary Brahman.*

> Maya, in her potential aspect, is the divine power of the Lord. She has no beginning. She is composed of the three qualities (*guna*), subtle, beyond perception. It is from the effects she produces that her existence is inferred by the wise. It is she who gives birth to the whole universe. She is neither being nor nonbeing, nor a mixture of both. She is neither divided nor undivided, nor a mixture of both. She is neither an indivisible whole, nor composed of parts, nor a mixture of both. She is most strange. Her nature is inexplicable. Just as knowing a rope to be a rope destroys the illusion that it is a snake, so Maya is destroyed by direct experience of the Brahman—the pure, the free, the one without a second.
>
> [*Viveka-chudamani*, p. 49]

That is You

The Upanishadic statement "That is you" (tat tvam asi) is viewed by exponents of nondualist Vedanta as a statement of the nondifference of the Atman *and the* Brahman. *The following excerpt discusses this statement from the nondualist perspective.*

> The scriptures establish the absolute identity of the Atman and the Brahman by declaring repeatedly: "That is you." The terms "Brahman" and "Atman," in their true meaning, refer to "That" and "you" respectively. In their literal, superficial meaning, "Brahman" and "Atman" have opposite attributes, like the sun and the glow-worm, the king and his servant, the ocean and the well, or Mount Meru and the atom. Their identity is established only when they are understood in their true significance, and not in a superficial sense.

"Brahman" may refer to God, the ruler of Maya and creator of the universe. The "Atman" may refer to the individual soul, associated with the five coverings which are effects of Maya. Thus regarded, they possess opposite attributes. But this apparent opposition is caused by Maya and her effects. It is not real, therefore, but superimposed. These attributes caused by Maya and her effects are superimposed upon God and upon the individual soul. When they have been completely eliminated, neither the soul nor God remains. If you take the kingdom from a king and the weapons from a soldier, there is neither soldier nor king. The scriptures repudiate any idea of a duality in the Brahman. Let a man seek illumination in the knowledge of the Brahman, as the scriptures direct. Then those attributes, which our ignorance has superimposed upon the Brahman, will disappear. . . .

Then let him meditate upon the identity of the Brahman and the Atman, and so realize the truth. Through spiritual discrimination, let him understand the true inner meaning of the terms "Brahman" and "Atman," thus realizing their absolute identity. See the reality in both, and you will find that there is but one. . . .

Just as a clay jar or vessel is understood to be nothing but clay, so this whole universe, born of the Brahman, essentially the Brahman, is the Brahman only—for there is nothing else but the Brahman, nothing beyond That. That is the reality. That is our Atman. Therefore, "That is you"—the pure, blissful, supreme Brahman, the one without a second.

[*Viveka-chudamani*, pp. 72–74]

Qualified Nondualism: Ramanuja's Interpretation

Ramanuja disagrees with the nondualist system of Upanishadic interpretation. In this passage, he contends that it is absurd to completely equate the absolute Brahman *with the individual* Atman. *As an exponent of devotionalism, Ramanuja rejects the nondualist system, since it would make devotion absurd. If the* Atman *and the* Brahman *were one, there would be no real basis for worship. Ramanuja contends that the Upanishadic statement "That is you" does not mean what nondualists think it does; rather, it indicates that there are two separate entities, the* Atman *and the* Brahman, *and that the former is wholly dependent upon the latter, like a wave in relation to the ocean. The wave appears to stand apart from the ocean, but its substance and being derive from the ocean, although it has at least a qualifiedly separate identity. Similarly, the* Atman *derives from the* Brahman, *but because the history of each* Atman *is distinctly its own, it contradicts reason and actual experience to claim that the* Atman *is completely identical with the* Brahman.

The opponents sum up their view as follows: Eternal, absolutely unchanging consciousness, whose nature is pure undifferentiated intelligence, free from all distinction whatsoever, due to error illusorily manifests itself . . . as divided into manifold distinctions: . . . .

This entire theory rests on a fictitious foundation of completely hollow and corrupt arguments that cannot be stated in definite logical alternatives. . . . The theory therefore must be rejected by all those who, by way of scripture, direct perception, and the other means of valid cognition—assisted by sound reasoning— have an insight into the true nature of things. . . .

Those who maintain the doctrine of a substance devoid of all difference have no right to assert that there is a proof for such a substance, because all means of valid cognition have for their object things that are affected by difference. . . . All consciousness implies difference. All states of consciousness have for their object something that is marked by some difference, as appears in the case of judgments like, "I saw this." And . . . you yourself admit that different attributes, such as permanence and oneness, actually belong to consciousness, and it cannot be shown that these are only Being in general. And even if this point were admitted, it is seen that a discussion of different views takes place, and you yourself attempt to prove your theory by means of the differences between those views and your own. It therefore must be admitted that reality is affected with difference well established by valid means of proof. . . .

But what all these [scriptural] texts deny is only plurality in the sense of contradicting that unity of the world which depends on its being in its entirety an effect of the Brahman, and having the Brahman for its inward ruling principle and its true Self. They do not, on the other hand, deny that plurality on the Brahman's part which depends on its intention to become manifold. . . .

Also, in texts, such as [the one that states,] "That is you," the coordination of the constituent parts is not meant to convey the idea of the absolute unity of an undifferentiated substance. On the contrary, the words "that" and "you" denote a Brahman distinguished by difference. The word "that" refers to the Brahman, which is omniscient, etc., which had been introduced as the general topic of consideration in previous passages of the same section. . . . Also, it is not possible that ignorance could belong to the Brahman, whose essential nature is understanding, which is free from all imperfections, omniscient, containing within itself all auspicious qualities, or that [the Brahman] could be the basis of all those defects and afflictions that spring from ignorance. . . . The text is thus making a statement about one substance distinguished by two aspects, and the fundamental principle of "co-ordination" is preserved. . . .

[*Shri-bhashya*, ch. 1]

Selections from Treatises on Dharma
(The Laws of Manu)

Actions and Their Results

The Laws of Manu *codify the hierarchy of medieval Indian society and outline the duties of the four primary social groups: (1)* brahmins, *the priests; (2)* kshatriyas, *the warriors and rulers; (3)* vaishyas, *tradespeople and merchants, and (4)* shudras, *or servants. Each of them is said to have a role to play in creating a stable and ordered society. Manu also outlines the duties for the four stages of life: the student, the householder, the forest-dweller, and the world renouncer. According to this scheme, liberation is recognized as the supreme goal of the religious life, but its pursuit should be postponed until the proper time, which is said to be when one has seen a grandson born (indicating that one's lineage will continue) and gray hairs have appeared on one's head (indicating that one has lived long enough to fulfill the requirements of dharma).*

12.3. Action, which springs from the mind, from speech, and from the body, produces either good or evil results; by actions are caused (the various) conditions of men, the highest, middling, and the lowest.

   4. Know that the mind is the instigator here below, even for [actions] that are connected with the body. . . .

   40. Those endowed with Goodness (*sattva*) reach the state of gods, those endowed with Activity (*rajas*) the state of men, and those endowed with Darkness (*tamas*) always sink to the condition of beasts; that is the threefold course of transmigrations. . . .

   95. All those traditions (*smriti*) and all those despicable systems of philosophy, which are not based on the Veda, produce no reward after death; for they are declared to be founded on darkness. . . .

   104. Austerity and sacred learning are the best means by which a brahmin gains supreme happiness; by austerity he destroys guilt, by sacred learning he obtains the cessation of (births and) deaths. . . .

   173. If (the punishment falls) not on (the offender) himself, (it falls) on his sons, if not on the sons, (at least) on his grandsons; but an iniquity (once) committed never fails to produce consequences for him who wrought it.

   174. He prospers for a while through unrighteousness, then he gains great good fortune, next he conquers his enemies, but (at last) he perishes (branch and) root. . . .

   240. Single is each being born; single it dies; single it enjoys (the reward of its) virtue; single (it suffers the punishment of its) sin. . . .

   31. For the sake of the prosperity of the worlds, he (the Lord) caused the brahmin, the kshatriya, the vaishya, and the shudra to proceed from his mouth, his arms, his thighs, and his feet. . . .

   87. But in order to protect this universe He, the most glorious one, assigned separate (duties and) occupations to those who came from his mouth, arms, thighs, and feet. . . .

10.1. The three twice-born castes, carrying out their (prescribed) duties, study (the Veda); but among them the brahmin (alone) shall teach it, and not the other two; this is an established rule. . . .

   3. On account of his pre-eminence, on account of the superiority of his origin, on account of his observance of restrictive rules, and on account of his particular sanctification, the brahmin is the lord of (all) castes.

   4. The brahmin, the kshatriya, and the vaishya castes are the twice-born ones, but the fourth, the shudra, has one birth only; there is no fifth (caste).

129

5. In all castes those (children) only which are begotten in the direct order on wedded wives, equal (in caste and married as) virgins, are to be considered to belong to the same caste (as the fathers). . . .

45. All those tribes in this world, which are excluded from the (community of) those born from the mouth, the arms, the thighs, and the feet (of the Brahman), are called Dasyus ["slaves"], whether they speak the language of the barbarians (*mleccha*) or that of the Aryans. . . .

[*Manu-smriti* selections]

The Four Stages of Life

6.87. The student, the householder, the forest dweller, and the world renouncer: these constitute the four separate orders. . . .

89. And in accordance with the precepts of the Veda and of the traditional texts, the householder is declared to be superior to all of them, because he supports the other three. . . .

7.352. Men who commit adultery with the wives of others, the king shall cause to be marked by punishments which cause terror, and afterwards banish.

353. For by (adultery) is caused a mixture of the castes among men; from that (follows) sin, which cuts up even the roots and causes the destruction of everything. . . .

2.36. In the eighth year after conception, one should perform the initiation (*upanayana*) of a brahmin, in the eleventh (year) after conception (that) of a kshatriya, but in the twelfth that of a vaishya. . . .

69. Having performed the (rite of) initiation, the teacher must first instruct the (pupil) in (the rules of) personal purification, conduct, of the fire sacrifice, and of the twilight (morning and evening) devotions. . . .

176. Every day, having bathed and being purified, he must offer libations of water to the gods, sages . . . worship the gods, and place fuel (on the sacred fire).

177. He should abstain from honey, meat, perfumes, garlands, substances (used for) flavoring (food), women, all substances turned acid, and from doing injury to living creatures, . . .

179. From gambling, idle disputes, backbiting, and lying, looking at and touching women, and from hurting others. . . .

199. Let him not pronounce the mere name of his teacher (without adding an honorific title), behind his back even, and let him not mimic his gait, speech, and deportment. . . .

201. By censuring (his teacher), though justly, he will become a donkey (in his next birth); by falsely defaming him, a dog; he who lives on his teacher's substance will become a worm, and he who is envious (of his merit), a (larger) insect. . . .

3.1. The vow (of studying) the three Vedas under a teacher must be kept for thirty-six years, or for half that time, or for a quarter, until the (student) has perfectly learned them.

3.2. (A student) who has studied in due order the three Vedas, or two, or even one only, without breaking the (rules of) studentship, shall enter the order of the householders. . . .

4. Having bathed, with the permission of his teacher, and performed according to the rule the rite on homecoming, a twice-born man shall marry a wife of equal caste who is endowed with auspicious (bodily) marks. . . .

75. Let (every man) in this (second order, at least) daily apply himself to the private recitation of the Veda, and also to the performance of the offering to the gods; for he who is diligent in the performance of sacrifices supports both the movable and the immovable creation. . . .

78. Because men of the three (other) orders are daily supported by the householder with (gifts of) sacred knowledge and food, therefore (the stage of) householder is the most excellent stage. . . .

2. A brahmin must seek a means of subsistence which either causes no, or at least little, pain (to others), and live (by that) except in times of distress.

3. For the purpose of gaining bare subsistence, let him accumulate property by (following those) irreproachable occupations (which are prescribed for) his (caste), without (unduly) fatiguing his body. . . .

11. Let him never, for the sake of subsistence, follow the ways of the world; let him live the pure, straightforward, honest life of a brahmin. . . .

[*Manu-smriti* selections]

Leaving Home Life

6.1. A twice-born *snataka,* who has thus lived according to the law in the order of householders, may, taking a firm resolution and keeping his organs in subjection, live in the forest, duly [observing the rules given below].

2. When a householder sees his (skin) wrinkled, and (his hair) white, and the sons of his sons, then he may resort to the forest.

3. Abandoning all food raised by cultivation, and all his belongings, he may depart into the forest, either committing his wife to his sons, or accompanied by her. . . .

8. Let him be always industrious in privately reciting the Veda; let him be patient in hardships, friendly, of collected mind, ever liberal, and never a receiver of gifts, and compassionate towards all living creatures. . . .

26. Making no effort (to procure) things that give pleasure, chaste, sleeping on the bare ground, not caring for any shelter, dwelling at the roots of trees. . . .

33. Having thus passed the third part of his life in the forest, he may live as an ascetic during the fourth part of his existence, after abandoning all attachment to worldly objects.

34. He who after passing from order to order, after offering sacrifices and subduing the senses, becomes, tired with (giving) alms and offerings of food, an ascetic, gains bliss after death. . . .

36. Having studied the Vedas in accordance with the rule, having begat sons in accordance with the sacred law, and having offered sacrifices according to his ability, he may direct his mind to (the attainment of) final liberation.

37. A twice-born man who seeks final liberation, without having studied the Vedas, without having begotten sons, and without having offered sacrifices, sinks downwards.

38. Having performed the *Ishti,* sacred to the Lord of Creatures, where (he gives) all his property as a sacrificial fee, having deposited the sacred fires in himself, a brahmin may depart from his house (as an ascetic). . . .

41. Departing from his house fully provided with the means of purification, let him wander about absolutely silent, and caring nothing for enjoyments that may be offered (to him). . . .

45. Let him not desire to die, let him not desire to live; let him wait for (his appointed) time, as a servant (waits) for the payment of his wages. . . .

49. Delighting in what refers to the Self, sitting (in yogic meditation), independent (of external help), entirely abstaining from sensual enjoyments, with himself for his only companion, he shall live in this world, desiring the bliss (of final liberation). . . .

65. By deep meditation let him recognize the subtle nature of the Supreme Self, and its presence in all organisms. . . .

85. A twice-born man who becomes an ascetic, after the successive performance of the above-mentioned acts, shakes off sin here below and reaches the highest Brahman.

[*Manu-smriti,* ch. 6]

Duties of the Four Social Classes

i. The Brahmin

4.74. Brahmins who are intent on the means (of gaining union with) the Brahman and firm in [discharging] their duties shall live by correctly performing the following six acts in their (proper) order.

75. Teaching, studying, sacrificing for oneself, sacrificing for others, making gifts and receiving them are the six acts of a brahmin. . . .

79. To carry arms for striking and for throwing (is prescribed) for kshatriyas as a means of subsistence; to trade, (to raise) cattle, and agriculture for vaishyas; but their duties are liberality, study of the Vedas, and performance of sacrifices.

80. Among the several occupations, the most commendable are: teaching the Veda for a brahmin, protecting (the people) for kshatriya, and trade for a vaishya.

81. But a brahmin, unable to subsist by his peculiar occupations just mentioned, may live according to the law applicable to kshatriyas, for the latter is next to him in rank.

82. If it is asked, "What should he do if he cannot maintain himself by either (of these occupations," the answer is), he may adopt the vaishya's mode of life, employing himself in agriculture and raising cattle.

83. But a brahmin, or a kshatriya, living by a vaishya's mode of subsistence, shall carefully avoid agriculture, (which causes) injury to many beings and depends on others. . . .

ii. The Kshatriya

18. Punishment alone governs all created beings, punishment alone protects them, punishment watches over them while they sleep; the wise declare punishment to be the law (*dharma*).

19. If (punishment) is properly inflicted after consideration it makes all people happy; but inflicted without consideration, it destroys everything.

20. If the king did not, without tiring, inflict punishment on those worthy to be punished, the stronger would roast the weaker, like fish on a spit. . . .

22. The whole world is kept in order by punishment, for a guiltless man is hard to find; through fear of punishment the whole world yields enjoyments. . . .

88. Not to turn back in battle, to protect the people, to honor the brahmins is the best means for a king to secure happiness.

89. Those kings who, seeking to slay each other in battle, fight with the utmost exertion and do not turn back, go to heaven. . . .

144. The highest duty of a kshatriya is to protect his subjects, for the king who enjoys the rewards just mentioned is required to do that duty. . . .

198. He should, (however), try to conquer his foes by conciliation by (well-applied) gifts and by creating dissension, used either separately or conjointly, never by fighting (if it can be avoided).

199. For when two (princes) fight, victory and defeat in the battle are, as experience teaches, uncertain; he should therefore avoid an engagement.

iii. The Vaishya

9.326. After a vaishya has received the sacraments and has taken a wife, he shall be always attentive to the business whereby he may subsist and to (that of) cattle.

327. For when the Lord of Creatures created cattle, he gave them to vaishyas; to the brahmins and to the king he entrusted all created beings.

328. A vaishya must never wish, "I will not keep cattle"; and if a vaishya is willing (to keep them), they must never be kept by other (castes).

329. (A vaishya) must know the respective value of gems, of pearls, of coral, of metals, of (cloth) made of thread, of perfumes, and of spices.

330. He must know how to plant seeds and the good and bad qualities of fields, and he must perfectly know all measures and weights. . . .

333. Let him exert himself to the utmost in order to increase his property in a righteous manner, and he should zealously give food to all created beings.

iv. The Shudra

8.334. Serving brahmins who are learned in the Vedas, who are householders, and who are famous (for virtue) is the highest duty of a shudra, which leads to beatitude.

335. [A shudra who is] pure, the servant of his betters, gentle in his speech, free from pride, and who always seeks a refuge with brahmins, attains (in his next life) a higher caste. . . .

413. But a shudra, whether bought or unbought, he may compel to do servile work; for he was created by the Self-existent to be the slave of brahmins.

414. A shudra, even though emancipated by his master, is not released from servitude; since that is innate in him, who can set him free from it? . . .

128. The more a (shudra), keeping himself free from envy, imitates the behavior of the virtuous, the more he gains . . . in this world and the next.

[Manu-smriti, chs. 4, 9, 8]

How Women Should Live

3.55. Women must be honored and adorned by their fathers, brothers, husbands, and brothers-in-law, who desire (their own) welfare.

56. Where women are honored, there the gods are pleased; but where they are not honored, no sacred rite yields rewards.

57. Where the female relations live in grief, the family soon wholly perishes; but that family where they are not unhappy ever prospers.

58. The houses on which female relations, not being duly honored, pronounce a curse, perish completely, as if destroyed by magic. . . .

60. In that family where the husband is pleased with his wife and the wife with her husband, happiness will assuredly be lasting. . . .

67. The nuptial ceremony is stated to be the Vedic sacrament for women (and to be equal to the initiation), serving the husband is (equivalent to) the residence in (the house of the) teacher, and household duties are (the same) as the (daily) worship of the sacred fire. . . .

5.147. By a girl, by a young woman, or even by an aged one, nothing must be done independently, even in her own house.

148. In childhood a female must be subject to her father, in youth to her husband, when her lord is dead to her sons; a woman must never be independent. . . .

150. She must always be cheerful, clever in household affairs, careful in cleaning her utensils, and economical in expenditure.

151. Him to whom her father may give her, or her brother with her father's permission, she shall obey as long as he lives, and when he is dead, she must not insult (his memory). . . .

154. Though destitute of virtue, or seeking pleasure (elsewhere), or devoid of good qualities, a husband must be constantly worshipped as a god by a faithful wife.

155. No sacrifice, no vow, no fast must be performed by women apart (from their husbands); if a wife obeys her husband, she will be exalted for that (reason alone) in heaven.

156. A faithful wife, who desires to dwell (after death) with her husband, must never do anything that might displease him who took her hand, whether he be alive or dead.

157. At her pleasure let her emaciate her body by (living on) pure flowers, roots, and fruit; but she must never even mention the name of another man after her husband has died. . . .

160. A virtuous wife who after the death of her husband constantly remains chaste, even if she has no sons, reaches heaven, just like those chaste men. . . .

164. By violating her duty towards her husband, a wife is disgraced in this world; (after death) she enters the womb of a jackal, and is tormented by diseases for her sin.

165. She who, controlling her thoughts, words, and deeds, never fights her lord, lives (after death) with her husband (in heaven) and is called virtuous. . . .

167. A twice-born man, versed in the sacred law, shall burn a wife of equal caste who conducts herself thus and dies before him with (the sacred fires used for) the Agnihotra and with the sacrificial implements.

168. Having thus, at the funeral, given the sacred fires to his wife who dies before him, he may marry again, and again kindle (the fires).

[*Manu-smriti,* chs. 3, 5]

The Four Main Castes/Summary

Twice-born

(Males participate in a sacred thread ceremony, considered a kind of second birth.)

Brahmins: Priests, whose dharma is to study and to teach the Vedas, and to perform the sacrifices. Created from the mouth of Purusha, the primordial man-god.

Kshatryas: Aristocratic warrior caste, whose dharma is to rule over and to protect society, by means of war, if necessary; also to study the Vedas. Created out of the arms of Purusha, the primordial man-god.

Vaishyas: Merchants and owners of farms, whose dharma is to sustain society and to study the Vedas. Created out of the thighs of Purusha, the primordial man-god.

Not twice-born

Shudras: Servants, laborers, whose dharma is to serve the other castes, especially the brahmins; traditionally not meant to study the Vedas. Created out of the feet of Purusha, the primordial man-god.

The Untouchables: Either the lowest subcaste of the Shudras or outside of the caste system altogether, who perform the most menial and degrading of tasks, often involving polluting substances.

The Four Stages of Life/Summary

(Traditionally meant for males of the three upper, twice-born castes alone)

Stage 1: The Student

Boys are initiated into this first stage when they undergo the sacred thread ceremony and become twice-born. The age at which this ceremony take place depends on one's caste—7 years old (the brahmins); 10 years old (the kshatriyas); 11 years old (the vaishyas). Period of life for studying the Vedas.

Stage 2: The Householder

Period of life for marrying, bearing children, earning a livelihood, sustaining society, and supporting students, forest dwellers, and world renouncers. One must remain a householder until one "sees his skin wrinkled, and his hair white, and the sons of his sons."

Stages 3 and 4: The Forest Dweller and World Renouncer

After having fulfilled all the duties of a householder, the man may now pass through these two increasingly detached ways of life. When he first retires to the forest, he leaves his belongings and may bring his wife with him; then he finally "give all his property as a sacred fee" and must now have "himself for his only companion." He sits in meditation, seeking moksha, or absorption into the Brahman.

Section Eight
Buddhism
Born in Northern India/Nepal but Rapidly Spreading into Asia

Study Guide on Buddhism/Section Eight

In order to answer the questions below, you will need to refer to the illustrations and readings for Section Eight. You will also need to refer to your notes from in-class lectures, and to what you learn from the film to be shown in class, *The Life of the Buddha* (BBC).

1. Outline the main events in the life of the founding Buddha, Siddhartha Gautama.

2. Why is he sometimes called the Buddha Shakyamuni?

3. Into what caste was Siddhartha born, and what was predicted at his birth?

4. What were the four "sights" that led the young Siddhartha to abandon life in the palace?

5. Explain the various ways in which the Buddha rejected the religion of the Hindu Brahmins in his own life path.

6. Why did the Buddha reject extreme asceticism? What did he advocate in its stead? pg 143

7. Explain which important key concepts Buddhism shares with Hinduism, and which important concepts Buddhism rejects. pg 148

8. Explain the Buddhist concept of *anatman*, providing some concrete examples of how this concept applies. pg 145

9. What are the "four noble truths" discovered by the Buddha? pg 145

10. How does the Buddhist concept of Nirvana differ from the Hindu concept of moksha? Be sure to include the terms, samsara, the Atman, anatman, and the Brahman in your answer. pg 147

11. Describe in detail the six realms of existence in traditional Buddhist cosmology. In which realm is it possible to achieve Nirvana, and why? For each of the other realms, explain why it is not possible to do so.

12. Describe the five "aggregates", or constantly changing parts, that make up a human being during a lifetime.

13. Explain the most important differences between Mahayana and Theravada Buddhism.

14. What is a Bodhisattva in Mahayana Buddhism? How does a Bodhisattva differ from a Buddha?

15. What is the "Buddha nature" in Mahayana Buddhism? How does it differ from the Atman of Hinduism?

The Founding Buddha or "Enlightened One"

THE BUDDHA SIDDHARTHA is one of his names because Siddhartha, meaning "every wish (or purpose) fulfilled," was his personal first name.

THE BUDDHA GAUTAMA is another of his names because Gautama was his surname, or family name.

THE BUDDHA SHAKYAMUNI was another of his names because he was born a prince of the Shakya clan.
He is therefore sometimes called "the sage of the Shakyas."

THE FOUNDING BUDDHA IS NOT THE SAME AS THE BUDDHA MAITREYA, OR FUTURE BUDDHA.
The Buddha Maitreya has not yet been born. He is a bodhisattva who will be reborn in the future, His rebirth will issue in an age of prosperity.
The Chinese version of the Buddha Maitreya is usually represented as fat and jolly and has Chinese features. This representation is based on
a Ch'an (Zen) monk who lived about a 1,000 years ago, and was known for his benevolent nature. Maitreya means "loving-kindness."

HALO
Unlike in depictions of Jesus, the
halo around the Buddha's head
is not meant to represent his
divine status, but rather the
light of the higher wisdom
he achieved.

MEDITATIVE STATE
The Buddha's half-shut
eyes and gentle smile
indicate a perfect state
of mindfulness.

ELONGATED EARLOBES
In most representations
the Buddha's earlobes are
elongated, the result of the
heavy gold earrings he had
worn when a prince.

MONASTIC CLOAK
The Buddha wears the heavy
and simple robe of an
ascetic monk.

THE WISDOM BUMP
Indicative of the higher wisdom the Buddha acquired after
reaching enlightenment.

MEDITATIVE POSTURE
The Buddha sits in the full lotus position, one of the
most ancient of Hindu yoga postures.

THE URNA
A third eye of higher conciousness located on
the Buddha's forehead.

INDIAN FEATURES
The founding Buddha was born and was
active in northern India and southern
Nepal.

PERFECT PROPORTIONS
The body of the Buddha reflects
perfect human proportions.

Selections from The Pali Canon*

The Life of the Buddha

According to traditional accounts, the Buddha was born a prince named Siddhartha Gautama in a small kingdom in what is today southern Nepal. His final incarnation was a culmination of a training program that spanned countless lifetimes, during which he gradually perfected the exalted qualities that would mark him as a buddha. Shortly after his birth, his father consulted a number of astrologers, all of whom declared that the newborn prince would become a great king and that he would rule the whole world with truth and righteousness. One astrologer, however, declared that if the prince were to see a sick person, an old person, a corpse, and a world renouncing ascetic, he would become dissatisfied with his life and become a wandering mendicant in order to seek final peace. These four things became known in Buddhism as the "four sights." The first three epitomize the problems inherent in the world, while the fourth points to the way out of the endless cycle of birth, death, and rebirth, which is characterized by suffering and loss.

According to the Extensive Sport Sutra (Lalitavistara-sutra), *Siddhartha's father, king Shuddhodana, decided to prevent his son from encountering any of the four sights and surrounded him with pleasant diversions during his early years. The prince, however, eventually convinced his father to let him visit a part of the city that lay outside the palace gates.*

Before allowing the prince to ride out in his chariot, Shuddhodana first ordered that the streets be cleared of all sick and old people, and that the prince not be allowed to see any corpses or world renouncers. Despite the king's efforts, however, at one point the path of the royal chariot was blocked by a sick man. Siddhartha had never before encountered serious illness, and he turned to Candaka, his charioteer, and asked,

> O charioteer, who is this man, weak and powerless?
> His flesh, blood, and skin withered, his veins protruding,
> With whitened hair, few teeth, his body emaciated,
> Walking painfully and leaning on a staff?

Candaka informed the prince that the man had grown old and that such afflictions were the inevitable result of age. He added,

> O prince, this man is oppressed by age
> His organs are weak; he is in pain, and his strength and vigor are gone.
> Abandoned by his friends, he is helpless and unable to work,
> Like wood abandoned in a forest. . . .
> Lord, this is not unique to his race or his country.
> Age exhausts youth and the entire world.
> Even you will be separated from the company
> Of your mother and father, friends and relatives.
> There is no other fate for living beings.

Siddhartha was amazed to find that most people see such sights every day but persist in shortsighted pursuits and mundane affairs, apparently unconcerned that they will inevitably become sick, grow old, and die.

In three subsequent journeys outside the palace, Siddhartha saw an old man and a corpse, and when he learned that eventually his young, healthy body would become weak and decrepit he fell into a profound

* From *Scriptures of the World's Religions* by J. Fieser and S. Powers. Copyright © 1998 McGraw-Hill Education. Reprinted by permission.

depression. On a fourth trip, Siddhartha saw a world renouncer, a man who stood apart from the crowd, who owned nothing and was unaffected by the petty concerns of the masses, and who radiated calm, serenity, and a profound inner peace. This sight lifted Siddhartha's spirits, since it revealed to him that there is a way to transcend the vicissitudes of mundane existence and find true happiness. Intrigued by the ascetic, Siddhartha asked Candaka what sort of man he was, and the charioteer replied,

> Lord, this man is one of the order of bhikshus [mendicants].
> Having abandoned sensual desires,
> He has disciplined conduct.
> He has become a wandering mendicant.
> Who views himself and the external world with the same regard.
> Devoid of attachment or enmity, he lives by begging.

Realizing the folly of remaining in the palace, Siddhartha resolved to renounce the world and find inner peace.

> Candaka, for countless ages I have enjoyed sensual objects
> Of sight, sound, color, flavor, and touch, in all their varieties;
> But they have not made me happy. . . .
> Realizing this, I will embark on the raft of dharma, which is steadfast,
> Endowed with the range of austerities, good conduct,
> Equanimity, effort, strength, and generosity,
> Which is sturdy, made of the firmness of effort, and strongly held together.

Siddhartha then declared his desire to become awakened in order to show other suffering beings a way to end suffering:

> I desire and wish that,
> After attaining the level of awakening,
> Which is beyond decay and death,
> I will save the world.
> The time for that has arrived.

Siddhartha left the palace and subsequently practiced meditation with several teachers, but none could show him a path leading to the cessation of suffering. At one point he fell in with five spiritual seekers who told him that the way to salvation lies in severe asceticism. He followed their practices, and eventually was only eating a single grain of rice per day. After swooning due to weakness, however, Siddhartha realized that extreme asceticism is just as much a trap as the hedonistic indulgence of his early years.

Thus he left his ascetic companions behind and resolved to find a path leading to the cessation of suffering. He recognized that he would have to discover the truth for himself. Before embarking on his final quest for truth Siddhartha made a solemn vow,

> As I sit here, my body may wither away,
> My skin, bones, and flesh may decay,
> But until I have attained awakening—
> Which is difficult to gain even during many ages—
> I will not move from this place.

Siddhartha stood in a spot that is now known as "the Circle of Awakening," located in modern-day Bodhgaya. Sitting under a tree, during the night Siddhartha entered into progressively deeper meditative states, in which the patterns of the world fell into place for him, and thus he came to understand the causes and effects of actions, why beings suffer, and how to transcend all the pains and sorrows of the world.

By the dawn of the next morning he had completely awakened from the misconceptions of ordinary people, and at this point Buddhist texts refer to him as "buddha," indicating that he was now fully awake and aware of the true nature of all things. Scanning the world with his heightened perception, the Buddha recognized that his realization was too profound to be understood by the vast majority of beings in the world, and so initially he decided to remain under the tree in profound equanimity, and to pass away without teaching what he had learned.

> Profound, peaceful, perfectly pure,
> Luminous, uncompounded, ambrosial
> Is the dharma I have attained.
> Even if I were to teach it,
> Others could not understand
> Thus, I should remain silent in the forest.

After the Buddha had made this statement, however, the Indian god Brahma appeared before him and begged him to teach what he had learned for the benefit of those few beings who could understand and profit from his wisdom. Moved by compassion for the sufferings of beings caught up in the round of cyclic existence, the Buddha agreed, and for the next 40 years he traveled around India, teaching all who cared to listen.

[*Lalita-vistara* selections]

The Buddha's Good Qualities*

From a Buddhist perspective, the Buddha is not only important as a person who taught a corpus of texts. The events of his life serve as an inspiration to devout Buddhists, who see him as the supreme example of how meditative realization should be put into practice in daily life. The following passage describes how he lived and related to people and things around him.

Renouncing the killing of living beings, the ascetic Gotama abstains from killing. He has put down the club and the sword, and he lives modestly, full of mercy, desiring in his compassion the welfare of all living beings.

Having renounced the taking of what is not given, the ascetic Gotama abstains from grasping after what does not belong to him. He accepts what is given to him and waits for it to be given; and he lives in honesty and purity of heart. . . .

Having renounced unchastity, the ascetic Gotama is celibate and aloof and has lost all desire for sexual intercourse, which is vulgar.

Having renounced false speech, the ascetic Gotama abstains from lying, he speaks the truth, holds to the truth, is trustworthy, and does not break his word in the world. . . .

Having renounced slander, the ascetic Gotama abstains from libel. When he hears something in one place he will not repeat it in another in order to cause strife . . . but he unites those who are divided by strife and encourages those who are friends. His pleasure is in peace, he loves peace and delights in it, and when he speaks he speaks words that make for peace. . . .

Having renounced harsh speech, the ascetic Gotama avoids abusive speech. He speaks only words that are blameless, pleasing to the ear, touching the heart, cultured, pleasing to people, loved by people. . . .

Having renounced frivolous talk, the ascetic Gotama avoids gossip. He speaks at the right time, in accordance with the facts, with meaningful words, speaking of the truth (*dhamma*), of the discipline (*vinaya*). His speech is memorable, timely, well illustrated, measured, and to the point.

The ascetic Gotama has renounced doing harm to seeds or plants. He takes only one meal per day, not eating at night, nor at the wrong time. He abstains from watching shows or attending fairs with song, dance, and music. He has renounced the wearing of ornaments and does not adorn himself with garlands, scents, or cosmetics. He abstains from using a large or high bed. He abstains from accepting silver or gold, raw grain or raw meat. He abstains from accepting women or girls, male or female slaves, sheep or goats, birds or pigs, elephants or cows, horses or mares, fields or property. He abstains from acting as a go-between or messenger, from buying and selling, from falsifying with scales, weights, or measures. He abstains from crookedness and bribery, from cheating and fraud. He abstains from injury, murder, binding with bonds, stealing, and acts of violence.

[*Digha-nikaya* 1.4–10]

Key Buddhist Concepts

The Middle Way

After almost fasting to death, the Buddha discovered the **Middle Way**, in between extreme asceticism and a life of luxury: "There are two extremes, which he who has given up the world ought to avoid…(1) A life given to pleasures and lusts: this is degrading, sensual, vulgar, ignoble and profitless; and (2) a life given to mortification (extreme self-denial): this is painful, ignoble and profitless."

The Four Noble Truths

1. All life is "**dukkha**." "Dukkha can be translated "**full of suffering**," "unsatisfactory," or "impermanent and conditioned" (i.e., dependent upon and affected by other things, and hence beyond our own control).

2. The **cause** of suffering, dissatisfaction, etc., is **desire**, or more literally, "**thirst**."

3. There is **a cure** for suffering and dissatisfaction, which is **Nirvana**, literally "**cooling**," or "extinguishing" of "thirst/desire."

4. The **means** to this cure or **to Nirvana** (the removal of desire/"thirst") involves wisdom, practice, and meditation: a careful following of the **eight-fold path** (the eight-spoked dharma wheel).

The Eight-Fold Path

A) Wisdom, which includes (1) right views/belief and (2) right intentions/aspiration.
B) Practice or moral living, which includes (3) right speech, (4) right action/conduct, and (5) right livelihood.
C) Meditation, which includes (6) right effort/endeavor, (7) right mindfulness/memory, and (8) right concentration/meditation.

Key Concepts of Hindu Philosophy Shared by the Buddha

Samsara: The phenomenal world and its cycle of birth, death, and rebirth.

Karma: The Law of the Universe of cause and effect—your moral actions always have consequences, whether in this life or the next; everything is interdependent and connected.

Key Concepts of Hindu Philosophy *Rejected* by the Buddha

The Atman: The Buddha totally rejected the notion of the Atman, self, or soul.

The Brahman: For the Buddha, there is no ultimate reality beyond samsara, or which is a source of samsara. Samsara is all there is, and the Buddha discouraged any speculation about how it got here while emphatically denying the existence of a creator God responsible for bringing samsara into being.

What the Buddha Taught Instead

Anatman or nonsoul/nonself. Central to Buddhist philosophy is the impermanence and interdependence of all things. Everything within samsara is always changing and in flux. Given that everything is interconnected via the law of karma (the law of cause and effect), when one thing changes, it produces changes in everything else along with it. Hence, there is no inner part of any sentient being that is independent of the body and, unlike the body, unchanging and permanent. Like everything else, sentient beings are always changing, inside and out.

Human beings and other sentient creatures are instead made up of five aggregates—(1) form, the physical elements that make up the body; (2) feeling or sensation of the physical as pleasant or unpleasant (or neither); (3) perception, rationally identifying what is perceived through the senses; (4) volition (the will), impulses, compulsions, ideas, opinions, mental habits, prejudices, dispositions, decisions, productive of karma, because it is these in particular that induce sentient beings to act; (5) consciousness, which arises from the four other aggregates.

Within each sentient being, these five aggregates are always in flux, ever changing, always interacting, and thus constantly being modified by contact with the others. It is the interaction of these five aggregates that creates the illusion of a self.

Note that, of the five aggregates, only one is physical; the other four are mental or spiritual. The four mental/spiritual aggregates, moreover, are never independent of the body, but always being modified by it and then modifying it in turn.

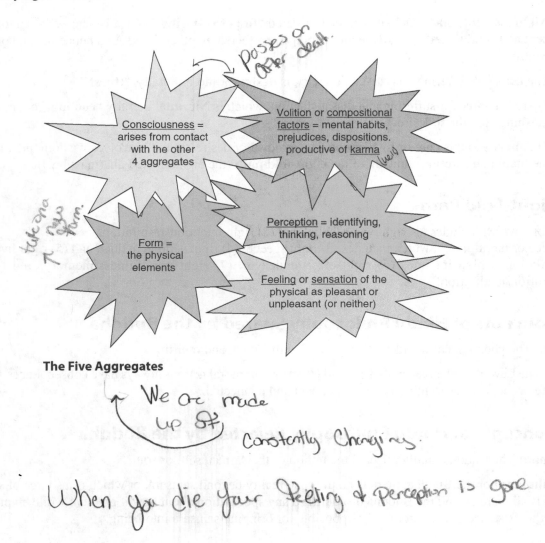

The Five Aggregates

[handwritten notes:] passes on after death. / take on a new form / We are made up of / Constantly Changing. / When you die your feeling & perception is gone

Nirvana Is a *State of Being*; Hence, It Is not the Same as the Hindu Notion of Moksha

The Buddha denied the existence of any ultimate reality beyond samsara and, indeed, questioned the notion that there is any essence or god that one could identify as the source, origin, or creator of samsara. The origin of the universe or samsara was, to the Buddha, an unanswerable and, indeed, an unimportant question, because what mattered was finding the solution to the suffering of existence.

If samsara is all that there is, then, how can one be liberated from samsara? What, then, is Nirvana?

Nirvana, according to the Buddha, is a *state of being*, in which all desire/craving/thirst has been quenched or extinguished. This state liberates a sentient being from a clinging to the five aggregates within samsara, and thus from the cycle of birth and rebirth; but it is *not* an absorption of one's Atman (which the Buddha denied existed) into some reality beyond samsara, called the Brahman (which the Buddha also denied existed).

What, then, is Nirvana?

First and foremost, it is the "extinction," or "quenching" of desire, and hence of suffering. It is the attaining of **a state of being within samsara (which is all there is)**. It is thus **both free of space and time but also within space and time**. It is the only state within samsara that is unconditioned and not subject to change, because it involves the complete letting go of any clinging to the five ever-changing and interdependent aggregates that make up a sentient being within samsara.

It should occasion no surprise that Nirvana is thus often characterized as "indescribable."

In particular, Western, logical categories, cannot serve to explain it.

It is for this purpose that koans are used in Zen Buddhism as a discipline in meditation. The word comes from the Japanese *kōan,* from *kō* public + *an* proposition. A koan is a paradox to be meditated upon that is used to train Zen Buddhist monks to abandon ultimate dependence on reason and to force them into gaining intuitive enlightenment. The effort to solve a koan is designed to exhaust the analytic intellect and the will, leaving the mind open for response on an intuitive level. There are about 1,700 traditional koans, which are based on anecdotes from ancient Zen masters. They include the well-known example "When both hands are clapped a sound is produced. What is the sound of one hand clapping?"

Nirvana

Nirvana is said to be the final cessation of suffering, a state beyond the cycle of birth and death. As such, it could be said to be the ultimate goal of the path taught by the Buddha, whose quest was motivated by a concern with the unsatisfactoriness of cyclic existence and a wish to find a way out of the round of suffering that characterizes the mundane world. Despite its importance, however, there are few descriptions of nirvana in Buddhist literature. The selection below is one of the most detailed analyses of what nirvana is and how one attains it.

Monks, there exists something in which there is neither earth nor water, fire nor air. It is not the sphere of infinite space, nor the sphere of infinite consciousness, nor the sphere of nothingness, nor the sphere of neither perception nor non-perception. It is neither this world nor another world, nor both, neither sun nor moon.

Monks, I do not state that it comes nor that it goes. It neither abides nor passes away. It is not caused, established, arisen, supported. It is the end of suffering. . . .

What I call the selfless is difficult to perceive, for it is not easy to perceive the truth. But one who knows it cuts through craving, and for one who knows it, there is nothing to hold onto. . . .

Monks, there exists something that is unborn, unmade, uncreated, unconditioned. Monks, if there were not an unborn, unmade, uncreated, unconditioned, then there would be no way to indicate how to escape from the born, made, created, and conditioned. However, monks, since there exists something that is unborn, unmade, uncreated, and unconditioned, it is known that there is an escape from that which is born, made, created, and conditioned. . . .

There is wandering for those who are attached, but there is no wandering for those who are unattached. There is serenity when there is no wandering, and when there is serenity, there is no desire. When there is no desire, there is neither coming nor going, and when there is no coming nor going there is neither death nor rebirth. When there is neither death nor rebirth, there is neither this life nor the next life, nor anything in between. It is the end of suffering.

[*Udana,* ch. 8.1–4]

Buddhist Cosmology:

THE GREAT WHEEL OF LIFE

The wheel contains four concentric circles:
(1) The innermost circle, or hub, within which are the three "poisons" that give rise to karma, good or bad.
(2) The karma produced by the three poisons, which results in beings descending and ascending among the six realms of samsara.
(3) The six realms of samsara, produced by karma.
(4) The twelve karma formations or links of dependent origination, which also keep us caught within samsara.

THE LORD OF DEATH

Yama, the lord of death, clutches the wheel of life in his fangs and claws, symbolizing impermanence as a fundamental aspect of existence and the inevitability of death in all six realms.

REALM OF THE DEMI-GODS OR DEVAS

In this realm, beauty, happiness, and pleasure temporarily transcend suffering. Once their good karma is exhausted, however, the beings in this realm die, as do all beings. Indeed, death is extremely painful for them, as it means losing their happy existence. A white bodhisattva reminds the beings in this realm that their time there is transitory.

REALM OF THE ASURAS OR TITANS

The beings in this realm are driven by their envy of the beings in the heavenly realm, and also of each other. They are often depicted as eating of the fruit of the wishing tree or as dressed in armour and engaged in warfare whether with each other or with the demi-gods or devas of the realm above them. A blue bodhisattva urges the beings in this realm to let go of their envy and end their warfare.

THE THREE POISONS

At the hub of the wheel are the three primary causes of what keep beings caught within samsara: Ignorance or delusion (the pig); aversion (the snake); and attraction (the bird).

KARMA WHEEL

Good karma (white) causes beings to ascend to higher realms, while bad karma (black) causes them to descend to lower realms.

THE HUNGRY GHOSTS

The beings inhabiting this realm are insatiably greedy, and constantly tormented by hunger and thirst because nothing can satisfy their desires. A red bodhisattva provides them with celestial food and reminds them of the virtues of generosity and sacrifice.

THE REALM OF THE HELLS

A large quantity of bad karma sends beings into this lowest and most painful of all realms. Yama sits in the center, surrounded by beings undergoing multiple forms of torment as a consequence of their bad deeds. There are cold and hot regions of this realm. An indigo bodhisattva holds a flame and a cup of water, reminding these beings that there is still light in the darkness and hope of eventual relief, for once they have exhausted their bad karma, they will escape this realm.

THE REALM OF HUMANS

This is the only realm in which beings are able to achieve enlightenment. It is only in this realm where one can control behavior and follow the eight-fold path. Not all humans choose to do so, however, and thus some of the people here are represented as seeking liberation, while others are depicted as driven by life's desires. A yellow bodhisattva teaches the four noble truths.

THE REALM OF ANIMALS

Animal life is more painful than human life because they are always in fear of being eaten by each other or by humans, and are also driven by instinct to cling to life. They also lack the intelligence required to learn the four noble truths and overcome their ignorance. A green bodhisattva urges them to seek higher wisdom so as to be reborn in the human realm.

THE TWELVE KARMA FORMATIONS

Moving clockwise around the outermost wheel: KARMA PRODUCING ACTIVITY (a potter shaping a vessel); UNCONTROLLED CONSCIOUSNESS (a monkey swinging aimlessly); WORDS AND IMAGES (two men riding in a boat; THE SIX SENSES (a house with 3 windows on each side), which include thought; CRAVING OR ATTACHMENT (a mother and child); JUDGEMENT BASED ON FEELING (an arrow piercing an eye); PHYSICAL CRAVING (a man with a bowl); CLINGING (a man picking fruit); IGNORANCE (a blind man); REBIRTH (a woman giving birth); BECOMING (a man and a woman having sex); OLD AGE AND DEATH (a very old man.)

Courtesy of Rick Taylor

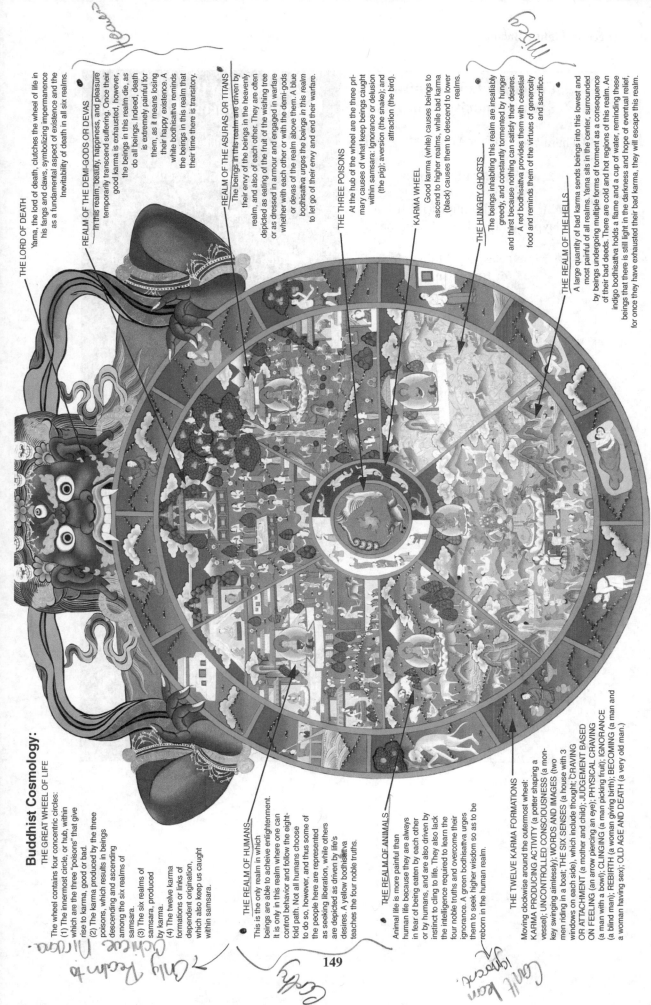

149

Theravada Buddhism (the minority group)	**Mahayana Buddhism (including Tibetan Buddhism)**
"Theravada" = "the Way of the Elders"	"Mahayana" = "the Greater Vehicle"
■ Southern Buddhism	■ Northern Buddhism
■ It is virtually impossible for a layperson to achieve liberation.	■ Laypeople, as well as monks and nuns, can achieve liberation.
■ More "classical," Indian form of Buddhism.	■ Much more influenced by local traditions and cultures, such as (in China) Taoism and Confucianism, and (in Japan) Shintoism.
■ The goals of life are self-reliance and self-liberation; nirvana can only be achieved through one's individual efforts, and thus this is the ultimate aim of each individual, with the goal of never being reborn within samsara. Only one bodhisattva is acknowledged —namely, Maitreya, the future Buddha.	■ The goal of life is self-liberation, but through the path of first becoming a bodhisattva = a being who has achieved liberation, but who delays his or her buddhahood out of compassion for his or her fellow sentient creatures, and thus chooses to be reborn in samsara, in order to help others achieve liberation. The Mahayana tradition thus recognizes many bodhisattvas, both male and female.
■ The Buddha Nature is not taught.	■ The Buddha Nature is a central teaching. It is an innate potential, within all human beings, for awakening and becoming a Buddha. This innate "Buddha-Mind" or "Buddha element" is eternal, incorruptible, and indestructible. It is not fully actualized in most people, and hence is not clearly seen and known in its full radiance. It is not the Atman of any individual person, however, but a single unified essence shared by all human beings.

Beyond Words: The Platform Sūtra*

Meditation Buddhism (Chinese Ch'ān, Japanese Zen) theoretically depends on direct transmission, and not upon scriptures. It thus traces its source back to the Buddha. However, it developed its own writings, the most esteemed of which is the Platform Sūtra – the only Chinese work to attain this title of Sūtra or Classic – which goes back to the records of the teaching of the Sixth Patriarch Hui-neng. With Meditation Buddhism the Buddhist trend towards direct experience rather than verbal truth is extended in an interesting and creative way.

Monk Hung-jen asked Hui-neng: 'Whence have you come to pay homage to me? What do you want from me?'

Hui-neng answered: 'Your disciple is from Lingnan [south of the Mountain Ranges, in the region of the present Canton]. A citizen of Hsinchou, I have come a great distance to pay homage, without seeking anything except the Law of the Buddha.'

The Great Master reproved him, saying: 'You are from Lingnan and, furthermore, you are a barbarian. How can you become a Buddha?'

Hui-neng answered: 'Although people are distinguished as northerners and southerners, there is neither north nor south in Buddha-nature. In physical body, the barbarian and the monk are different. But what is the difference in their Buddha-nature?'

The Great Master intended to argue with him further, but, seeing people around, said nothing. Hui-neng was ordered to attend to duties among the rest. It happened that one monk went away to travel. Thereupon Hui-neng was ordered to pound rice, which he did for eight months.

One day the Fifth Patriarch [Hung-jen] suddenly called all his pupils to come to him. As they assembled, he said: 'Let me say this to you. Life and death are serious matters. You people are engaged all day in making offerings [to the Buddha], going after blessings and rewards only, and you make no effort to achieve freedom from the bitter sea of life and death. Your self-nature seems to be obscured. How can blessings save you? Go to your rooms and examine yourselves. He who is enlightened use his perfect vision of self-nature and write me a verse. When I look at his verse, if it reveals deep understanding, I shall give him the robe and the Law and make him the Sixth Patriarch. Hurry, hurry!'

At midnight Shen-hsiu, holding a candle, wrote a verse on the wall of the south corridor, without anyone knowing about it, which said:

Our body is the tree of Perfect Wisdom,
And our mind is a bright mirror.
At all times diligently wipe them,
So that they will be free from dust.

The Fifth Patriarch said: 'The verse you wrote shows some but not all understanding. You have arrived at the front of the door but you have not yet entered it. Ordinary people, by practising in accordance with your verse, will not degenerate. But it will be futile to seek the Supreme Perfect Wisdom while holding to such a view. One must enter the door and see his self-nature. Go away and come back after one or two days of thought. If you have entered the door and seen your self-nature, I shall give you the robe and the Law.'

Shen-hsiu went away and for several days could not produce another verse.

Hui-neng also wrote a verse . . . which says:

The tree of Perfect Wisdom is originally no tree.
Nor has the bright mirror any frame.
Buddha-nature is forever clear and pure.
Where is there any dust?

Another verse:

The mind is the tree of Perfect Wisdom.
The body is the clear mirror.
The clear mirror is originally clear and pure.
Where has it been affected by any dust?

Monks in the hall were all surprised at these verses. Hui-neng, however, went back to the rice-pounding room. The Fifth Patriarch suddenly realized that Hui-neng was the one of good knowledge but was afraid lest the rest learn it. He therefore told them: 'This will not do.' The Fifth Patriarch waited till midnight, called Hui-neng to come to the hall, and expounded the Diamond Sutra. As soon as Hui-neng heard this, he understood. That night the Law was imparted to him without anyone knowing it, and thus the Law and the robe [emblematic] of Sudden Enlightenment were transmitted to him. 'You are now the Sixth Patriarch.' said the Fifth Patriarch to Hui-neng. 'The robe is the testimony of transmission from generation to generation. As to the Law, it is to be transmitted from mind to mind. Let people achieve understanding through their own effort.'

The Fifth Patriarch told Hui-neng: 'From the very beginning, the transmission of the Law has been as delicate as a hanging thread of silk. If you remain here, some one might harm you. You had better leave quickly.'

Hui-neng [having returned South] said: 'I came and stayed in this place [Canton] and have not been free from persecution by government officials, Taoists, and common folk. The doctrine has been transmitted down from past sages; it is not my own idea. Those who wish to hear the teachings of the past sages should purify their hearts. Having heard them, they should first free themselves from their delusions and then attain enlightenment.'

Great Master Hui-neng declared: 'Good friends, perfection is inherent in all people, it is only because of the delusions of the mind that they cannot attain enlightenment by themselves. They must ask the help of the enlightened and be shown the way to see their own nature. Good friends, as soon as one is enlightened, he will achieve Perfect Wisdom.

'Good friends, in my system, meditation and wisdom are the bases. First of all, do not be deceived that the two are different. They are one reality and not two. Meditation is the substance (*t'i*) of wisdom and wisdom is the function (*yung*) of meditation. As soon as wisdom is achieved, meditation is included in it, and as soon as meditation is attained, wisdom is included in it. Good friends, the meaning here is that meditation and wisdom are identified. A follower after the Way should not think wisdom follows meditation or vice versa or that the two are different. To hold such a view would imply that the Dharmas possess two different characters. To those whose words are good but whose hearts are not good, meditation and wisdom are not identified. But to those whose hearts and words are both good and for whom the internal and external are one, meditation and wisdom are identified. Self-enlightenment and practice do not consist in argument. If one concerns himself about whether [meditation or wisdom] comes first, he is deluded. Unless one is freed from the consideration of victory or defeat, he will produce the [imagining of] Dharmas and the self, and cannot be free from the characters [of birth, stagnation, deterioration, and extinction].

'Good friends, there is no distinction between sudden enlightenment and gradual enlightenment in the Law, except that some people are intelligent and others stupid. Those who are ignorant realize the truth gradually, while the enlightened ones attain it suddenly. But if they know their own minds and see their own nature, then there will be no difference in their enlightenment. Without enlightenment, they will be forever bound in transmigration.

'Good friends, in my system, from the very beginning, whether in the sudden enlightenment or gradual enlightenment tradition, absence of thought has been instituted as the main doctrine, absence of phenomena as the substance, and nonattachment as the foundation. What is meant by absence of phenomena? Absence of phenomena means to be free from phenomena when in contact with them. Absence of thought means not to be carried away by thought in the process of thought. Nonattachment is man's original nature. [In its ordinary process] thought moves forward without a halt; past, present, and future thoughts continue as an unbroken stream. But if we can cut off this stream by an instant of thought, the Dharma-body will be separated from the physical body, and at no time will a single thought be attached to any Dharma. If one single instant of thought is attached to anything, then every thought will be attached. That will be bondage. But if in regard to all Dharmas, no thought is attached to anything, that means freedom. This is the reason why nonattachment is taken as the foundation.

'Good friends, to be free from all phenomena means absence of phenomena. Only if we can be free from phenomena will the reality of nature be pure. This is the reason why absence of phenomena is taken as the substance.

'Absence of thought means not to be defiled by external objects. It is to free our thoughts from external objects and not to allow Dharmas to cause our thoughts to rise. If one stops thinking about things and wipes out all thought, then as thought is terminated once and for all, there will be no more rebirth. Take this seriously, followers of the Path. It is bad enough for a man to be deceived himself through not knowing the meaning of the Law. How much worse is it to encourage others to be deceived! Not only does he fail to realize that he is deceived, but he also blasphemes against the scripture and the Law. This is the reason why absence of thought is instituted as the doctrine.

'All this is because people who are deceived have thoughts about sense-objects, With such thoughts, pervasive views arise, and all sorts of defilements and erroneous thoughts are produced from them.

'However, the school instituted absence of thought as the doctrine. When people are free from [erroneous] views, no thought will arise. If there are no thoughts, there will not even be "absence of thought". Absence means absence of what? Thought means thought of what? Absence means freedom from duality and all defilements. Thought means thought of Thusness and self-nature. True Thusness is the substance of thought and thought is the function of True Thusness. It is the self-nature that gives rise to thought. [Therefore] in spite of the funtioning of seeing, hearing, sensing, and knowing, the self-nature is not defiled by the many sense-objects and always remains as it truly is. As the Vimalakīrti Scripture says: "Externally it skillfully differentiates the various Dharma-characters and internally it abides firmly in the First Principle".

'Good friends, in this system sitting in meditation is at bottom neither attached to the mind nor attached to purity, and there is neither speech nor motion. Suppose it should be attached to the mind. The mind is at bottom an imagination. Since imagination is the same as illusion, there is nothing to be attached to. Suppose it were attached to purity, man's nature is originally pure. It is only because of erroneous thought that True Thusness is obscured. Our original nature is pure as long as it is free from erroneous thought. If one does not realize that his own nature is originally pure and makes up his mind to attach himself to purity, he is creating an imaginary purity. Such purity does not exist. Hence we know that what is to be attached to is imaginary.

'This being the case, in this system, what is meant by sitting in meditation? To sit means to obtain absolute freedom and not to allow any thought to be caused by external objects. To meditate means to realize the imperturbability of one's original nature. What is meant by meditation and calmness? Meditation means to be free from all phenomena and calmness means to be internally unperturbed. If one is externally attached to phenomena, the inner mind will at once be disturbed, but if one is externally free from phenomena, the inner nature will not be perturbed. The original nature is by itself pure and calm. It is only because of causal conditions that it comes into contact with external objects, and the contact leads to perturbation. There will be calmness when one is free from external objects and is not perturbed. Meditation is achieved when one is externally free from phenomena and calmness is achieved when one is internally unperturbed. Meditation and calmness mean that externally meditation is attained and internally calmness is achieved.'

'All scriptures and writings of the Mahāyāna and Hīnayāna schools as well as the twelve sections of the Canon were provided for man. It is because man possesses the nature of wisdom that these were instituted. If there were no man, there would not have been any Dharmas. We know, therefore, that Dharmas exist because of man and there are all these scriptures because there are people to preach them.

'Among men some are wise and others stupid. The stupid are inferior people, whereas the wise ones are superior. The ignorant consult the wise and the wise explain the Law to them and enable them to understand. When the ignorant understand, they will no longer be different from the wise. Hence we know that without enlightenment, a Buddha is no different from all living beings, and with enlightenment, all living beings are the same as a Buddha. Hence we know that all Dharmas are immanent in one's person. Why not seek in one's mind the sudden realization of the original nature of True Thusness?'

The Great Master said to Chi-ch'eng [pupil of Shen-hsiu]: 'I hear that your teacher in his teaching transmits only the doctrine of discipline, calmness, and wisdom. Please tell me his explanation of these teachings.'

Chi-ch'eng said: 'The Reverend Shen-hsiu said that discipline is to refrain from all evil actions, wisdom is to practise all good deeds, and calmness is to purify one's own mind. These are called discipline, calmness, and wisdom. This is his explanation. I wonder what your views are.'

Patriarch Hui-neng answered: 'His theory is wonderful, but my views are different.'

Chi-ch'eng asked: 'How different?'

Hui-neng answered: 'Some people realize [the Law] more quickly and others more slowly.'

Chi-ch'eng then asked the Patriarch to explain his views on discipline, calmness, and wisdom, The Great Master said: 'Please listen to me. In my view, freeing the mind from all wrong is the discipline of our original nature. Freeing the mind from all disturbances is the calmness of our original nature. And freeing the mind from all delusions is the wisdom of our original nature.'

Master Hui-neng continued: 'Your teacher's teaching of discipline, calmness, and wisdom is to help wise men of the inferior type but mine is to help superior people. When one realizes his original nature, then discipline, calmness, and wisdom need not be instituted.'

Chi-ch'eng said: 'Great Master, please explain why they need not be instituted.'

The Great Master said: 'The original nature has no wrong, no disturbance, no delusion. If in every instant of thought we introspect our minds with Perfect Wisdom, and if it is always free from Dharmas and their appearances, what is the need of instituting these things? The original nature is realized suddenly, not gradually step by step. Therefore there is no need of instituting them.'

Chi-ch'eng bowed, decided not to leave Ts'aoli Mountain, but immediately became a pupil and always stayed close by the Master.

Glossary/Introduction to Religion

Adam **(in Hebrew)** = *A human being*, or *humankind* in general; derived from the Hebrew *adamah* = ground.

Agnostic = One who *does not know* whether or not a God or gods/goddesses exist(s); from the Greek, *agnōsis*—or *gnōsis* (knowledge) with the *alpha-privitive* (which expresses negation); hence, literally, "without knowledge."

Aesthetic = Concerned with beauty or the appreciation of beauty.

Aggregate = A bundle, or heap, of particles massed together.

Allah = From the Arabic definite article, "the" (*Al-*), added to the Arabic word for "God" (*ilah*) = meaning literally, "*The* God," or "The [One-and-Only] God," or "The [One True] God." Not only Arab Muslims but also Arab Christians and Jews call God by this name, considered to be his proper name. God can have many other names denoting his various attributes, however. In Islam, there are traditionally ninety-nine such other names.

Anatman = *Non-soul*, or *non-self*, a central Buddhist teaching. There is no inner part of any sentient being that is independent of the body and, unlike the body, unchanging and permanent. Like everything else, sentient beings are always changing, inside and out.

Anglican = A member of the Church of England, called an "Episcopalian" in the United States; a Protestant denomination founded by Henry VIII in 1534. Anglicans are found in other colonies of England, such as Canada and Australia. Mark, in *I Heard the Owl Call My Name*, is a Canadian Anglican priest. Unlike Catholic clergy, Anglican clergy can marry.

Animal Sacrifice = The sacrifice of an animal to a god or gods was very common among many religions of the ancient world; with a few exceptions, it usually involved eating the meat.

Animism = The oldest form of religion, practiced by many native cultures, including the North American natives; involving a belief that all aspects of nature—including trees, fish, food plants, birds, animals, the sun and moon and stars—are inhabited by a great number of spirits of about equal rank to the spirits that inhabit human beings. Animism emphasizes the equality and oneness of human beings with the natural world. The traditions of animistic religions tend to be passed down in oral form.

Anthropomorphic = Literally, "human-like"; from the Greek, *anthrōpos* (human being) and *morphos* (shape or form).

Arminianism = Is a teaching regarding salvation associated with the Dutch theologian Jacob Arminius (1560–1609), which rejected the Calvinist notion of double predestination and affirmed freedom of human will and that salvation has been offered to all. Arminians therefore hold that human beings may resist the grace of God and that believers may fall from grace.

Aryan = Derived from the Sanskrit *ārya* ("noble"), originally a reference to the Indo–Iranian people who, it was believed, came to settle in the Indus Valley, and *not* Nordic, blonde-haired and blue-eyed people, as later propagated by the Nazis. Nevertheless, according to the original theory, the Aryans did have lighter skin than the natives of the area they came to inhabit and introduced the caste system, setting themselves at the top of it. Today, this theory is disputed.

Ascetic = A person who chooses to live a simple life of self-denial, abstaining from sexual activity and living either alone or in community with other ascetics.

Asceticism = Practicing self-denial and abstention from sexual activity. Asceticism can be more or less extreme, ranging from living a simple life to denying oneself to the point of fasting to death. The Buddha ultimately rejected such an extreme form of asceticism.

Asherah **(plural,** *Asherim***)** = A Canaanite fertility goddess, widely worshipped in both the northern kingdom of Israel and the southern kingdom of Judah during the First Temple Period. She was probably understood to be the wife or consort of the high God, Yahweh.

Asuras = In Buddhism, anti-gods or demigods, who populate the lower heavens, the second highest realm of existence. They enjoy a similar existence to the gods of the highest realm, but are plagued by jealousy of the latter and wage fruitless wars against them.

Atheist = One who categorically denies the existence of a God or gods/goddesses. From the Greek, *atheos*, or *theos* (god) with the *alpha-privitive* (which expresses negation); hence, literally "godless."

Atman = from Sanskrit, *ātman*, meaning "breath," or "spirit"; in Hinduism, the individual self, or soul. The Atman is immortal and is the part of sentient beings that is reborn after death, albeit in a different physical form. The Atman thus undergoes repeated birth and death and rebirth within samsara. Monistic Hindus understand the Atman to be identical to the Brahman, whereas dualistic Hindus understand them as distinct, with the goal of meditation being the absorption of the individual Atman into the Brahman.

Avatar = The incarnation on earth of a Hindu deity, especially Vishnu, in human or animal form.

Babylonian Exile = The destruction of Jerusalem and the First Temple by the Babylonians in 586 BCE followed by the exile of many of the Jews to Babylonia until Cyrus the Persian permitted them to return to Jerusalem in 539 BCE.

BCE/B.C.E. = "Before the common era," previously BC.

Bible = From the Greek word, *ta biblia*, literally "little books." Thus, the Bible is by definition *not a single book*, but a *collection of books* considered authoritative by a given group of Jews or Christians. It is essentially a Jewish or Christian Biblical Canon. The Jewish, Catholic, Orthodox, and Protestant Bibles are all different one from the other.

Bishop = In the Anglican, Catholic, Orthodox, and some Methodist and Lutheran churches, a member of the clergy ranked higher than a priest, who oversees the various churches of a specific geographical area and their priests.

Bodhisattva = In Buddhism, a being who has achieved liberation or Nirvana, but who delays his or her Buddhahood, out of compassion for his or her fellow sentient creatures, and so chooses to be reborn within samsara in order to help others achieve liberation.

Brahma = The creator god within the Hindu trinity, which also includes Vishnu, the preserver, and Shiva, the destroyer. Brahma has four heads representing the four Vedas.

Brahman = The supreme existence or ultimate reality, the spiritual source of the finite world or samsara. For dualistic Hindus, it is also located beyond samsara. For monistic Hindus, the Brahman is *all there is* and is identical to the Atman; hence, samsara is an illusion, the product of *maya*. For monotheistic Hindus, the Brahman is identified as the one God. The Buddha *denied* the existence of the Brahman, or of any ultimate reality that is the source of samsara or that exists beyond it, and of a creator God of any kind.

Brahmins = The highest caste of Hinduism, the priests, whose dharma is to study and to teach the Vedas, and to perform the various rituals and sacrifices. Created from the mouth of *Purusha*, the primordial man-god.

Byzantine = The Byzantine Empire was the predominantly Greek-speaking continuation of the Roman Empire during Late Antiquity and the Middle Ages, which practiced Eastern Orthodox Christianity. Its capital city was Constantinople, named after the emperor, Constantine.

Buddha = "Enlightened one," anyone who has achieved Nirvana or "enlightenment," or who will achieve it in the future; hence, the founding Buddha, Siddhartha Gautama, was only the first Buddha.

Buddha Siddhartha Gautama Shakyamuni = The founding Buddha, whose proper name was Siddhartha (every wish/purpose fulfilled) and family name was Gautama, prince of the Shakya tribe or clan.

Buddha Maitreya = The future Buddha; a bodhisattva who will be reborn in the future, sometimes called the "laughing Buddha."

Calvinism = The teaching of John Calvin (1509–1564), which emphasizes the absolute sovereignty of God and predestination. Those whom God has elected cannot resist his grace, nor can they fall from grace. Those whom God has not elected are barred from His grace and were created for damnation. It is for the elect alone that Jesus died.

Canaanite = The designation of the people who lived in Palestine before the Israelites.

Canon = A collection of books accepted as authoritative by a religious community.

Catholic = Literally, "universal"; from the Greek, *kata* (according to) and *holos* (the whole). Together with the Orthodox Church, with which it was once united, the Catholic Church is one of the oldest main branches of Christianity.

CE/C.E. = "The common era," previously AD.

Clergy = The body of individuals in the Christian church that have been ordained to perform religious duties.

Confucianism = A Chinese philosophical system that developed from the teachings of Confucius (551–479 BCE) and his disciples.

Constantine the Great = The Roman emperor who made Christianity the official religion of the Empire and convened the Council of Nicaea in 325 CE, which created the first version of the Nicene Creed.

Constantinople (later Instanbul) = Founded by Constantine the Great and later became the capital of the Byzantine, Greek Eastern Orthodox Empire; sometimes called Byzantium.

Cosmogony = Beliefs/theories about how the universe originated, and about how it came to have the structure it presently has; from the Greek, *cosmos* (universe) and *gonē* (birth or origin).

Cosmology = The study of the structure of the universe; from the Greek, *cosmos* (universe) and *logos* (study of).

Crusader = A member of the Roman Catholic medieval military order charged with reclaiming the Holy Land from the Muslims who had occupied it since the mid seventh-century CE; called "the Franks" by Byzantine Christians.

Dharma = "Duty" or "truth"; behavior or doctrine (teaching) that is in accordance with the fundamental cosmic principles of the universe.

Diaspora = The settlements of Jews in various places outside the Holy Land of Israel after the Babylonian Exile. Any Jew living outside Israel was and is a Diaspora Jew. From the Greek, *dia* (throughout) + *speirein* (to sow).

Doctrine = From Latin, *doctrina*, literally "teaching"; a belief or set of beliefs held and taught by a religious group.

Essenes = One of the sects of Judaism during the time of Jesus and Paul, before the destruction of the Second Temple in 70 CE; cf., Pharisees and Sadducees.

Filioque = Latin for "**and the Son**," a clause added to the Nicene Creed (325 CE) at the Council of Toledo in Spain in 589 CE by the Western, Catholic church. Without the *filioque* clause, the third person of the Trinity, the Holy Spirit, "proceeds from the Father" alone; with the clause, the Holy Spirit "proceeds from the Father **and the Son** (filioque)." One of the major causes of the Great Schism between the Latin and Catholic churches in 1054.

First Temple Period = The period of Jewish history from the time that Solomon built the first Jerusalem temple in 950 BCE until it was destroyed by the Babylonians in 586 BCE.

Ganesh = The Hindu god with the elephant head, son of Shiva and Parvati. He is the god of wisdom and learning, and a remover of obstacles.

Great Schism = The division of the church in 1054 into the western, Latin Roman Catholic Church and the eastern, Greek Orthodox church.

Hadith = Literally in Arabic, "talk," or "speech"; stories about Muhammad's deeds and sayings recounted by his followers.

Hajj = The pilgrimage to Mecca, which all Muslims who are able make at least once in their lifetime; one of the Five Pillars of Islam.

Hamatsa = A kind of wild, animal-like, cannibal man, in the native North American traditions of the northwest. The ceremony of the Hamatsa dance involves taming the Hamatsa to the point of becoming human again. In addition to the Hamatsa himself, the complex cast of characters involved in this dramatic ritual dance includes a number of bird-monsters that were terrifying eaters of human flesh.

Hanuman = The great ape god, general of the monkey army, and loyal servant of Prince Rama, who assists the prince in rescuing his wife Sita and defeating Ravana.

Hanukkah = The eight-day Jewish celebration every year commemorating the retaking and cleansing of the Second Temple by Judas Maccabee in 163 BCE after it had been defiled by the Seleucid king Antiochus IV Epiphanes.

Henotheism = The raising of one god to the position of high god, while acknowledging the existence of other lesser gods and goddesses, which may also be worshipped. From the Greek, *theos* (god) and *henos* (one), meaning literally "one [most high] god."

High Places = Open-air altars to Yahweh, typically constructed on hills, where animal sacrifices took place. They were located all through the northern kingdom of Israel and the southern kingdom of Judah in the First Temple Period.

Hijāb = Literally in Arabic, "screen," or "curtain." It is a head covering worn by many Muslim women, usually covering their hair, neck, and chest, with the purpose of dressing modestly. There is considerable debate among Muslims about whether or not it is mandated by the Qur'an. It *is* required by the Saudi Arabian authorities for women going on the *Hajj*.

Hijrah = Literally in Arabic, "flight." The migration of Muhammad and his followers from Mecca to Yathrib (later called Medina) in 622 CE, which marks year one of the Muslim calendar.

Iblis = The name of *Shaytan*, or the devil, in Islam; a *jiin* who disobeyed Allah's command to bow down to Adam, the first human being.

Imām = Literally in the Arabic, "leader," or "guide"; the leader of prayer and worship in a mosque among Sunni Muslims. Among Shi'ites, however, there have only been seven or twelve *imāms*, beginning with Ali and all belonging to the bloodline of Muhammad.

Incarnate = Literally from the Latin "to be made flesh."

Incarnation = In Christianity, Jesus Christ during his lifetime, who was God in human form; the descent of God, or the second member of the divine Trinity, to earth by being made flesh by being born of Mary who conceived by the Holy Spirit. In Hinduism, a god, especially Vishnu, who descends to earth by being embodied in flesh in animal, human, or superhuman form. With reference to reincarnation, incarnation can also refer to one of the series of forms and lifetimes that an individual undergoes in the cycle of life, death, and rebirth.

Īsh (**in Hebrew**) = A man, or male human being; husband.

Īshah (**in Hebrew**) = A woman, or female human being; wife.

Islam = Literally in the Arabic, "surrender" or "submission" [to Allah].

Jainism = A religion originating in India characterized in particular by its utter devotion to *ahimsa* (non-violence).

Jihād = Literally in the Arabic, "struggling," or "exertion." It can sometimes be a reference to Holy War, when in defense of Islam; but most often it is a reference to striving hard in the service of Allah.

Jiin = Creatures made of smokeless fire. Unlike the angels that are made of light and always obey Allah, like humans Jiin have free will and can obey or disobey Allah.

Josiah's Reform = The king of Judah who reformed the religious practice, or cult, of his kingdom by insisting on the worship of Yahweh alone (monolatry) and that sacrifices to Yahweh could only be conducted in the Jerusalem temple (centralization of the cult).

Ka'bah = Literally in Arabic, "cube." It is the holy shrine in Mecca, toward which all Muslims pray.

Koan = From the Japanese *kōan*, from *kō* public + *an* proposition. A koan is a paradox to be meditated upon that is used to train Zen Buddhist monks to abandon ultimate dependence on reason and to force them into gaining intuitive enlightenment. A famous example is: "When both hands are clapped a sound is produced. What is the sound of one hand clapping?"

Kosher = (Of food, or conditions under which food is sold, cooked, or eaten) satisfying the requirements of Jewish law.

Kshatryas = The second highest of the main castes of Hinduism, the aristocratic warrior caste, whose dharma is to rule over and to protect society, by means of war, if necessary; also to study the Vedas. Created out of the arms of *Purusha*, the primordial man-god.

Laity = The group of all members of a religion who are not members of the clergy or monks or nuns. From the Greek, *laos*, meaning "people."

Lay people = Members of a religion who are not monks or nuns or priests. The adjective, "lay," is also from the Greek, *laos* (people).

Liturgy = The prescribed ceremonies and words repeated in a worship service. From the Greek, *leitourgia* (public service).

Lunar Calendar = A calendar based on the phases of the moon; it does not agree exactly with the solar calendar. The religious practices of both Jews and Muslims are based on a lunar calendar.

Luther, Martin = A Catholic monk who, with his posting of ninety-five theses against abuses in the Church in 1517, became the founder of the Protestant Reformation.

Maccabean Revolt = The revolt of the Jews in 165 BCE against the Seleucid King, Antiochus IV Epiphanes, who viciously persecuted them, attempted to force them to abandon their religious practice and adherence to Torah, and defiled the Jerusalem temple with a pagan god.

Mahayana = "The Greater Vehicle"; the form of Buddhism predominant in Northern Asia, including China, Mongolia, Vietnam, North and South Korea, Taiwan, Japan, Bhutan, and Tibet. Tibetan Buddhism is a form of Mahayana Buddhism. This form of Buddhism is much more strongly influenced than Therevada Buddhism by local traditions, such as (in China) Taoism and Confucianism, and (in Japan) Shintoism.

Maimonides = One of the most influential and prolific Jewish scholars of the Middle Ages (1135–1204), who lived and wrote in Muslim-occupied Spain and Egypt. His work is still studied closely in Rabbinic schools to this day.

Mayim **(in Hebrew)** = Waters; literally, two waters, as the form is dual, perhaps in order to distinguish the water above the *shamayim* (Hebrew for heavens or sky) from the water below it in the Priestly Account of Creation (Genesis 1).

Mecca = The birthplace in Saudi Arabia of the prophet, Muhammad, and location of the Ka'bah, toward which Muslims pray.

Medina = Literally in Arabic, "city of the prophet." The town of Yathrib in Saudi Arabia was thus renamed after Muhammad and his followers fled Mecca to settle there in 622 CE.

Mishnah = Literally, "repetition," from the Hebrew verb, *shanah* (to repeat). Traditionally, the compilation in writing of the Oral Torah around 200 CE by Rabbi Judah ha-Nasi ("the Prince").

Moksha = Liberation, the goal of Hindu meditation. For dualistic Hindus, it is the release of the Atman from samsara and its absorption into the Brahman. For monistic Hindus, is discarding the illusion that there is any duality in the Brahman and coming to a full understanding that the Brahman *is* the Atman, and vice versa, that they are one. The Hindu notion of moksha is *not* the same as the Buddhist notion of Nirvana.

Monastery = A building or complex within which a community of male or female ascetics (monks or nuns) live.

Monastic = Pertaining to the lifestyle of male and/or female ascetics (monks or nuns).

Monk = A male ascetic, who usually takes vows of chastity, poverty, and obedience, and who often lives in a community of other monks (a monastery), apart from the rest of society.

Monolatry = The insistence that only one god is worthy of worship, while still acknowledging that other gods and goddesses exist. From the Greek, *monos* (only [one]) and *latreō* (to worship).

Monotheism = The belief that only one God exists. From the Greek, *theos* (God) and *monos* (only [one]).

Mosque = A Muslim place of worship; the direction of Mecca is typically indicated.

Muhammad = From the Arabic, meaning "highly praised"; the great prophet of Allah and founder of Islam; *not* his actual birth name, which is unknown.

Muslim = Literally in the Arabic, "one who surrenders/submits" [to Allah].

Nicene Creed = The formal statement of Christian faith (= creed) put together by the Council of Nicaea in 325 CE.

Nirvana = According to the Buddha, it is the "extinction," or "quenching" of desire, and hence of suffering. It is *not* Hindu moksha, or the absorption of one's Atman (which the Buddha denied existed) into some reality beyond samsara, called the Brahman (which the Buddha also denied existed). Instead, it is a <u>*state of being*</u> that is paradoxically both *within* space and time (samsara) and yet *free of* space and time (samsara).

Nun = A female ascetic who usually takes vows of chastity, poverty, and obedience, and who often lives in a community of other nuns, apart from the rest of society.

Ordain = To make someone a minister, priest, rabbi, etc., conferring upon that person the authority associated with that office.

Orthodox = Literally, "right belief"; from the Greek, *orthos* (straight or right) and *doxa* (opinion or belief). Together with the Catholic Church, with which it was once united, the Orthodox Church is one of the oldest main branches of Christianity.

Pantheon = From the Greek, *pan* ("all") and *theōn* ("of the gods") = all the gods and goddesses of a particular religion.

Pantheism = From the Greek, *pan* ("everything") and *theos* (God), the belief that God and the universe are identical = literally, everything is God and God is everything.

Parvati = Wife of the Hindu god Shiva; and mother and creator of the god Ganesh.

Pharisees = One of the sects of Judaism during the time of Jesus and Paul, before the destruction of the Second Temple in 70 CE; cf., Essenes and Sadducees. They were advocates of Oral Torah and thus the main precursors to the rabbis.

Polytheism = Belief in and also the worship of many gods and goddesses. While there may be a hierarchy of some kind among these gods and goddesses, no single god is raised as a high god, way above all the others, as in henotheism.

Pope = From the Greek word, *papas*, a child's word for "father"; in the Catholic Church, the Bishop of Rome and thus the supreme head of the entire Catholic Church because, according to Catholic doctrine, he is the successor of the first Bishop of Rome, Jesus' disciple Simon, whom he nicknamed Cephas (which in Aramaic means "rock") or Peter (*Petros*, which in Greek means "rock"), the "rock" upon which the church was initially founded.

Potlatch = From a native North American word, meaning "to give." Potlatches are lavish feasts, held for various occasions, including the handing on of family privileges. Traditional dances are performed and gifts are generously distributed to the guests.

Predestination = The doctrine that all that will happen has already been decided and predetermined by God from before creation, especially with regard to the salvation of some and not others.

Priest = In general, a person authorized to perform the sacred rites of a given religion; in Judaism, a descendent of Aaron authorized to perform the various rituals associated with the worship of God, especially animal sacrifice; in Hinduism, a member of the highest caste authorized to teach the Vedas and to perform the various religious rituals, including animal sacrifice; in Christianity, the leader of worship in the Catholic, Orthodox, and Anglican (Episcopalian) churches.

Priestly Account of Creation = The account of creation found in Genesis 1 of the Hebrew Bible, thought to have been composed by Jerusalem priests sometime after the Babylonian Exile. God is not called Yahweh in this account.

Primary Text = A document written at the time or by the person being studied; for example, the letter to the Galatians was written by Paul himself, and thus is a primary text for the study of Paul and the time of Paul (the first century CE).

Protestant = Literally, "one who protests"; a member or follower of any of the Western Christian churches that are separate from the Roman Catholic and Orthodox Churches and follow the principles of the Reformation, which began with Martin Luther's posting of ninety-five theses in 1517. There are many Protestant denominations, including the Baptist, Presbyterian, Lutheran, Methodist, and Anglican (Episcopalian) churches. Protestantism is one of the three main branches of Christianity today.

Ptolemies = The Macedonian Hellenistic (i.e., Greek) dynasty that ruled over Egypt, founded by Ptolemy I at the death of Alexander in about 323 BCE and ending with the defeat of Cleopatra VII by the Roman general, Octavian (later Caesar Augustus) in 30 BCE. The Ptolemies also ruled over Palestine until 198 BCE.

Qur'an = From the Arabic, "to recite," because Muhammad originally delivered Allah's message to the people orally. It was soon written down, however, during the last 23 years of his life. It is the holiest book of Islam, written in Arabic.

Rabbi = From the Hebrew word for "teacher"; a person trained in the laws and rituals of Judaism and ordained to be the leader of a synagogue.

Rama = A prince, the seventh avatar or incarnation of Vishnu, and slayer of the demon, Ravana.

Ramadan = The month of fasting, from dawn to dusk each day, observed by all Muslims who are able; one of the Five Pillars of Islam.

Ravana = A Hindu demon-god, having ten heads and twenty arms, incapable of being destroyed by the gods. He is slain by Prince Rama, the avatar or incarnation of Vishnu in human form, because he abducted the prince's wife, Sita.

Reincarnation = The belief, shared by Hindus and Buddhists and other eastern religions that, when a sentient being dies, it is then reborn in a new incarnation or body, and thus it is _reincarnated_. In Hinduism, it is the soul or Atman that is reborn in a new physical form. This is not, however, the belief of Buddhists, who deny the existence of an Atman.

Religion = Very difficult to define, given its diversity in the world; most definitions that have been attempted are problematic in one way or another, either being too narrow or too broad.

Sadducees = One of the sects of Judaism during the time of Jesus and Paul, before the destruction of the Second Temple in 70 CE; cf., Essenes and Pharisees. The Sadducees were mainly priests and rejected Oral Torah, insisting that only the written Torah is binding.

Samsara = In Hinduism, Jainism, and Buddhism, and other eastern religions, the phenomenal world and the cycle of reincarnation (life, death, rebirth, life, death, rebirth, life, death, etc.).

Sanskrit = The ancient language of India, in which the Hindu scriptures, the Vedas, are written, and in which the classical Indian epic poems are written, and from which many modern northern Indian languages are derived.

Second Temple Period = History of the Jews from the rebuilding of the Jerusalem temple in about 520 to 515 BCE, after Cyrus the Persian allowed the Jews to return to Jerusalem at the end of the Babylonian Exile, to its destruction by the Romans in 70 CE.

Seleucids = The Macedonian Hellenistic (i.e., Greek) dynasty founded by Seleucus I after the death of Alexander the Great. It ruled much of Asia Minor from 312 to 64 BCE, and in the earlier part of this period also over the Persian part of Alexander's conquests. The Seleucids captured Palestine from the Ptolemies in 198 BCE.

Sheol = In the Hebrew Bible, the dark pit under the ground, similar to the early Greek notion of Hades, where everyone goes,whether righteous or wicked, when they die. Once in Sheol, one is no more than a shade, without thought or feeling of any kind.

Shi'ite = The sect of Islam that attributes a special spiritual status to Ali, a cousin and son-in-law of Muhammad, and which does not recognize the first three caliphs of Sunni Muslims.

Shintoism = The traditional religion of Japan; literally, "the way of the gods"; the worship of many Japanese deities, from the chief of whom the emperor is descended.

Shiva = The god of destruction in the Hindu Trinity, which also includes Brahma, the creator god, and Vishnu, the preserver god. Although a god of destruction, Shiva is also a god of recreation; hence, he is the god of the constant cycle of reincarnation.

Shudras = The lowest cast of Hinduism, the servants and laborers, whose dharma is to serve the other castes, especially the brahmins; traditionally not meant to study the Vedas. Created out of the feet of *Purusha*, the primordial man-god.

Sita = Wife of Prince Rama, kidnapped by the demon Ravana.

Sentient Being = Any living creature possessing feeling, perception, and consciousness, however simple.

Shamayim **(in Hebrew)** = The heavens or sky; the name God gave to the dome he created to separate the water above it from the water below it; thus, the word is closely related to the Hebrew word for waters, *mayim*.

Solar Calendar = A calendar based on the time it takes the earth to revolve around the sun.

Sunni = The sect of Islam that rejects attributing a special spiritual status to Ali, recognizing him merely as the fourth caliph of the caliphate in general.

Supernatural = Of or relating to events or beings, which cannot be explained by science or the known laws of nature.

Surah = A section of the Qur'an, varying in length from almost 300 to 3 verses, arranged within the Qur'an from longest to shortest. There are 114 surahs in the Qur'an.

Synagogue = A Jewish congregation engaged in communal prayer, worship, and study of Torah, and also the building within which such an assembly takes place; from the Greek, *synagōgē*, lit., "a gathering together."

Talmud = Literally, "instruction"; from the Hebrew, *talmūd*. Two Talmuds exist, produced by two different groups of Jewish scholars: the Babylonian Talmud (ca. 600 CE) and the Palestinian Talmud (ca. 400 CE). Each contains passages from the Mishnah with accompanying "commentary," or Gemara.

Tao = In Chinese philosophy, meaning literally, "the way"; the absolute principle underlying the universe, combining within itself the principles of yin and yang and signifying the way, or code of behavior, that is in harmony with the natural order.

Taoism = A Chinese mystical philosophy traditionally founded by Lao-tzu in the sixth century BCE that teaches conformity to the Tao by unassertive action and simplicity.

Theodicy = Literally, "God's righteousness"; from the Greek, *theos* (God) and *dike* (justice or righteousness). The term is usually employed with reference to attempts to defend God's righteousness in the face of the prosperity of the wicked and the suffering of the good, especially given the promises of Deuteronomy 28 that those who obey the covenant will be rewarded and those who disobey will be severely punished *in this lifetime*. But the issue of theodicy reached a particular crisis during the Maccabean Revolt when, for the first time ever, Jews were dying in order to keep Torah!

Therevada = "The Way of the Elders"; the more classical, Indian form of Buddhism predominant in the southern part of Asia, in the countries of Burma, Thailand, Laos, Cambodia, and Sri Lanka.

Torah = Literally, "teaching" or "instruction"; from the Hebrew, *torah*. The Written Torah consists of the first five books of the Hebrew Bible, often called the Pentateuch (from the Greek for "five scrolls") by Christians = Genesis, Exodus, Leviticus, Numbers, Deuteronomy. The Oral Torah developed later and was finally compiled in writing in the Mishnah in *ca.* 200 CE.

Trinity = In Christianity, the union of three distinct persons, the Father, Son, and Holy Spirit within one Being, the Godhead; in Hinduism, the three gods, Brahma of creation, Vishnu of preservation, and Shiva of destruction (and recreation).

Untouchables = In traditional Hinduism, either the lowest sub-caste of the Shudras, or outside of the caste system altogether. These individuals performed the most menial and degrading of tasks, often involving polluting substances.

Vaishyas = The third highest caste of Hinduism, the merchants and owners of farms, whose dharma is to sustain society and to study the Vedas. Created out of the thighs of *Purusha*, the primordial man-god.

Vedas = Hindu scriptures, from Sanskrit, *vēda*, meaning "knowledge."

Vishnu = The preserver god, a member of the Hindu Trinity, along with Brahma the creator and Shiva the destroyer. Vishnu has been incarnated in various forms nine times. Two of these avatars or incarnations are Krishna and Prince Rama.

Yahweh = The divine name; the personal name of the Jewish God. This name is never pronounced by observant Jews. It probably stems from the Hebrew for "He is," or "He causes to be."

Yahwist Account of Creation = The account of creation found in Genesis 2-3, in which God is routinely called, "Yahweh God" (the "Lᴏʀᴅ God" in most English translations). It was probably written before the Priestly Account of Creation, during the First Temple Period, as it is far less influenced by Babylonian cosmology and reflects the rain-fed agriculture of Palestine, with the temporary abode of the first human couple, the Garden of Eden, planted "to the east" in Babylonia.

Yang = In Chinese philosophy, the active male, creative principle of the universe, associated with heaven, heat, and light.

Yin = In Chinese philosophy, the passive female, sustaining principle of the universe, associated with earth, dark, and cold.

Zoomorphic = Literally, "animal-like." From the Greek, *zōon* (animal or living thing) and *morphos* (shape or form).